Setting Requirements for Maintenance Manpower in the U.S. Air Force

Carl J. Dahlman • Robert Kerchner • David E. Thaler

Prepared for the
United States Air Force

Approved for public release; distribution unlimited

RAND
Project AIR FORCE

The research reported here was sponsored by the United States Air Force under Contract F49642-01-C-0003. Further information may be obtained from the Strategic Planning Division, Directorate of Plans, Hq USAF.

ISBN: 0-8330-3132-5

Cover photo courtesy of U.S. Air Force Link,
TSgt Cedric H. Rudisill, photographer.

RAND is a nonprofit institution that helps improve policy and decisionmaking through research and analysis. RAND® is a registered trademark. RAND's publications do not necessarily reflect the opinions or policies of its research sponsors.

Cover design by Stephen Bloodsworth

Published 2002 by RAND
1700 Main Street, P.O. Box 2138, Santa Monica, CA 90407-2138
1200 South Hayes Street, Arlington, VA 22202-5050
201 North Craig Street, Suite 102, Pittsburgh, PA 15213-1516
RAND URL: http://www.rand.org/
To order RAND documents or to obtain additional information,
contact Distribution Services: Telephone: (310) 451-7002;
Fax: (310) 451-6915; Email: order@rand.org

This report assesses the methodology that the United States Air Force uses to determine the size and composition of active-duty enlisted manpower in wing-level aircraft maintenance organizations. The focus is on maintenance apprentices, journeymen, and craftsmen in operational units, such as fighter, aircraft generation, and maintenance squadrons. In particular, the study evaluates the operation and application of the Logistics Composite Model (LCOM); the appropriateness of man-hour availability rules; and the representation of certain Air Force activities that neither LCOM nor availability rules completely address.

This study is the result of a direct tasking to RAND by General Michael Ryan, former Chief of Staff of the United States Air Force. Project AIR FORCE conducted the research in the Resource Management Program under the auspices of the Directorate of Manpower, Deputy Chief of Staff for Plans and Programs, and the Directorate of Maintenance, Deputy Chief of Staff for Installations and Logistics.

This study should be of interest to a broad Air Force audience, including decisionmakers and analysts in the manpower, maintenance, personnel, and operations communities. It should also be of interest to planners and programmers in the other services and in the Office of the Secretary of Defense as well as to outside observers of defense planning and military preparedness. Research was completed in July 2001.

PROJECT AIR FORCE

Project AIR FORCE, a division of RAND, is the Air Force's Federally Funded Research and Development Center (FFRDC) for studies and analysis. It provides the Air Force with independent analyses of policy alternatives affecting the development, employment, combat readiness, and support of current and future aerospace forces. Research is performed in four programs: Aerospace Force Development; Manpower, Personnel, and Training; Resource Management; and Strategy and Doctrine.

CONTENTS

FIGURES

TABLES

Over the last decade, the Air Force has faced challenges that were not foreseen when the Cold War ended. A significant portion of the force has become engaged in contingency operations that have on occasion included fairly intensive combat operations. Added to this stress has been the necessity to support peacekeeping operations even after hostilities have ceased. As the force has declined in number, forward deployments have created an unplanned level of stress.

Coupled with these increases in deployments has been an economy beckoning with good jobs and benefits. Experienced people have been leaving the force in unexpected and unwelcome numbers. The result has been a mismatch between taskings and available personnel.

Given current taskings, three distinct factors can cause a shortfall in personnel. First, the analytical methods used to determine requirements could be incomplete or biased downward. Second, there could be too few authorized positions to perform the tasks if not all requirements are funded. Third, even when authorizations match the tasks, there could be too few qualified personnel to fill all authorizations. These factors and their permutations could come into play simultaneously: The requirements could be understated *and* underfunded with authorizations, *and* there may not be enough qualified people to fill these authorizations.

The purpose of this study is twofold: to review the methodology that the Air Force uses to determine active-duty enlisted manpower requirements in aircraft maintenance, and to investigate whether there are indications that these requirements—and the authorizations based on them—are underestimated. The investigation is informed by explorations of the challenges these maintainers—who constitute about 29 percent of active-duty Air Force enlistees—face in the field. The underlying research aims to identify steps the Air Force can take to provide more complete information to its decisionmakers in their efforts to remedy the shortfalls described herein. The research does not identify specific remedies to shortfalls but can provide a foundation for assessing remedial concepts.

In the course of our analysis, we developed an expository framework, depicted in Figure S.1, to help illuminate the processes for determining maintenance manpower requirements. The processes are decomposed into three boxes: a red box, a blue box, and a white box, where the colors serve no other purpose than to categorize various issues. Each box represents the number of hours programmed or available to perform the activities associated with that box. The three boxes together comprise the total number of hours in a day (24 hours) or in a month (730 hours). The boxes are in reality unequal in size, although they are equally sized in Figure S.1.

The red box depicted in Figure S.1 contains hours derived from the Logistics Composite Model (LCOM). LCOM is a statistical simulation model that the Air Force uses to estimate the monthly man-hours and shift manning required to accomplish direct maintenance tasks. The blue box contains hours derived from Air Force- and major command (MAJCOM)-wide standards and policies that prescribe the average number of monthly hours individuals can be expected to be away from their primary duties. The associated regulations state the average number of hours individuals are unavailable (holidays,

RAND*MR1436-S.1*

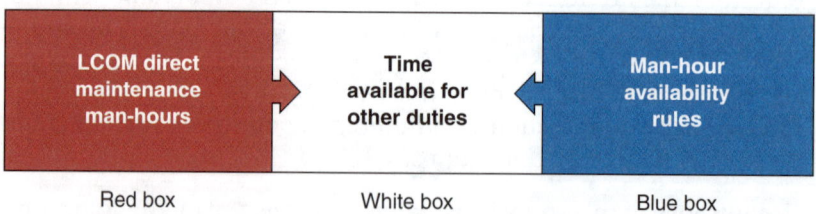

Red box   White box   Blue box

Figure S.1—A Framework for Discussing Processes for Determining
Maintenance Manpower Requirements

weekends, sick leave, etc.) and specify a number of overhead tasks they are expected to accomplish during duty hours, thereby setting ceilings for the hours available for primary duties (which include LCOM-simulated direct maintenance tasks). Finally, the white box represents valid Air Force tasks that maintainers must accomplish during the remainder of the duty day that are not directly represented in either the red box or the blue box.

INADEQUACIES IN EXISTING MANPOWER PROCESSES

The overarching conclusion of the research in this report is that maintenance manpower requirements are indeed underestimated. In general, the research indicates that Air Force manpower processes do not adequately account for all valid tasks that maintainers in the field must perform. These tasks are as follows:

- To meet the operational requirements of the combatant commanders (including contingencies and rotational deployments);

- To sustain the long-term health of the Air Force (including producing sorties for pilot training, providing on-the-job training [OJT], and conducting life-cycle maintenance of equipment); and

- To perform other duties that the Air Force considers appropriate and necessary.

Manpower processes do not adequately account for some key operational requirements of the combatant commanders—namely, the rotational deployments that encourage split operations. Such processes are not built on data that represent the true peak workload the Air Force desires as a basis for estimating the requirement for maintenance man-hours. They also fail to appropriately address the requirement of the long-term health of the force—especially OJT—at a time when the experience mix is becoming less favorable. Finally, they do not sufficiently represent other Air Force tasks that take maintainers away from duties associated with their occupational specialties. These inadequacies are manifested in each of the three boxes described above.

The Red Box: LCOM-Related Shortfalls

The quality of the data used in LCOM is only minimally adequate.
Overall, LCOM is a sophisticated model that is capable of portraying
in significant detail the process of servicing and maintaining aircraft
to meet various flying schedules. However, LCOM is a highly data-
intensive model. The greatest limitation to the model in its current
use lies in the lack of availability of high-quality data on break rates
and fix times. Available automated information systems in maintenance (Core Automated Maintenance System [CAMS], GO-81) are
not sufficiently consistent and accurate to give the detailed data necessary to run the model as designed. To mitigate this problem,
LCOM analysts perform field audits with maintenance personnel to
generate more complete data. These audits, which are by necessity
more impressionistic than statistical, are clearly a second-best alternative, but they do provide a sufficient basis on which to run LCOM.

In addition, LCOM as it is currently applied may not represent peak
maintenance demands. A fundamental concept is that the model
runs should be based on the most demanding operational requirements, and this may in fact be the case in terms of sortie rates. However, the inadequate statistical data for LCOM—the efforts associated
with field audits notwithstanding—may omit some peak maintenance demands. Data points from the 1999 Kosovo conflict suggest
that the rate at which equipment breaks can be higher during high-
intensity operations than indicated by the data used for LCOM.

LCOM scenarios are deficient. The scenarios that feed LCOM do not
adequately represent the current environment under which maintainers must operate. In the fighter world, the most stressful demands that arise seem to relate to preparation for, workload during,
and recovery from split operations (split ops)—yet this is not reflected in official Air Force manpower estimates. Split ops usually
refer to overseas deployments in which a squadron is required to
deploy only a portion of its aircraft, pilots, and maintainers. In this
context, the deploying part of the squadron naturally takes the best
equipment and more experienced people to minimize any risks inherent in an operational environment. The nondeploying part of the
squadron remains at home station and continues normal peacetime
operations, but it does so with less reliable aircraft and less experienced technicians who need training while continuing to meet a fly-

ing schedule for the pilots who stay behind. Training at home station usually suffers as a result.

LCOM analysis does not explicitly account for OJT or experience mix. More generally, the man-hours dedicated to OJT are not systematically included in LCOM analysis. OJT is a crucial activity for sustaining the long-term health of the Air Force's personnel inventory, particularly in such technically demanding fields as maintenance. OJT constitutes an important part of the duty day for junior maintainers as well as for the senior maintainers who must train them.

Moreover, LCOM analysis does not explicitly take experience mix into account. Changes in experience mix (i.e., the ratio of senior to junior technicians in a unit) affect the productivity of a unit as well as its ability to conduct OJT. For example, when experience declines (i.e., when the ratio of senior maintainers to junior maintainers drops), the ability to generate sorties and repair aircraft declines as well. At the same time, the ratio of trainees to teachers rises. In the real world, senior maintainers compensate for deteriorating experience mix by working longer hours. Were LCOM to incorporate the important effects of falling experience in units, it would mean an increase in the manpower requirement.

The official maintenance policies that LCOM incorporates do not always reflect reality. LCOM analyses must adhere to official policies controlling the maintenance processes modeled in LCOM. These include policies and goals related to cannibalization, time-change technical orders (TCTOs), and mission-capable rates. Actual rates in the field often fail to meet the standards set in Air Force policy. When this happens, it drives a higher manpower requirement that is not satisfied in programming.

While the shortfalls in the red box outlined above raise questions about the manpower estimates derived from LCOM, no better substitute for LCOM has yet been identified. Moreover, the analysis in this report finds that LCOM is not the only, or even the most important, problem associated with current manpower processes. This means that even if the Air Force were able to rectify all the problems involved in the application of LCOM, a manpower shortfall would remain as a result of problems in other areas.

The Blue Box: Shortcomings in Rules Governing Man-Hour Availability

Man-hour availability is averaged across the entire Air Force. One set of Air Force man-hour availability rules is applied to all positions—officer and enlistee, chief master sergeant and airman basic, avionics specialist and security police. This implies that a junior 3-level maintainer (i.e., an apprentice) is expected to spend the same amount of time per month in formal education and training as his wing commander. Generally, the hours assumed for activities during nonavailable periods may severely underestimate the hours maintainers actually dedicate.

In addition, the blue box includes time set aside for activities associated with "indirect labor" during primary duty hours. Indirect labor includes attendance at meetings, administrative duties such as performance evaluation and personnel management, and cleanup of work areas. Indirect labor hours are determined by—and differ between—the MAJCOMs. These rules, too, fail to differentiate between officers and enlistees or among ranks, experience levels, or occupations.

The generality offered in the blue box seems inconsistent with the extreme detail in the red box.

Acceptable working hours are defined and enforced in programming but not in execution. In defining the programmed hours airmen are supposed to be available for primary duties, Air Force regulations also define an allowable overtime of 7.7 percent (11.7 hours per month, or about half an hour per workday). For many maintenance occupations, this overtime is regularly exceeded in execution when maintainers work ten or more hours per day even under normal conditions. While this is not inherently a problem caused by manpower processes, it is important to note that there is no standardized process either for tracking the hours maintainers work under various conditions or for establishing limits to prevent excessively long hours.

OJT is not included as a blue box activity. Neither Air Force regulations on man-hour availability nor MAJCOM assumptions about indirect labor explicitly include the time it takes to teach and learn via OJT, a key element of the maintainer's skill progression. The "education and training" reference in the man-hour availability rules speaks mainly to formal training and coursework; only three hours *per month* are set aside for this purpose, representing a pittance in an OJT-intensive field such as maintenance. Activities under indirect labor include the development and preparation of training standards and materials but not the training itself.

The White Box: Ample Time for Residual Activities?

Key activities appear in the white box by default. Neither the LCOM analyses in the red box nor the man-hour availability rules in the blue box take residual activities into account. Manpower analysts and programmers have been content simply to assume that the time left over after calculating hours in the red and blue boxes would be sufficient to allow maintainers to complete all other tasks during their normal duty day. This assumption has not been questioned owing to a lack of focused oversight over these other tasks.

Activities defaulted to the white box include the following:

- **OJT.** In one fighter wing and two mobility wings we surveyed, senior maintainers averaged 15 to 20 percent of their duty days teaching OJT. Junior maintainers spent between one-quarter and one-third of their time learning. The capacity for OJT declines as the experience mix deteriorates. OJT often serves as a bill payer when units come under stress: Time spent on OJT decreases in favor of the completion of other pressing tasks.

- **High operational tempo (OPTEMPO).** Duty hours increase substantially and task emphasis changes during deployments (especially split ops), inspections, surges, and exercises. These periods can total five to six months per year in fighter wings and somewhat less in mobility wings. Surveys indicate that during high-OPTEMPO periods, hours worked per day rise by 12 to 21 percent; hours dedicated to production increase by 40 to 50 percent. Training invariably suffers, however, with dedicated hours declining by 28 to 36 percent.

- **Additional direct maintenance.** Activities such as cannibalization can be quite labor-intensive. One mobility wing reported that three experienced technicians were assigned simply to manage the C-5 designated as the source for cannibalized parts. Sixty other maintainers were averaging ten hours per week tracking cannibalization actions.

- **Out-of-hide positions.** Some positions are necessary for the smooth operation of the organization but are not funded in programming. Organizations fill these positions by moving personnel out of their primary occupations. As the largest occupational group in many operational units, maintainers—who are usually experienced technicians—bear the lion's share of the burden. A recent Air Staff study indicated that 4 percent of assigned maintainers occupy out-of-hide positions. This puts added stress on those who remain in direct maintenance positions.

The white box may be "bursting at the seams." The lack of focused oversight over the direction of a significant portion of the maintainer's duty day is leading to a form of "mission creep": the uncontrolled addition of tasks that is creating an overtasked workforce, especially among midlevel and senior personnel. The pressure on maintainers is compounded by deteriorating experience, which has led to a decline in productivity and to an increase in the requirement for OJT capacity. Yet the Air Force lacks insight into the actual level of effort maintainers apply to these tasks. As a result, maintainers in the field accomplish their missions only by working longer hours and by postponing some activities.

RECOMMENDATIONS

This report concludes with a number of recommendations for improving the processes involved in determining maintenance manpower requirements. There are suggestions about adjusting Air Force policies and conducting new data collection and analysis. What follows are the highest-priority recommendations, many of which are designed to alleviate the problems associated with the white box.

Make OJT an explicit requirement. Activities that lack standards and metrics tend to become bill payers for other, more observable activities. OJT is one of the activities that experience pressure during high-OPTEMPO periods or when demands for pilot training are high. OJT deserves a focused effort to define standards for training tasks, progression gates, and times to upgrade. OJT must be tracked in order to assess and manage the long-term health of the maintenance force and to make adjustments to manpower requirements as the experience mix changes. With additional standards for trainee-to-trainer ratios, OJT should be made an explicit task in LCOM analyses and/or man-hour availability rules.

Limit actual overtime by policy or by targeted increases in authorizations. The Air Force must gain more control over the volume of hours its maintainers work. Excessive overtime over extended periods can increase stress (excluding overtime at deployed locations, when the mission and the separation from family may make maintainers more willing to work long hours) and can contribute to declining retention rates. The first step is to ascertain how much time is currently demanded of maintainers in the field. To bring overtime down, the Air Force can mandate limits if it is willing to accept that some lower-priority tasks may go unfulfilled. Alternatively, it can increase authorizations for senior maintainers in busier specialties, such as that of crew chief. The need to increase authorizations could be limited by flushing experienced maintainers out of the so-called out-of-hide positions and returning them to the flight line and the back shop.

Inject greater specificity into man-hour availability rules. Standards for nonavailable and indirect labor hours should be reviewed for maintenance occupations and should differentiate grades, specialties, and levels of experience. This can be expected to affect manpower requirements. Greater specificity would help make these rules more consistent with the level of detail that LCOM generates.

Develop a richer scenario set for LCOM that addresses the prevailing conditions that maintainers see during peacetime. The goal of modeling the most stressful scenarios in LCOM is an appropriate one. High-OPTEMPO demands—particularly the demands at home station during split ops—should be captured in official LCOM analyses. The "peacetime" activities of contingency deployments and other demands may constitute the most stressful scenarios. They could drive a manpower requirement that would be prohibitively expensive to underwrite. Still, the Air Force should be well aware of this requirement even if it cannot be fully funded.

While there appears to be a potential shortfall in manpower authorizations in the maintenance force, the remedy is not necessarily to increase authorizations. Corrective policies may eventually include higher authorizations, but other avenues must also be pursued. Personnel actions to increase the fill rate through a combination of increased retention and higher training load in technical schools are two candidates. Various ways of increasing the availability of maintainers, based on critical analyses of the tasks they are performing, are equally important. Most significantly, the Air Force must begin a focused and sustained effort to address the problems we have identified in all areas of the manpower requirements process and to couple these changes with appropriate attention to how personnel policies should be better aligned with functional requirements.

ACKNOWLEDGMENTS

The authors would like to express their appreciation for the support of a number of individuals and organizations during the conduct of this research. The authors thank Lieutenant General Michael Zettler, Brigadier General Teresa Gabreski, Colonel Glen Locklear, Major Martha Pruitt, and Chief Master Sergeant Matthew McMahan of the Air Force Directorate of Installations and Logistics for their helpful insights into the maintenance community and their critical reviews of the final briefing of this work. Colonel William Booth and Major Andrew Baker of the Air Force Directorate of Manpower and Organization were stellar in their reviews of the research, draft reports, and briefings; their knowledge, perspectives, and candor were extremely valuable in the framing of research results. Additional thanks go to the principal LCOM analysts, Don White (ACC), David Albers (AMC), Senior Master Sergeant Charles Chisholm (AFSOC), and Fred Juarez (AFMIA), who spent a great deal of their time and energy leading the authors through the intricacies of the model and forthrightly presenting its pros and cons. The authors also greatly appreciate the counsel of Colonel Greg Flierl, former chief of the Air Force Readiness Center, who helped guide the authors during the earlier stages of research that led up to the current effort. C. Robert Roll, director of the Resource Management Program within Project AIR FORCE, provided helpful suggestions and guidance as the research was developed, conducted, and documented. RAND colleagues Raymond Conley and Edward Keating conducted technical reviews of the report that greatly improved its cohesion and clarity.

Finally, the authors would like to express their great appreciation and respect to the maintainers of the 388th Fighter Wing, the 60th Air

Mobility Wing, and the 305th Air Mobility Wing. They expressed the real-world experiences that the authors attempted to relate throughout this report. These airmen and maintainers like them throughout the Air Force are dedicated, hard-working individuals whose main concern is getting the job done right. The authors write this report with these maintainers' well-being and sense of mission foremost in their minds.

ACRONYMS

2LM	Two-level maintenance
3LM	Three-level maintenance
A1C	Airman first class
AB	Airman basic
ACC	Air Combat Command
ADSS	Analysis Decision Support System
AETC	Air Education and Training Command
AFI	Air Force Instruction
AFLMA	Air Force Logistics Management Agency
AFMIA	Air Force Management Improvement Agency
AFSATCOM	Air Force satellite communications
AFSC	Air Force specialty code
AFSOC	Air Force Special Operations Command
AGS	Aircraft generation squadron
AMC	Air Mobility Command
Amn	Airman
AMW	Air mobility wing

APU	Auxiliary propulsion unit
A/R	Attrition reserve
ART	Air reserve technician
ASD	Average sortie duration
BAI	Backup aircraft inventory
CAFSC	Control Air Force specialty code
CAMS	Core Automated Maintenance System
CINC	Commander-in-chief
CMR-E	Combat mission ready experienced
CMR-N	Combat mission ready inexperienced
CMSgt	Chief master sergeant
CRS	Component repair squadron
CUT	Cross-utilization trained
DCF	Deceleration factor
EAF	Expeditionary Aerospace Force
ECM	Electronic countermeasure
ECS	Environmental control system
EMS	Equipment maintenance squadron
FL	Flight lead
FO/FOD	Foreign object/foreign object damage
FS	Flying squadron
FW	Fighter wing
GS	General schedule
HF	High frequency

HSC	Home station check
IFF	Identification friend or foe
IP	Instructor pilot
LANTIRN	Low-Altitude Navigation and Targeting Infrared for Night
LCOM	Logistics Composite Model
LMI	Logistics Management Institute
LORAN	Long-Range Aid to Navigation
MAF	Man-hour availability factor
MAJCOM	Major command
MC	Mission commander, mission-capable [rate]
MDS	Mission design series
MQT	Mission qualification training
MRT	Mission-ready technician, maintenance repair team
MSgt	Master sergeant
MTBF	Mean time between failures
M-UTE	Manpower utilization rate
NCO	Noncommissioned officer
NMCM	Non–mission capable due to maintenance
NMCS	Non–mission capable due to supply
NOC	Not otherwise coded
OJT	On-the-job training
ONA	Operation Noble Anvil
OPTEMPO	Operational tempo

PACAF	Pacific Air Forces
PAFSC	Primary Air Force specialty code
PCS	Permanent change of station
PIQ	Pilot initial qualification
PMAI	Primary mission aircraft inventory
PME	Precision measurement equipment
PTO	Power takeoff
QA	Quality assurance
RAM	Radar absorptive material
REMIS	Reliability and Maintainability Information System
RR	Removal rate
RSP	Readiness spares package
SCM	Space cargo modified
SEI	Special experience indicator
SGF	Sortie generation flight
SGR	Sortie generation rate
SMSgt	Senior master sergeant
SORTS	Status of Resources and Training System
SrA	Senior airman
SSF	Sortie support flight
SSgt	Staff sergeant
STDEV	Standard deviation
TCTO	Time-change technical order
TNMCM	Total non–mission capable due to maintenance

TNMCS	Total non–mission capable due to supply
TRG	Targeting [pod removals]
TSgt	Technical sergeant
UHF	Ultrahigh frequency
UPT	Undergraduate Pilot Training
USAFE	United States Air Forces in Europe
UTC	Unit type code
VHF	Very high frequency
VTM	Variance-to-mean [ratio]
WMP5	War Mobilization Plan, Volume 5
WUC	Work unit code

Chapter One

INTRODUCTION

BACKGROUND

Over the last decade, the United States Air Force has faced challenges that were not foreseen when the Cold War ended. A significant portion of the force has become engaged in contingency operations that have on occasion included fairly intensive combat operations. Added to this stress has been the necessity to support peacekeeping operations even after hostilities have ceased. As the force has declined in number, forward deployments have created an unplanned level of stress.

Coupled with these increases in deployments has been an economy beckoning with good jobs and benefits. Experienced people have been leaving the force in unexpected and unwelcome numbers. The result has been a mismatch between taskings and available personnel.

Given current taskings, three distinct factors can cause a shortfall in personnel. First, the analytical methods used to determine requirements could be incomplete or biased downward. Second, there could be too few authorized positions to perform the tasks if not all requirements are funded. Third, even when authorizations match the tasks, there could be too few qualified personnel to fill all authorizations. These factors and their permutations could come into play simultaneously: The requirements could be understated *and* underfunded with authorizations, *and* there may not be enough qualified people to fill these authorizations.

1

Figure 1.1 depicts in a generalized format the Air Force process that leads from requirements for maintenance manpower to personnel available for duty. The Logistics Composite Model (LCOM) is a statistical simulation model that the Air Force uses to estimate the monthly man-hours and shift manning required to accomplish direct maintenance tasks. Manpower standards and policies are applied to derive requirements for manpower spaces. Spaces are then authorized in the Air Force corporate structure on the basis of fiscal guidance and programmatic funding. The manpower function can be a source of manning shortfalls in two general areas. First, the data, standards, and assumptions that the manpower community (that which sets manpower spaces) uses to determine manpower requirements could be understated, thereby causing authorizations to be too low. Second, the requirements might be appropriate to the taskings, but funding may not be available to authorize the manpower to meet the requirements.

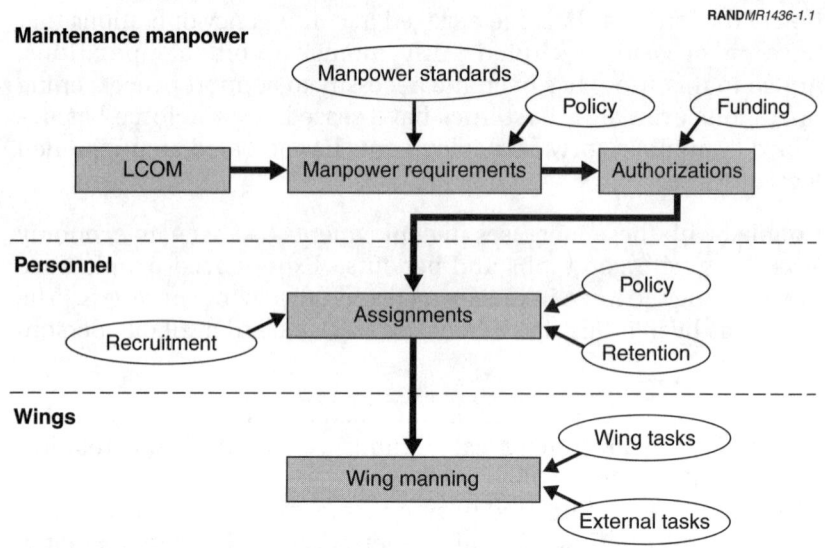

Figure 1.1—Air Force Process for Turning Maintenance Manpower Requirements into Available Personnel in the Field

The Air Force personnel community assigns "faces," or individuals, to the spaces that have been authorized. It establishes recruiting and retention goals and then uses the assignment system to ensure an efficient and equitable distribution of appropriate personnel across Air Force organizations. This distribution is governed both by operational demands and by personnel policies. For example, front-line units receive priority in the assignment of personnel, but personnel who have served unaccompanied tours abroad get priority in choosing the location of their next assignments. The personnel function can be a second source of shortfalls in manning. Even when the manpower function matches manpower requirements to tasks and the corporate structure fully funds the requirements in authorizations, the personnel community might not be able to fill those requirements with qualified people owing to recruiting and retention problems.

Individuals are assigned to wings on the basis of the personnel community's efforts to match assignments with authorized positions. Commanders in the receiving wing, squadron, and flight then have some leeway as to the actual duties they assign to these individuals. A commander must make his own assessment of his unit's challenges—i.e., the organizational needs of the unit, operational demands from combatant commanders, and the like—and must then respond to those challenges as he sees fit. As such, he may use assigned individuals in ways that are valid but that the personnel community had not intended. Thus, the wing and its subordinate organizations can be a third source of manning shortfalls in certain positions—whether in response to internal or external demands.

OBJECTIVES AND APPROACH

The purpose of this study is twofold: to review the methodology that the Air Force uses to determine manpower requirements in aircraft maintenance, and to investigate whether there are indications that these requirements—and the authorizations based on them—are underestimated. Thus, the study focuses on the manpower function depicted in Figure 1.1. However, the investigation is informed by explorations of the personnel and wing functions as well. The underlying research aims to identify steps the Air Force can take to provide more complete information to its decisionmakers in their efforts to remedy the shortfalls described herein. The research does not identify specific remedies to those shortfalls but can provide a foundation for assessing remedial concepts.

In the course of our analysis, we developed an expository framework to help illuminate the process for determining maintenance manpower requirements. This framework, depicted in Figure 1.2, is also used as an organizing tool for this report. The process is divided into three boxes colored red, white, and blue. Each box represents the number of hours programmed or available to perform the activities associated with that box. The three boxes together comprise the total number of hours in a day (24 hours) or in a month (730 hours). The boxes are in reality unequal in size, although they are equally sized in Figure 1.2.

The red box depicted in Figure 1.2 contains hours derived from LCOM. LCOM helps the manpower community translate sortie scenarios, logistics practices, and policy guidelines into the maintenance manning needed to generate sorties and repair aircraft. The blue box contains hours derived from Air Force- and major command (MAJCOM)-wide standards and policies that prescribe the average number of monthly hours individuals can be expected to be away from their primary duties. The associated regulations state the average number of hours individuals are unavailable (holidays, weekends, sick leave, etc.) and specify a number of overhead tasks they are expected to accomplish during duty hours, thereby setting ceilings for the hours available for primary duties (which include LCOM-simulated direct maintenance tasks). Finally, the white box represents valid Air Force tasks that maintainers must accomplish

RAND*MR1436-1.2*

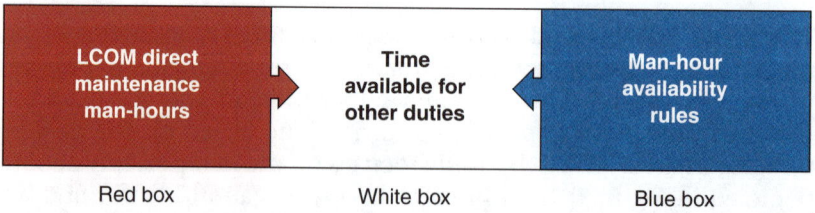

Figure 1.2——A Framework for Discussing Processes for Determining
Maintenance Manpower Requirements

during the duty day that are not adequately covered in either the red box or the blue box. These are activities we identify as lacking adequate discrimination and oversight in Air Force maintenance manpower processes and end up in the white box by default. Since the sizes of the red and blue boxes determine the size of the white box as a residual (within the context of a 24-hour day), it becomes critical to assess whether the white box is large enough to fit all the residual tasks. If this is not the case, some tasks go undone and/or people work overtime.

ORGANIZATION OF THE REPORT

Chapter Two of this report briefly describes the context for maintenance manning during the 1990s and into the 21st century. Subsequent chapters employ the framework introduced above to assess the maintenance manpower process. Chapter Three describes the inner workings of LCOM and discusses how its inputs relate to its outputs. Chapter Four illustrates how LCOM determines the size of the red box and provides an assessment of the adequacy of the model and its current application. Chapter Five discusses the instructions and regulations that determine the size and composition of the blue box and suggests a number of shortcomings in this part of the methodology. Chapter Six analyzes the remaining activities related to the white box and estimates whether failure to incorporate these activities in manpower processes could help drive a mismatch between requirements and resources. Chapter Seven provides a preliminary evaluation of manpower shortfalls based on observed duty hours and the deterioration in maintainer experience. Finally, Chapter Eight enumerates several recommendations for gaining insight into the practical requirements levied on maintainers in the field and the implications for improving Air Force maintenance manpower processes.

The three boxes that form the process for determining maintenance manpower requirements are disparate in nature; each box could stand on its own as a separate study aimed at specific audiences. In this report, there is a technical evaluation of LCOM and its application, a review of Air Force standards for man-hour availability, and an examination of the challenges facing maintainers in the field. Senior decisionmakers may gain more insight from some sections of the report, and analysts of manpower and aircraft maintenance may be more interested in others. In recognition of the different audiences reading this report, Chapters Three to Six conclude with summaries that can help readers gain general insights into the attendant subject matter. The appendices then give more detail than can be found in the chapters. We take the position that there is a great deal of overlap among these areas and that they should be viewed as an integrated whole as contributors to setting requirements.

Chapter Two

THE MAINTENANCE FORCE IN CONTEXT:
SUPPLY AND DEMAND

This chapter provides some context for subsequent discussions on the details of manpower processes. How has the character of the maintenance force changed over the past several years? What are these maintainers tasked to do? What has prompted the Air Force leadership to ask questions about the manpower process at the close of the 1990s?

Active-duty, enlisted maintainers constitute some 29 percent of the total active-duty enlisted force. The Air Force uses a five-digit Air Force specialty code (AFSC) to identify each enlisted occupational specialty.[1] The majority of the enlisted maintenance force bear AFSCs beginning with "2A" (e.g., 2A3X3, F-16 crew chiefs, or 2A6X1, engine troops). This report also includes weapon and munition troops (2W), maintenance analysts (2R), and precision measurement technicians (2P) in the maintenance career field.

The fourth digit in the AFSC (signified by the "X" in the examples above) denotes the level of qualification or skill that an individual has reached. This digit can be a 1, 3, 5, 7, 9, or 0, going from the most junior to the most senior airmen. This report focuses on the heart of the workforce in operational units: 3-level apprentices, 5-level journeymen, and 7-level craftsmen. Maintainers usually leave tech school and enter the first assignment in an operational unit as 3-levels. After some 15 to 24 months of on-the-job training (OJT) and

---

[1]See U.S. Department of the Air Force, *Classifying Military Personnel (Officers and Airmen),* Air Force Instruction (AFI) 36-2101, Washington, D.C., May 1, 1998.

formal learning, 3-levels qualify to become 5-levels. After several years of education, training, and experience, 5-levels become 7-levels. These skill levels are also tied to rank or grade. As technicians become more seasoned, they take on greater supervisory and teaching responsibilities.

SUPPLY: TRENDS IN MAINTENANCE MANNING

The size and composition of the Air Force's maintenance force has changed dramatically over the past several years. Figure 2.1 depicts the total number of authorized and assigned 3-level, 5-level, and 7-level maintainers from FY 1994 to FY 2000.[2] Authorized positions are shown as dashed lines and assigned personnel as solid lines. Lines with circular data points signify 3-levels; lines with square data points are 5-levels; and lines with an "x" at each data point are 7-levels.

Overall, authorizations declined by 12.5 percent in concert with the broader downsizing of the force in the 1990s. The 7-level maintainers took a 20 percent cut in authorizations, and 3-level spaces diminished by 16 percent. Five-level manpower, which constituted the majority of maintenance authorizations, was reduced by only 8 percent. In terms of skill-level cuts as a percentage of total cuts, 3-levels took the smallest portion (26 percent); 5-levels and 7-levels took nearly equal cuts (36 and 38 percent, respectively). The authorized experience mix remained relatively constant during this period, with about a 20-59-21 split between 3-, 5-, and 7-levels.

The most prominent trend in Figure 2.1 is the widening gap between authorized and assigned 5-levels. The number of assigned technicians as a percentage of those authorized (the "fill rate") has declined steadily from 97 percent in FY 1994 to 75 percent in FY 2000. Conversely, assigned 3-levels and 7-levels in FY 2000 exceed what is

---

[2]The numbers of assigned personnel in Figure 2.1 are by control AFSC. The personnel system employs control AFSCs to make enlisted assignments. An individual's control AFSC is "a management tool used to make airman assignments, to assist in determining training requirements, and to consider individuals for promotion" (AFI 36-2101, p. 50). Conversely, an airman's primary AFSC is "the awarded AFSC in which an individual is best qualified to perform duty" (AFI 36-2101, p. 51). For the purposes of looking across the Air Force, we use control AFSCs. Later, when we address capabilities within wings, we use primary AFSCs.

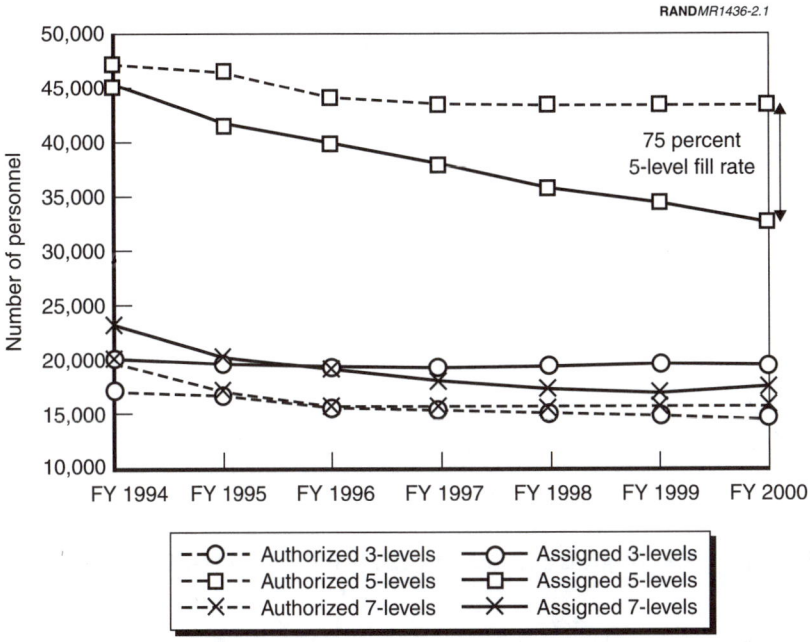

Figure 2.1—Number of Authorized vs. Control Assigned 3-, 5-, and 7-Level
Maintainers (2A, 2P, 2R, 2W0, 2W1) by Experience Level,
FY 1994 to FY 2000

authorized—by 34 percent and 11 percent, respectively. Still, because of the preponderance of 5-levels in the force, total assignments
diminished by 22 percent, representing a greater decline than that
seen in authorizations. Moreover, 3-levels increased as a percentage
of the total assigned force from less than 23 percent in FY 1994 to
about 28 percent in FY 2000. Five-levels dropped from 51 percent to
47 percent, while 7-levels hovered between 24 and 26 percent.

As the numbers of assigned 5-levels have declined, so too has their
average level of experience. Figure 2.2 depicts the average number of
months 5-levels have been qualified at their skill level. This has
diminished from about 42 months in FY 1994 to 30 months in FY
2000. Average experience actually rose between FY 1994 and FY 1996
and then dropped by 39 percent. As senior 5-levels have been replaced with junior 5-levels, the maintenance force has lost significant

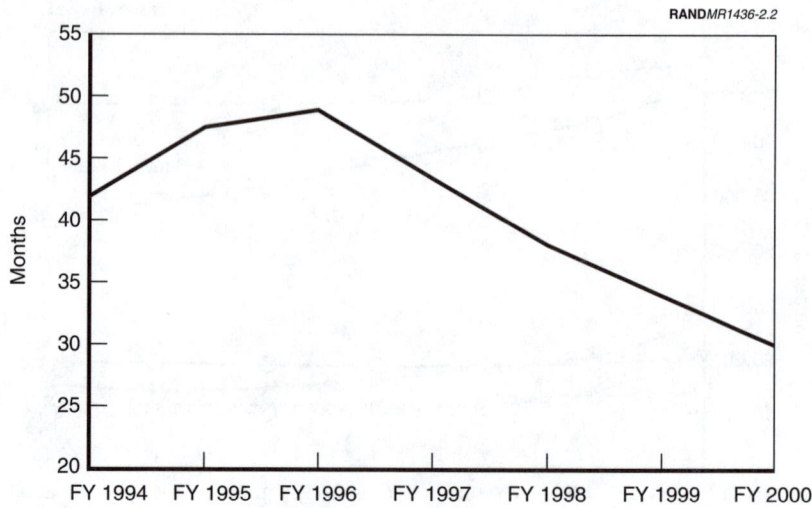

Figure 2.2—Months as Primary 5-Level Maintainer (2A AFSCs Only)

experience over the period. In other words, not only has the fill rate of 5-levels declined, but erosion of the knowledge base, as indicated by falling experience among the remaining 5-levels, has further aggravated the decline in numbers.

Figure 2.1 therefore encapsulates what has become a major problem for the management of the maintenance force as well as for ensuring that the capacity of the force to meet the demands on it is preserved. We will show in this report that current manpower requirement tools pay inadequate attention to the problems associated with skill mix because the effects of such problems are insidious and sometimes difficult to ascertain or measure with available data. An ever-younger force such as that shown in Figure 2.1 is less productive and requires more experienced trainers than a more mature one. We will discuss these issues in detail later in this report.

A major source of this problem is the retention rate of second-term enlisted airmen. For a variety of reasons—including a strong economy and frustration with recurring deployments—the Air Force has had trouble retaining its more experienced journeymen.[3] As greater numbers of these more senior 5-levels leave the service, they are replaced by junior technicians who must take on a greater share of the responsibility for maintaining and generating aircraft as well as for training 3-levels.

DEMAND: WHAT MAINTAINERS ARE REQUIRED TO ACCOMPLISH

U.S. Air Force wings and squadrons are tasked "to provide capabilities required by the combatant commanders to execute their assigned missions. This is derived from the ability of each unit to deliver the outputs for which it was designed."[4] Thus, one evaluates readiness in terms of the relationship between the tasks assigned to a unit and its ability to perform these tasks. In practical terms, as depicted in Figure 2.3, units in the Air Force must accomplish two

RAND*MR1436-2.3*

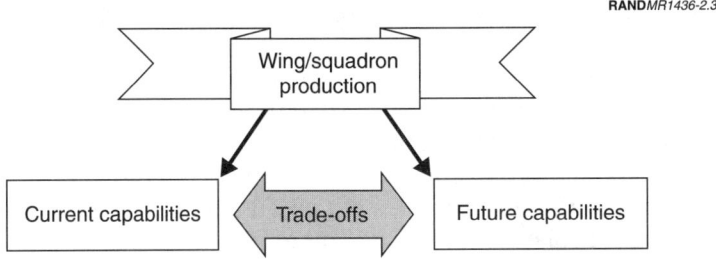

Figure 2.3—Two Overarching Tasks for Air Force Units

---

[3]Average retention rates for second-term enlistees approximate 70 percent, below the Air Force goal of 75 percent. Retention rates for maintainers are below the average.

[4]The DoD definition of unit readiness. See US. Department of Defense, *Department of Defense Dictionary of Military and Associated Terms,* Joint Publication 1-02, April 12, 2001, available at http://www.dtic.mil/doctrine/jel/new_pubs/jp1_02.pdf.

overarching tasks: to *maintain operational readiness* and to *rejuvenate the human and physical capital of the force.*

Operational readiness is the ability to provide current military capabilities to meet the near-term operational requirements of combatant commanders. If the wing had to go to war now, how well would its capabilities match up with the demands levied by the combatant commanders-in-chief (CINCs)? Are enough personnel qualified to execute required wartime tasks? Is the equipment in good working condition with an adequate level of supplies? Can the requisite number of effective sorties be generated? On the other hand, rejuvenating human and physical capital refers to training and upgrading junior personnel and maintaining the basic health of fleets of aircraft and equipment. This is to ensure that future commanders will continue to have an experienced, capable force from which to draw.

Over the past decade, the character of the demand has changed in many ways. During the Cold War, operational readiness was associated with the capacity to deter and defeat an adversary in a single, large-scale war. Today, the term also includes the capability to engage in small-scale contingencies and to service long-term rotational deployments. For the Air Force, the requirements of large-scale war differ considerably from those of rotational deployments in that complying with the latter does not entail halting peacetime requirements—particularly the requirement to rejuvenate the force.

Unfortunately, the rejuvenation of human and physical capital tends to be addressed less directly in planning and programming. DoD and Air Force guidance on and management of readiness traditionally emphasize operational readiness, and the requirements for maintaining this readiness are explicit. The production of future capabilities through the rejuvenation of human capital by OJT is not normally recognized as a separate and equally important tasking that is embedded in units. Yet unless the continued rejuvenation of the military's human and physical capital (their knowledge base and equipment base, respectively) is carefully managed and sustained, future commanders may have to go into battle with a less experienced manpower pool and with less reliable equipment.

Simultaneous with producing some current output, every organization—commercial or governmental, service or goods producing—
trains its personnel and maintains its equipment to sustain the organization over time. What sets military organizations apart is that
they are characterized by a high rate of personnel flow-through
combined with the need to build highly specific technical skills that
require years to develop. Moreover, the military cannot hire skilled
labor from the outside (with the exception of some personnel with
previous military service). Military careers are short, averaging no
more than five to six years in the Air Force's enlisted force and ten to
eleven years in the officer corps, and assignments to various duties
are shorter still.[5] By design, this drives a requirement for a level of
OJT that has no parallel either in most of the private sector or in
other governmental institutions. Because this is such an integral element of military activities, one tends to give it less attention than it
deserves.

In the Air Force, the knowledge of how to conduct successful air and
space operations must be continually re-created by assigning units
the responsibility for OJT in many occupations, combined with formal training outside of units as appropriate and necessary. Thus, in
flying units, senior pilots teach junior pilots how to become effective
warfighters and train their own successors as flight leads and instructor pilots. The same holds true in aircraft maintenance, where senior
maintenance personnel spend a great deal of their time teaching
young enlisted airmen to become qualified maintainers and—as with
pilots—train their own successors as senior enlisted managers and
trainers.

Life-cycle maintenance of equipment is also a key activity that helps
sustain a capable force over the long term. Outside observers often
think of maintenance in terms of generating sorties and repairing
broken parts. However, a great deal of effort goes into the inspection
and refurbishment of airframes and their components to ensure that
aircraft remain "healthy" well into the future. Although many of
these activities take place in central depots, a significant number of
them fall on operational units to complete. A number of technicians

---

[5]Average years of service are drawn from personnel files provided by the Air Force
Personnel Center.

in squadrons are dedicated to life-cycle maintenance; they sometimes draw maintainers from the flight line or from back shops when necessary.

Figure 2.3 not only illustrates the general principle that units are tasked to produce current and future capabilities but also notes that there are inevitable trade-offs between these capabilities. When resources are insufficient both to generate operational readiness and to meet individual training goals, the latter invariably suffer. For example, when part of a fighter squadron deploys overseas on a rotation, the commander will send his more experienced pilots and technicians. Those remaining at home station must continue their training regimen with a much less favorable ratio of trainers to trainees, and training often falls behind as a result. This occurs despite the fact that training is always stressed as critical by the leadership of all military units. Therefore, the degree to which training—especially the training of junior personnel—falls behind serves as a good leading indicator of readiness problems.[6]

In addition to operational readiness and rejuvenation of the force, there are ancillary tasks that maintainers—and personnel in other occupations—execute. Numerous administrative duties must be performed that are rather peripheral and sometimes unrelated to direct maintenance, yet most such duties are essential to the smooth operation of a military organization. These duties can include attending ceremonies, managing computer networks, performing charity work, overseeing hazardous waste removal, and coordinating VIP visits.

Given these requirements, the maintenance force should be sized to do the following:

- Meet the operational requirements of the combatant commanders (including contingencies and rotational deployments);

---

[6]For an elaboration of this argument, see Carl J. Dahlman and David E. Thaler, "Ready for War But Not for Peace," in Zalmay Khalilzad and Jeremy Shapiro (eds.), *Strategic Appraisal: United States Air and Space Power in the 21st Century,* MR-1314-AF, Santa Monica: RAND, 2002.

- Sustain the long-term health of the Air Force (including producing sorties for pilot training, providing OJT, and conducting life-cycle maintenance); and

- Perform other duties the Air Force considers appropriate and necessary.

These are requirements that the reader should keep in mind in subsequent chapters. They should be seen as criteria for evaluating existing manpower processes in the Air Force.

Let us now turn to a discussion of LCOM and its associated processes.

Chapter Three

THE RED BOX: HOW THE LOGISTICS COMPOSITE MODEL WORKS

LCOM is used to determine manpower requirements associated with direct maintenance activities—i.e., the red box. This chapter thus begins with a brief description of LCOM. In it, we present some elements of the model's structure and describe how the LCOM simulation is used in practice. We also report results we have obtained from some test runs we performed on two weapon systems. These test runs were made to examine the sensitivity of the model's input requirements to alterations in the demand for the production of sorties.

THE LCOM SIMULATION

The Scope of LCOM and LCOM Use in the Air Force

The LCOM simulation models Air Force direct maintenance activities at the wing level, or the process of preparing and repairing aircraft that fly and break or become due for scheduled maintenance.[1] The fundamental concept is that there is an operational requirement for sorties from a particular weapon system, whether that system is composed of fighters, bombers, transports, tankers, or special capability aircraft. Each time a sortie is demanded, an aircraft is called from a pool of ready aircraft. Upon returning from the sortie, various

---

[1]We base the following description of the model on our examination of two working versions which were provided to us by the Air Force Management Improvement Agency, the Air Combat Command, and the Air Mobility Command.

parts or systems may require maintenance. Given a break on some system, LCOM models the repair process that enables the aircraft to be returned to the ready pool.

From the perspective of determining maintenance manpower requirements, LCOM is used to simulate base-level direct maintenance. It is not currently used to model depot-level maintenance, although this might be a reasonable use for the simulation. LCOM analyses of base-level maintenance have been performed for many of the MAJCOMs, with most of the analytical know-how residing in the Air Combat Command (ACC), the Air Mobility Command (AMC), and the Air Force Management Improvement Agency (AFMIA). However, other organizations, including the Air Force Special Operationsl Command (AFSOC), also maintain an LCOM capability. LCOM has other potential uses, most notably as a tool for evaluating maintenance process improvement concepts.[2]

LCOM responds to demands for maintenance tasks by providing the resources needed to perform the tasks and then by performing the tasks. If resources are not available, a task will be deferred or another task will be preempted (in accordance with a set of business rules) to provide the needed resources. The completion of a task may in turn generate the requirement for one or more additional tasks. Upon completion of all tasks, the aircraft is returned to the ready pool, thereby completing the cycle. Thus, given specified manpower, parts, and equipment resources, an LCOM run permits a determination of which sortie demands can be serviced from the pool of available aircraft. The basic objective for LCOM analysts is to determine the minimum resources that permit nearly all mission requirements to be met.

How LCOM Models Aircraft Maintenance

LCOM is considered a *dynamic simulation* model because it explicitly represents the states of the resources it models—aircraft, people, parts, and equipment—as they change over time to meet sortie demands through aircraft maintenance. The heart of the model is

---

[2]We in fact advocate LCOM's use in this way, but a detailed discussion is beyond the scope of this document.

therefore a representation of real-world maintenance processes. Statistics such as sortie generation rate (SGR) are computed by tracking each simulated sortie and then computing the number of successfully accomplished sorties at the end of the simulation period.[3]

Figure 3.1 shows a highly simplified view of the LCOM simulation process. This simple diagram shows aircraft drawn from the pool and sent out on sorties; these sorties trigger postflight maintenance. If something is broken, maintenance/repair actions are taken to make the aircraft available for its next sortie. In addition, the model keeps an aircraft out of the ready pool for scheduled maintenance when a specified number of sorties, flying hours, or calendar days accumulate. This basic representation of the LCOM process leaves out many important additional items but should suffice to make it clear that there is an actual flow of aircraft and parts through a network representing wing-level operational flying and aircraft maintenance activities, following appropriate cause-and-effect rules.

RAND*MR1436-3.1*

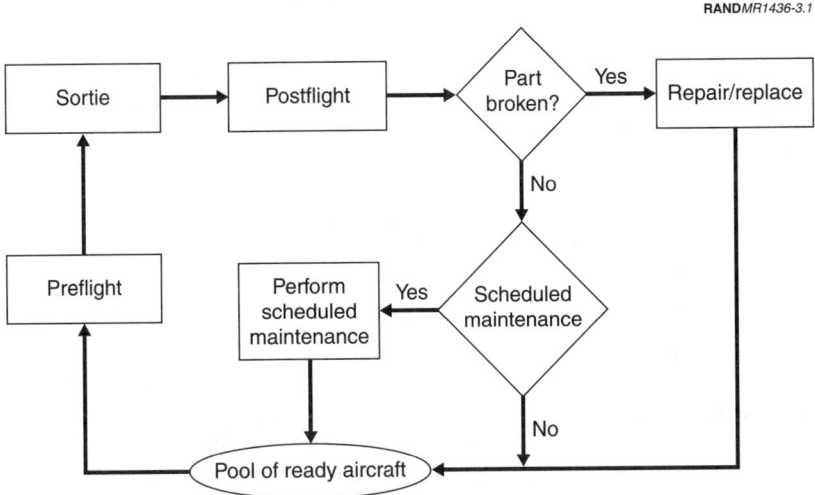

Figure 3.1—Simple Overview of the LCOM Process

[3]This simulation approach is in contrast to a closed-form model, in which the simulation outputs—e.g., SGR—are explicit functions (including table lookups) of the model input parameters.

Maintenance Networks

A work center in LCOM is organized around a set of discrete tasks, often down to a five-digit work unit code (WUC) level of detail, manned with people of appropriate skills. Work centers in actual maintenance units generally correspond to maintenance flights— e.g., sortie generation flights (SGFs) or avionics flights. A five-digit WUC is usually a specific part on an aircraft. Table 3.1 lists three

Table 3.1

Selected Work Centers and Associated Air Force Occupational Skills for the C-5

SORTIE GENERATION FLIGHT

Accomplishes launch, recovery, and servicing of aircraft along with minor scheduled inspections, home station checks (HSCs), and other maintenance necessary to return aircraft to operating activity. Performs unscheduled maintenance on engine, pneudraulic, electrical/environmental, and avionics aircraft systems. Accomplishes time-change technical order (TCTO) and indirect work such as supervision, administration, training, equipment maintenance, meting, supply, and cleanup.

AFSC:
Crew Chief 2A5X1
Communication/Navigation 2A4X2
Guidance and Control 2A4X1
Electro-Environmental 2A6X6
Pneudraulics 2A6X5
Jet Engine Mechanics 2A6X1

PROPULSION FLIGHT

Inspects, repairs, and tests engines. Inspects and repairs engines on aircraft during major inspections. Accomplishes TCTO and indirect work such as supervision, administration, training, equipment maintenance, meting, supply, and cleanup.

AFSC:
Jet Engine Mechanics 2A6X1

AVIONICS FLIGHT

Performs diagnostic analysis and intermediate maintenance on communication-navigation, electronic warfare, guidance control, and airborne photographic/sensor systems. Calibrates and repairs Type 4 precision measurement equipment (PME). Inspects and repairs avionics systems on aircraft during major inspections and refurbishment. Accomplishes TCTO and indirect work such as supervision, administration, training, equipment maintenance, meting, supply, and cleanup.

AFSCs:
Guidance and Control 2A4X1
Communication/Navigation 2A4X2
Electronic Countermeasures (ECMs) 2A1X7

---

work centers associated with tasks on the C-5 airlifter at the five-digit WUC level. In principle, then, a work center is represented in LCOM as a collection of WUCs and other service actions at the appropriate level (which may vary between different applications of the model in actual practice) and the associated occupational specialty codes that describe the types of manpower required to perform each task. Work centers are thus implicitly represented, while tasks are explicitly represented.

In LCOM, an AFSC such as 2A5X1 (crew chief for heavy aircraft) can for analytical purposes be viewed simply as a representation of a resource that performs maintenance on a set of five-digit work unit and service codes. That is to say, when something in an aircraft breaks during a sortie or when an aircraft has to be serviced before or after a sortie, the model allocates the work in accordance with network specifications that channel actions to the appropriate work center and the appropriate AFSC within that work center.

It is useful to note that each AFSC is associated with a specific work center.[4] That is, a task performed by a specific AFSC in one work center cannot automatically be performed by someone who has the same AFSC but has been assigned to a different work center. However, LCOM inputs do provide for explicit substitutions. If for some reason a person with that AFSC is not available in that work center, the network description may specify an allowable substitute from another work center or another AFSC within the same work center (assuming they are cross-utilization trained, or CUT). If no substitute labor resource is specified or none specified is available, LCOM will defer the action until later.

The availability of labor substitutes is intuitively important: When substitution is possible, bottlenecks that might otherwise arise can be averted. It is not clear that substitutes either from another loca-

---

[4]The data do not explicitly group tasks and resources by work center; instead, such grouping is implicit. Personnel who are members of the same AFSC but who belong to different work centers will be given slightly different designations—for example, 2A5A1 and 2A5B1, where the fourth character serves to distinguish distinct labor pools. Tasks for work center "X" would then specify that individuals of AFSC 2A5A1 were required, while another work center, "Y," would specify the need for AFSC 2A5B1. A completely shared labor pool would be specified simply by having the same AFSC— say, 2A5A1—designated as a labor resource for tasks from multiple work centers.

tion or from a different AFSC are represented according to actual practice. This is not an error on the part of the builders of LCOM data sets but rather is based on a mandate to use "official policy" as opposed to field practice.[5] The net effect is generally to raise LCOM's estimate of manpower requirements, sometimes significantly. This is to be expected a priori. Field practice may diverge from policy for good reason—often when local commanders see opportunities to take advantage of process improvements that official policy has not yet adopted.

The network in LCOM thus represents the business rules and organizational structure of maintenance at the wing level. The network describes what is being done, by whom, and the order of tasks that are assigned to fix a broken aircraft. Networks branch according to what action or actions are necessary. Different branches will be taken depending on which component has failed or whether or not a failure can be duplicated. Multiple branches can be taken simultaneously in the model—for instance, when more than one component has failed. In the network, business rules are reflected, such as how people may move or not move from an underutilized workstation to one that has a queue building up. The availability of test stations and supplies is also represented in the model's network, albeit with less detail, especially in supply. In general, the network representation in LCOM is highly flexible and includes many specialized features that are useful for representing base-level operations.

Constraints apply to the flow of tasks through the maintenance network. Any task generally requires some combination of parts, labor, and equipment resources, and unless the required resources are available, either the task will be delayed or another task will be preempted to make its resources available to the higher-priority task.

Monte Carlo Simulations

Chance is present in the real world and plays a major role in the aircraft maintenance world. Phenomena that are subject to the vagaries of chance include maintenance-specific items such as failures, repair times, and parts availability. Exogenous drivers such as sortie

---

[5]However, this policy is not applied uniformly.

demands and deployment requirements may also have major stochastic components.

The effects of chance are important. For instance, a run of bad luck will sometimes occur in which the breaks that are handled by a given maintenance work center come at a short-term rate that is much higher than average. The LCOM simulation uses what are known as Monte Carlo methods to capture this effect. Monte Carlo methods represent stochastic processes—in the case of LCOM, particularly breaks caused by sorties and labor hours to fix breaks—through statistical distributions from which random samples are drawn to represent real-world events.[6] This allows the model to represent the backlogs that occur when maintenance actions pile up as a result of a run of bad luck. If these backlogs are either too large or too frequent, the sortie schedule cannot be met. The LCOM analyst will then assign additional resources in the model to the work center in question even though the original manpower and/or equipment resources could meet the average throughput requirement.

The use of Monte Carlo methods is essential to sizing the maintenance force to a level that can handle these runs of bad luck. By quantifying the size and frequency of fluctuation-induced backlogs, LCOM can identify the specific maintenance man-hours required to raise the probability of meeting the most demanding maintenance scenarios to any desired level that the Air Force is willing to accept. Clearly, this is a strong advantage of LCOM—assuming that certain conditions regarding data availability and the proper analysis of the statistical properties of those data have been satisfactorily met.

How LCOM Uses Monte Carlo Methods

Like most Monte Carlo simulations, LCOM treats stochastic phenomena by deciding which possible outcome of each random process actually occurred.[7] That is to say, the sequence of events that

---

[6]For a simple description of these methods, see Reuven Y. Rubinstein, *Simulation and the Monte Carlo Method,* Wiley Series in Probability and Mathematical Statistics, New York: John Wiley & Sons, 1981.

[7]It is in principle possible to write a Monte Carlo simulation that follows multiple possible branches. For systems with real-world complexity, however, this technique is generally infeasible and in any event can be viewed as just a mechanism (albeit a

takes place in any one run of a Monte Carlo simulation represents a randomly selected single sequence out of an enormous (or even infinite) number of possibilities. Generally (as well as in the case of LCOM), the choice of a particular event outcome is made by a controlled random selection in which the probability of a particular outcome being chosen is intended to equal that outcome's frequency in the real world. Put another way, the statistical properties of the distributions from which random factors are pulled must be representative of the particular events that are being modeled. These properties include the class of distribution and the parameters that determine its mean and variance. These are central issues in LCOM.

Monte Carlo simulation techniques are essential for treating complex systems that include stochastic processes. However, a single run of a Monte Carlo simulation represents only one of a multitude of possible outcomes. The usual practice for most analyses that use Monte Carlo models is to generate many replications of the simulation run in order to understand the range of possible outcomes (and their likelihoods). This requirement to perform and statistically analyze the results of many runs is a significant burden. A full discussion of this issue is beyond the scope of this study,[8] but it is well understood that alternative approaches, which typically use some sort of "average value" concept, can produce enormously inaccurate answers when any non linear (e.g., threshold) behavior is present in the system. Illustrating this point is a simple example of broken parts queuing for maintenance: If the broken parts all arrive at the average rate—i.e., the (fleet) mean time between failures (MTBF)—then a capability to repair at just this rate will clearly suffice. However, the simulation would completely miss the need to provide for additional capacity to handle cases when several parts break at a rate that exceeds the MTBF.

LCOM analysts have adapted their application of the model to take advantage of the recurring nature of events in aircraft maintenance. First, they will run the model for a simulated period of 180 days or

clever one) for reducing the number of runs needed to get an adequate statistical sample.

[8]A good reference on Monte Carlo methods can be found in George S. Fishman, *Monte Carlo: Concepts, Algorithms, and Applications*, Springer Series in Operations Research, New York: Springer, 1996.

longer. This approach replicates events each day for many days, generating a series of replications automatically; in models that track only single events, this can be done only by running the model through many replications. Each type of event subject to randomness takes place many times during the typical LCOM simulated time period of 180 days or longer. Thus, similar situations recur many times, and as a result, the single LCOM run effectively provides the equivalent of multiple replications.[9] Second, after an LCOM has been solved through calibration of the inputs, it can then be run repeatedly with different initial random number seeds to check the robustness of the simulation. These two adaptations of the standard methodology in LCOM seem methodologically appropriate.

LCOM Monte Carlo Techniques for Generating Aircraft Breaks

It is important to devote some discussion to LCOM's mechanism for generating aircraft breaks. As intimated in the last section, it is nonuniformity, or variation in the occurrence of breaks, that generates the extra stresses and peak demands that the maintenance system must be sized to service. The way LCOM generates breaks should reproduce the real-life patterns that result in peak demand periods. Only to the extent that the frequency and magnitude of the peaks in LCOM are realistic can one be satisfied that a scenario is realistically stressing the (simulated) maintenance system.

Aircraft parts break down in different ways, as illustrated in Figure 3.2. The type A part has a relatively well defined lifetime, with most failures occurring in a narrow range after a certain initial time has passed. The type B part has a constant per-unit-time failure probability, resulting in a characteristic exponential distribution. The type C part is a combination in which there is a relatively high initial failure rate, perhaps corresponding to a common manufacturing defect, after which surviving parts have a relatively well defined lifetime. These failure patterns illustrate only some of the possibilities.

---

[9]Simple tests using C-130 data confirm this. For example, the standard deviation, across 360-day runs, of manpower utilization was only 0.25 percent. The standard deviation of "percent used for unscheduled maintenance" was 1.4 percent for an AFSC (2A7X3) that spent 68 percent of its time on unscheduled maintenance.

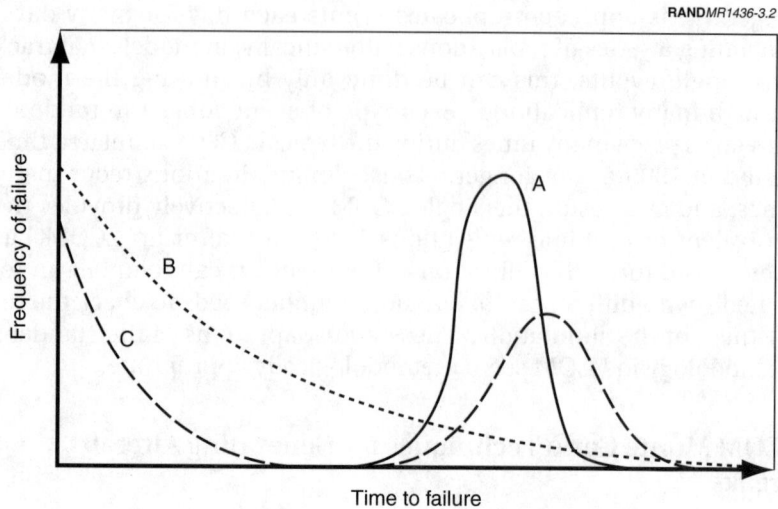

RAND*MR1436-3.2*

Figure 3.2—Various Notional Failure Patterns

Additionally, the "time" axis is a stand-in for whatever the aging mechanism might be. Calendar time is one case, but the mechanism might be flying hours, number of landings, number of times "high-G" turns have been executed, and many others.

The most straightforward way to capture this variety in a simulation would be to determine the break distribution for each part and then simulate the breaks for each individual part, tracked by serial number. However, this approach would be associated with a major data-gathering burden, and in fact the break mechanisms of some parts may not be well understood. LCOM thus takes an alternative approach.

LCOM does not attempt to model the break mechanisms of individual aircraft or individual parts. Instead, the model relies on a fleetwide clock to determine when a particular part, represented by a WUC, will break on some aircraft in the fleet. Clocks count down according to flying hours and/or sortie count, and when a clock is triggered by the total count, the aircraft whose sortie triggered the clock is designated as that in need of repair. This may mean that a particular aircraft could in principle fail for the same part on several successive sorties while another, by luck of the draw, could go without that part failure for a long time. However, this does not appear to be a problem for current LCOM applications, because tracking a realistic break history on any one aircraft is not important for the LCOM purposes; the critical issue is to get a fair representation of the demand for maintenance actions.

The fleetwide break clocks are modeled as stochastic processes according to an exponential distribution. To illustrate this, suppose that a part wears out, on average, once every S sorties. After a failure occurs, a random number is drawn from an exponential distribution with mean S. This random draw initiates a "failure clock." Each time a sortie is flown, the clock is decremented. When it counts down to zero, the aircraft that flew the last sortie is chosen to fail. Since the individual part failure modes clearly do not follow exponential distributions, this practice needs to be justified. The explanation is that the exponential distribution is not applied to each individual aircraft system or even to each aircraft, but rather to the fleet as a whole. If failures in different aircraft are *independent events,* the interval between failures for the fleet can reasonably be assumed to follow an exponential distribution.

This presumption is not generally true in the real world. For instance, the process of queuing for repair can result in a more uniform subsequent break distribution than that given by the exponential distribution. We examined the impact of the "exponential fleet clock" used in LCOM on actual results and found it to be of minor but not negligible importance. Details are discussed in Appendix A.

LCOM Monte Carlo Techniques for Generating Fix Times

LCOM also uses a Monte Carlo approach to determine the labor hours required to remove and repair a line- or shop-reparable unit. In principle, this approach is based on the same logic that applies to breaks, so that instances of unexpectedly high fix times can be guarded against through appropriate additions of manpower. To illustrate this point, suppose that two tasks, each having a lognormal task time distribution with a mean of 1.0 hour and a standard deviation (σ) of 0.29 hour, are performed in parallel. It can be shown that the mean time to finish both tasks is 1.21 hours, not 1.0 hour; such an increase is intuitively obvious, since if either of the tasks has a longer-than-average fix time, the joint process will take longer than average. In the case of parallel tasks with quite different mean durations, however, the total time is essentially given by the mean duration of the longer task; in this case, the variance plays almost no role. As a numeric example, for two parallel tasks where one has a mean of 1.0 hour and a σ of 0.29 hour, and the other a mean of 0.5 hour and a σ of 0.145 hour, the mean duration of the two tasks in parallel is still 1.00, to two decimal places.

Our empirical experiments with LCOM (described later in this chapter) indicate that in practice the variance in fix times does not cause additional queuing in LCOM. On the other hand, increasing the mean fix time will cause queuing, as would be expected. One reason the variance in fix times plays little role in determining LCOM maintenance man-hours is that parallel tasks with approximately equal average durations occur only infrequently. This appears to be due to the specific nature of the networks in LCOM rather than to an inherent characteristic of task networks in general.

An alternative hypothesis for the insignificance of fix-time variance is that wing-level maintenance is deliberately organized to avoid losing sorties due to variance in work time. For example, the time set aside for servicing aircraft before and after sorties is intentionally made generous to accommodate unexpectedly long task durations. Indeed, this is usually taken even to the point of preparing a backup aircraft if unexpected breaks or longer servicing times prevent the first aircraft from flying. Back shops can usually rely on parts inventories for aircraft in need of replacement parts; in other words, back shops work to put serviceable items on the shelf for use when needed. By providing buffers, wing level maintenance organizations can prevent the variance in fix times from affecting the sortie schedule.

DRIVERS OF LCOM OUTPUTS AND ASSOCIATED ISSUES

Several factors constitute primary drivers of LCOM outputs. This section briefly discusses each factor; additional details on some are presented later in this report.

Scenarios

The scenario provides the exogenous demand on the simulated wing level operations. Nearly all maintenance actions in the model are initiated by sorties: pre- and postflight servicing, fixing breaks, and performing scheduled maintenance. The sortie rate demanded is therefore the primary determinant of the overall number of maintenance actions required, but other factors, such as the regularity of the flying schedule (a variable schedule causes peak loads in maintenance) are also important. A basic precept in determining maintenance manpower requirements is that such requirements should be based on the most stressing realistic scenarios. If the scenarios used in LCOM do not represent the most demanding cases, then LCOM will underestimate the requirement for maintenance man-hours and may also understate the true requirement for manpower positions in various specialties.

Policy Constraints

LCOM analysts are instructed to use only "official" values for certain parameters that have a significant impact on the resulting workload.[10] As a matter of necessity, however, these official values are often violated in daily activities throughout the Air Force. For example, LCOM analysts often adjust spares to achieve a state in which a certain percentage of aircraft, as determined by maintenance policy, are non–mission capable due to supply (NMCS)—despite the widely known fact that actual NMCS rates often significantly exceed policy-determined levels. By implication, then, LCOM often overestimates the availability of aircraft and underestimates the extra workload caused by cannibalization of parts from aircraft in NMCS status. Another example is that LCOM analyses do not assume that deploying or warfighting support elements are "filled out" with equipment and personnel from nondeploying units; LCOM analysis is bound by policy to assume that units go to war as they are resourced even when it is well known that this is not the actual practice during either contingencies or wars.

---

[10]Based on conversations with LCOM analysts, who are well aware of the discrepancies between the official values they are directed to use and reality.

In the real world, fiscal constraints prevent the Air Force from funding in accordance with some of its policies. It is an important question whether LCOM business rules should reflect desired policies or whether the model should be calibrated to reflect realistic values. This question has become increasingly critical during a time when the Air Force must contemplate many concurrent deployments and contingencies, not just major wars. In principle, it seems both feasible and desirable that LCOM simulations provide values for desired levels of various variables, as set in policy, as well as for actual values as they are observed in various weapon systems over a recent year or two. This would allow for simulations of any changes in maintenance man-hours resulting from funding and other causes that make it impossible to achieve stated policy objectives. Comparative simulations of this kind should be done for variables that affect direct maintenance man-hours and could be helpful in assessing not just unfunded requirements but also potential sources for efficiencies. As we discuss below, however, many other factors that affect the working environment of maintainers must be analyzed outside LCOM entirely; an enhanced policy simulation capacity in LCOM is only one avenue to pursue.

Maintenance Action Rates

As one would expect, LCOM runs show that average maintenance man-hours scale linearly with maintenance action rates, at least until throughput constraints become binding.[11] In other words, a 10 percent across-the-board increase in the break rates of all systems will result in a 10 percent increase in required maintenance man-hours. However, moderate man-hour changes may not alter the manpower requirements at all. This would most commonly be the case because minimum crew-size requirements are determining the manpower requirement.[12] Given the presence of such manpower rules, LCOM turns out, in practice, to be a highly nonlinear model in manpower— that is to say, a 10 percent increase in break rates may not increase manpower requirements at all even though maintenance man-hours

---

[11]Based on LCOM runs we have made, varying maintenance action rates.

[12]This was clearly seen, for instance, in an analysis we performed using the C-130 LCOM model provided to us by AMC.

increase by 10 percent. It is important to note, however, that in these cases the impact on direct maintenance man-hours still affects the size of the red box, and thus has an effect on the size of the residual white box as well. Hence, a more complete analysis that includes all tasks assigned to maintainers might show an impact on manpower requirements even for relatively small changes in required maintenance man-hours.

Maintenance action rates also drive LCOM outputs by affecting the frequency and magnitude of maintenance backlogs. Even though average maintenance demands can be met, backlogs are generated because of fluctuations both in sortie demands and in maintenance action requirements. Thus, it is important to understand how LCOM generates variation in maintenance actions.

Scheduled maintenance and unscheduled maintenance have significantly different effects on backlog issues. In LCOM, aircraft are represented by tail number, so the time history of individual aircraft can be tracked for the entire simulation period. This allows for a determination of when each aircraft undergoes scheduled maintenance. Maintenance intervals can be based on either flying hours or calendar time. This is comparatively predictable and, more important, comparatively regular, so in the context of a given scenario, scheduled maintenance is not a major source of variation in the occurrence of aircraft maintenance actions. Even though a fleet clock is often used for scheduled maintenance (see Appendix A), the demand for scheduled maintenance will not be subject to much variation. This is because a nonstochastic mechanism, counting down to a fixed (nonrandom) number of flying hours or calendar hours, is used.

In contrast to scheduled maintenance, breaks are an important source of variation in aircraft maintenance. Aircraft are composed of many integrated systems and consist of thousands of replaceable pieces that are welded, bolted, or screwed together—all of which can potentially fail, and many of which fail often. One of the main concerns in LCOM simulations is the completeness and reliability of the break data. In order to allocate maintenance actions to the right work center and AFSC, LCOM needs high-quality data on the probability of failure of each WUC resulting from both sorties and maintenance actions on the aircraft.

Fix Times

The number of maintenance man-hours required to return an aircraft to the pool of available aircraft is the product of a WUC failing and the time it takes to repair that WUC given a failure. Fix times are stochastic in LCOM. Normally, a lognormal distribution is used for fix times. This implies that while the fix time has some average for a given WUC, there is a significant chance that the fix will take much longer than average. Conversely, relatively few maintenance actions take much less time than average. Some effort is made in LCOM audits to estimate the variance of fix times, which can depend both on the particular fixer and on the particular instance of a task. Our sensitivity analysis indicates that in practice, only mean fix times are significant drivers of manpower requirements.

Business Rules

The LCOM network description includes many business rules that determine the flow of tasks through the maintenance network. These rules have significant effects on the efficiency of maintenance activities, and thus their accurate representation is important when determining manpower requirements. Some relevant business rule areas include the following:

Task manpower requirements. The LCOM network descriptions include manpower required for each task by AFSC and work center as well as allowable manpower substitutions.

Task priorities and scheduling. In LCOM, tasks are typically associated with rigid priority rules that govern their choice and timing (and their preemption in the presence of resource conflicts). The use of LCOM "attributes" can add a degree of flexibility, but they are apparently inadequate to represent the complexities of smart scheduling practices.[13]

Cannibalization is a practice used when parts are not available from local stores; the part is removed or "cannibalized" from another

---

[13]For example, we observed several cases in which workarounds were used to "capture the effect" of intelligent scheduling of curing and engine run-ups rather than having LCOM explicitly represent actual practice.

aircraft. Policy regarding cannibalization is also represented in the model, and we have noted the discrepancy between officially stated maintenance policy and real-life practice—a difference that is not reflected in LCOM. As for other classes of business rules, the LCOM capability is not as flexible as real-world practice. For example, rigid limits are imposed on the number of aircraft that are allowed to be available for cannibalization as well as on the number of "holes" (engines in the inventory that are broken) allowed per aircraft. Additionally, it is unclear whether the time and resources associated with tasks such as panel removals for access are double-counted for cannibalization.

HOW LCOM IS USED TO DETERMINE SHIFT MANNING REQUIREMENTS

LCOM Is Part of an Analytical Process

It is important to understand that the LCOM simulation does not directly determine maintenance manpower requirements. Rather, it determines, through a manually controlled "optimization process," the shift manning requirements needed to satisfy the input scenario's sortie demands. LCOM analysts then convert this maintenance shift manning into what tables in LCOM reports label as "manpower requirements." This section discusses the process of determining shift manning requirements.

Figure 3.3 depicts this process. Generally, an initial run is made with no constraints on either parts or labor, but this has nothing to do with the optimization process per se. Rather, it serves as a shake-down for the input data sets and as a means of ensuring that the simulation, given unlimited access to all resources, can satisfy the sortie scenario's requirements. The first real step in estimating the minimum resources required to meet the sortie schedule is to constrain spare parts until a target NMCS rate is achieved. This step consists of an iterative series of runs, making adjustments to spare parts inventories until the desired NMCS rate is achieved.

Once spares have been constrained, the final step is to limit manpower. This is done in principle by constraining each individual AFSC/work center combination until further reduction would drive

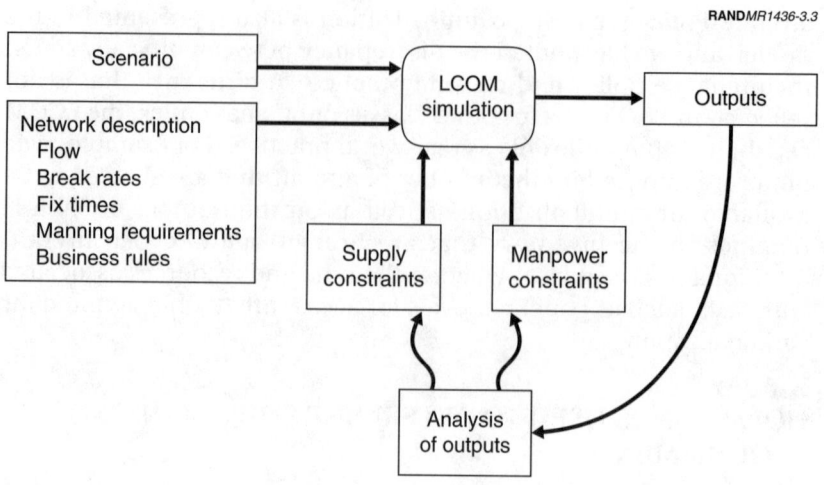

Figure 3.3—The LCOM Manual Optimization Process

sortie production below acceptable targets. It is not precisely clear what this means. *Some* reduction in sortie rate due to a personnel reduction must be acceptable depending on the magnitude of the trade-offs, as depicted notionally in Figure 3.4. For instance, would one want to man to a level that can produce the required sorties even in the event of an unlucky confluence of failures, the like of which occurs less than once a year? Suppose this would require adding several people to one shift for 365 days to meet a peak demand that occurs only once? If the resulting improvement would be only one sortie, the answer is probably no. In other words, actual LCOM calibrations must include the application of a subjective sanity criterion so that obvious absurdities are avoided. Figure 3.4 illustrates this principle. As this figure shows, there is a cost associated with driving down the risk of an unsatisfied sortie demand. At a certain point, the cost of protecting against an additional minuscule reduction in risk is not worthwhile.

The impact on sortie production also depends on stochastic factors, so to examine the issue with LCOM, one must presumably replicate a run many times with different random-number seeds. As noted above, our understanding of the practice here is that different

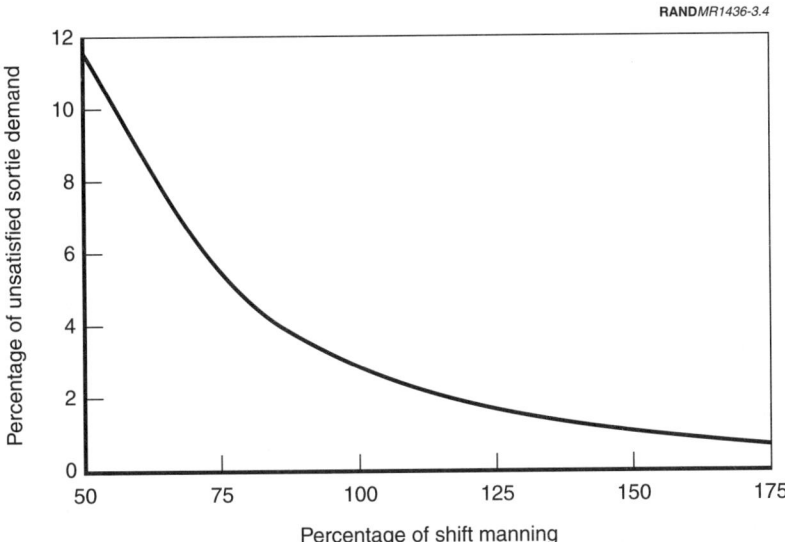

RAND*MR1436-3.4*

Figure 3.4—Notional Risk as Shift Manning (Cost) Increases

random-number seeds may be used at the end of other constraining steps as a check on the outcomes.

The shift manning that results from this process should be cognizant of minimum crew-size requirements and other special rules for certain positions. In an engine swap, for example, most steps may require only one or two technicians, but the lowering of the old engine and the hoisting of the new one may require four or five for safety reasons. Another example is that there are certain requirements, such as providing a specialist for end-of-runway presence, that are invariant with sortie rates, break rates, and fix times. LCOM input requires that the analyst specify the minimum crew size and the number of technicians for each task. It is possible, however, that a limiting task is so rare that it is not picked up even in many repetitions of LCOM runs. Such rare minimum manning requirements must thus be captured by processing the LCOM task requirement data offline. As previously noted, it is also important to confirm that such manning requirements are in fact necessary; could an alternative AFSC, with appropriate task training, round out the crew?

Using the LCOM Simulation Outputs

As noted earlier, the result of this sequence of steps is a set of shift mannings. However, more than one manpower allowance is needed to fill the requirement for a person on any one shift. The reason is that in wartime, all shifts must be fully manned 24 hours per day, seven days a week, every day of the month. The Air Force does not require a full shift of every person every day for a whole month, and therefore the requirement for one manpower slot on a shift during wartime requires the allotment of more than one person to that shift.

Finally, it should be noted that where resources are successively constrained to meet a sortie generation requirement, the LCOM calibration process does not represent "optimization" in the true sense of the word. The process takes the networks and tasks associated with each AFSC as given and obeys minimum crew-size and other policy rules in such a way as to ensure that sortie requirements can be met. The goal is to ensure that there are sufficient resources to meet the output goal while only approximately minimizing the manpower requirement objective.[14] Other factors—for example, cost—are also important, but there could easily exist methods of reaching the sortie production goal that would cost the Air Force less when all relevant areas (manpower, test stands, parts, cannibalizations, etc.) are considered. A full cost optimization would consider the marginal costs of all resources as well as their marginal contribution to the sortie requirement. Such a model would also allow various inputs to be traded against one another; for example, the value of capital investments to reduce man-hours could be examined, or the costs and benefits of reassigning tasks across work centers and AFSCs could be assessed.

LCOM is not intended to produce this type of optimization. It is, at heart, a manpower planning tool that can be expected to ensure only that the manpower resources provided are not constraining the sor-

---

[14]Note that the solution found by this process is not unique. For instance, there are alternative ways of applying parts constraints that lead to the same overall NMCS target rate, and there are alternative shift mannings that lead to the same overall sortie generation capability. We have not looked at how much the "equivalent" shift mannings differ from each other, nor have we tried to determine whether a rigorously optimal manpower requirement minimization would differ significantly from the solutions found using the current process.

tie generation requirement. Thus, the use of LCOM to determine manpower requirements is better described as a satisficing process, not an optimizing one.

RUNNING WITH THE MODEL: DATA AND EXPERIMENTS

LCOM is a highly detailed simulation. Its resulting ability to capture the impacts of the interplay of resource constraints, sortie demands, and breaks can in principle help yield estimates of maintenance manpower requirements that are more accurate than those supplied by simpler models. However, this capability comes with an enormous appetite for data. Limits on data accuracy imply limits on the accuracy of the manpower requirements developed by LCOM. This section discusses these data issues and also reports on some experimental test runs we performed.

Relationship Between Input and Output

LCOM represents maintenance as using resources—labor, spare parts, test stands, etc.—to produce an output: the repair and servicing of aircraft. Adding more of one of the inputs will result in an increased output per workday. In economic terminology, this effect is called the *marginal product of the input.* For small changes in the inputs, there will be a linear relationship between inputs and outputs—implying that the marginal product is a constant. This means that an increase of an input by x percent will result in an increase in the output by the same x percent.

Note that because of threshold effects—for instance, minimum crew-size requirements—the marginal product is zero or close to zero for a certain interval. If the required maintenance can be performed virtually all the time by a four-person team working full time at a workstation, then adding another person just to meet a requirement that rarely occurs will not raise the output of the team except when that rare task arises. In that case, the marginal product of the last person is virtually zero, although his presence can be critical at the time the rare task is needed to get the aircraft back to the ready pool. In such a case, a considerable change in an input can be made before there is an impact on some output variable, although other output variables might well change with even small changes to the input in question.

The converse does not apply: If a minimum crew-size constraint is operative, then the removal of even a single person from a shift can disrupt operations. That is to say, when a minimum crew-size constraint is binding, the marginal product will be zero only for positive changes in personnel.

We performed several experiments using a C-130 data set obtained from AMC. AMC LCOM analysts state that this data set is characteristic of a "final" LCOM run. That is, both parts and labor are fully constrained and the sortie demands are realistic. In other words, the data set is characteristic of the end point of the calibration process described in the previous section. Some of our basic findings are as follows:

Maintenance man-hours scale as expected with task frequency. All break rates were doubled, and the result was that unscheduled maintenance man-hours increased by 66.9 percent and scheduled maintenance man-hours by 1.5 percent. This is more or less consistent with first-order expectations of 100 percent and 0 percent.

There is very little sensitivity to task duration variances. This is also expected. There are certainly theoretical situations in which variation in task duration can matter. In practice, however, such conditions do not seem to characterize the C-130 network. As an example, one might expect to see an increase in the variance of task duration result in lost sorties in situations where the average preflight preparation time is close to the mission lead time. However, such tight time lines should not be allowed to arise in a real wing and thus are not expected to occur in LCOM data models of wing operations. In our tests, doubling the task duration standard deviations had no statistically significant impact on sortie generation. As noted above, mean task times are very important in determining maintenance man-hours required, but task time variance does not appear to be relevant.

Changing mean task durations by small amounts produced a response close to the first-order expectation of an elasticity equal to one in many outputs.[15] With a 10 percent increase in all task durations, the elasticities in Table 3.2 were observed.

_____

[15]A degree of elasticity is obtained by converting a marginal product into percentage terms.

Table 3.2

Percentage Change in Output for a 10 Percent Increase in Mean Task Duration

Average Presortie	Average Postsortie	Manpower Utilization Rate (M-UTE)	Man-Hours/ Flying Hours
0.74	0.90	0.97	1.14

It is important to assess how much of the information gathered for the LCOM runs that drive manpower requirements is actually relevant to determining those requirements. We performed LCOM test runs on two aircraft types, the C-130 and the F-15C/D. These aircraft types were selected in part because of data-set availability and in part because they allowed us to examine both a large aircraft and a fighter.

C-130 Results

There is significant indication that, at least for the C-130 data provided to RAND by AMC, LCOM manpower requirements are determined primarily by minimum crew-size considerations. We base this conclusion on the observation that sortie demand can be increased significantly while manpower is held unchanged. In other words, important factors that *might* be—and that one may *expect* to be—constraining the maintenance system do not, in practice, appear to be constraining the C-130 model from meeting its target sortie requirements. While there are some increases in maintenance manhours, these are insufficient to require additional shift personnel. Minimum crew sizes, an input variable to LCOM, are sufficiently large that output can be increased within existing limits.

To examine the degree to which sortie demand is constraining the system, we adjusted the input data to increase the demand for missions by up to 160 percent of the baseline sorties in the model. In fact, the daily demand for missions in the C-130 LCOM model is stochastic[16] owing to the random draw nature of the actual number

---

[16]This is actually a choice made by the developers of the input data. For the C-130, such a stochastic approach was used. For F-15C/D data that we have also examined, a deterministic mission demand was used.

of missions demanded and because of the variable number of air-craft demanded for each mission type. Hence, as we gradually in-creased the expected demand for sorties in 10 percent increments to 160 percent of the baseline, the actual demand increases differed somewhat from these expected values.

Figure 3.5 shows the fraction of missions and sorties accomplished as we increased the actual mission and sortie demands. The gray ellipses represent individual cases of associated mission and sortie demands. In general, for a given case the percentage increase in sor-tie demand (versus the baseline) differs from the percentage increase in mission demand. This is because different missions have different sortie counts, and the randomness of mission selection made it diffi-cult to control the exact mix. Note that the percentage of missions accomplished is generally larger than the percentage of sorties ac-complished. This is true because some missions can be flown with less than the nominal requested number of aircraft.

The primary observation is that over the one-year period simulated, sorties could be produced in much higher numbers than the baseline

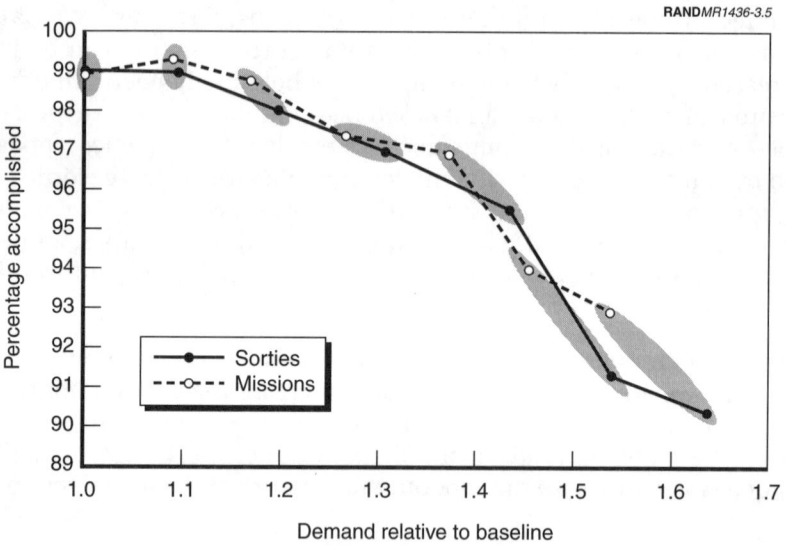

Figure 3.5—Mission Sortie Accomplishment as Scheduling Load Increases

scenario demanded. Even for a 60 percent increase in demand, over 90 percent of the sorties were accomplished, with an overall mission accomplishment rate of 93 percent.

The test also demonstrated that limits on manpower utilization rates (M-UTEs) are only a minor factor in determining the C-130 maintenance manpower levels contained in the available data set.[17] M-UTEs express the direct maintenance man-hours expended by a particular AFSC as a percentage of total primary duty hours. Figure 3.6 shows the average M-UTE as well as the maximum M-UTE that any one AFSC attained for the sortie demand increases we imposed on the model. The top line in Figure 3.6 indicates that utilization rates do not reach AMC's maximum allowable direct labor utilization level of 60 percent until sortie demand is increased by 30 percent,

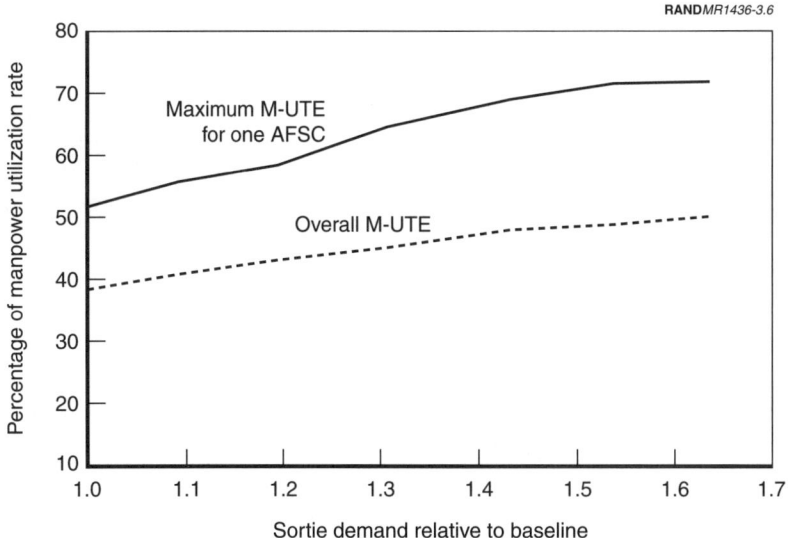

Figure 3.6—M-UTEs vs. Sortie Demand

---

[17]As will be discussed further in Chapter Four, each MAJCOM in the Air Force may set its own rules regarding what constitutes excessive M-UTEs. In AMC, the rule is 60 percent of available working hours; in ACC, it is 78 percent. As noted, actual M-UTEs rarely reach these levels.

and then only for two AFSCs (2A1X3 and 2A4X1).[18] Even for a 60 percent increase in sortie demand the maximum utilization rate is less than 72 percent, and only three AFSCs (2A1X3, 2A4X1, and 2A5X1) exceed 60 percent.

Other measures show signs of stress in the wing as sortie demand increases. The NMCS rate rises from 5.5 percent to 10.1 percent with a 30 percent increase in sortie demand, and for a 60 percent increase the NMCS rate increases to 16.3 percent. Also, the percentage of aircraft that are operationally ready falls from 51.5 percent (baseline) to 35.5 percent (+30 percent sortie demand) to 23.3 percent (+60 percent sortie demand). However, these are indirect measures of fleet health, and the NMCS rate is reasonable even for the +60 percent demand case. The fact that even for the 60 percent demand increase so much additional sortie production can be maintained over an entire year is a strong indicator that there is excess system capacity in the baseline case.

In order to examine the sustainability issue more carefully, we ran the +60 percent sortie demand case for a second simulated year. There was evidence of some deterioration as compared with the initial year. Table 3.3 shows that there is a statistically significant degradation for all measures except the maximum single-AFSC M-UTE. On the other hand, the degradation was not very large; by and large, the wing's performance did not deteriorate by a significant amount in our extended simulation.

The clear conclusion of our experiment is that the final manpower calibration in the LCOM C-130 model is not tightly constrained. Why, then, are the manpower levels set where they are? From our analysis, it appears that minimum crew-size requirements are generally responsible. As expected, the simulation may determine maintenance man-hours, which are determined mainly by the mean fix time for each WUC, but minimum crew sizes are determined outside the LCOM simulation entirely.

We examined several of the AFSCs listed in Table 3.4 to check this hypothesis. The 2A5R1 AFSC proved to be the extreme example of minimum crew size determining shift manning. There is a single

---

[18]See Table 3.4 for a list of AFSC names.

Table 3.3

Degradation over Time of an Overdriven C-130 Wing

	Year 1 (%)		Year 2 (%)		Significance of Difference (standard deviations)
	Value	Standard Deviation	Value	Standard Deviation	
Percentage of scheduled missions accomplished	93.80	0.27	91.56	0.41	3.5
Percentage of scheduled sorties accomplished	90.06	0.23	88.20	0.47	3.5
NMCS rate	16.01	0.17	17.73	0.44	3.7
Percentage operationally ready	21.46	0.41	19.07	0.67	3.0
M-UTE	50.57	0.27	51.66	0.29	3.7
Maximum M-UTE in one AFSC	75.10	1.27	76.50	1.12	0.8

Table 3.4

LCOM C-130 Shift Mannings

AFSC	Name	Shift 1	Shift 2	Shift 3
2A1X2	Avionics Guidance and Control System	2	0	0
2A1X3	Communication and Navigation Systems	3	0	0
2A1X7	Electronic Warfare Systems	3	0	0
2A4X1	Aircraft Guidance and Control	3	2	2
2A4X2	Aircraft Communication and Navigation Systems	2	2	2
2A5I1	Aerospace Maintenance	8	7	7
2A5R1	Aerospace Maintenance	6	2	2
2A5T1	Aerospace Maintenance	1	0	0
2A5X1	Aerospace Maintenance	16	16	16
2A6I1	Aerospace Propulsion	4	4	0
2A6S5	Aircraft Hydraulic Systems	4	0	0
2A6S6	Aircraft Electrical and Environmental Systems	4	0	0
2A6X1	Aerospace Propulsion	6	6	3
2A6X4	Aircraft Fuel Systems	6	6	4
2A6X5	Aircraft Hydraulic Systems	4	4	4
2A6X6	Aircraft Electrical and Environmental Systems	3	3	2
2A7X1	Aircraft Metals Technology	10	10	10
2A7X3	Aircraft Structural Maintenance	4	2	0

task (CARGODR) requiring six 2A5R1s, but it is extremely rare. In fact, it occurred only once over a year's simulation, arising in the case of the baseline sortie demand. Moreover, the next-largest crew-size requirement for 2A5R1 is only three, and a task requiring three 2A5R1s occurred only seven times in a year. Finally, the utilization of 2A5R1 is very low, totaling only 22 percent. This situation certainly seems to be a candidate for a process improvement. Are six 2A5R1s really needed, or can, say, CUT workers from other AFSCs meet some of the manpower requirement for the "high manpower" tasks?

The 2A5X1 (aerospace maintenance) AFSC had shift manning levels of 16/16/16, yet it had only a 43 percent M-UTE for the baseline sortie demand and did not exceed 60 percent until the sortie demand was increased by 60 percent. The largest single task manning requirement was seven, and this was required only slightly more than once per week. Three tasks had this requirement: ACTOW1, DWSH-TOW, and FULLJACK.[19] Based on the average duration and number of occurrences of each task, we calculate that two such tasks overlap—and thus require 14 people—less than once every ten days.[20] This begs the question of whether seven 2A5X1s are actually required or if other AFSCs with low utilization rates could substitute during those rare high-manpower-demand cases.

Next, consider the 2A1X7 AFSC (electronic warfare). It has a single shift of size three and an M-UTE (42 percent) that increases only modestly with sortie demand. The 2A1X7 AFSC has a number of lengthy tasks (I76A, I76B, I76J, I76N) that require all three people. These tasks collectively occur only 125 times in an entire year, but because of their duration (an average of 7.75 hours) and the fact that there is only a single shift of 2A1X7, these tasks alone induce a utilization rate of 33 percent.[21] It thus seems completely appropriate to retain a minimum shift size of three.

---

[19]Unfortunately, the LCOM data sets do not include a description of what is actually performed for these tasks.

[20]ACTOW1 occurred 248 times in one year and lasted 3.2 hours. DWSHTOW occurred 235 times and lasted 0.55 hour. FULLJACK occurred four times and lasted 1.463 hours. The calculation of overlap assumes that all tasks occur independently with these rates and durations.

[21]Task man-hours = $125 \times 7.75 \times 3$(task manning) = 2906. Shift hours = $365.25 \times 8 \times 3$(shift manning) = 18766. M-UTE = task man-hours/shift hours = 0.33.

The 2A6S5 AFSC has a single shift size of four and, like 2A1X7, has a low (24.5 percent) utilization rate that does not change substantially with sortie demand. However, this AFSC never requires more than two people to perform any task. An overlap calculation similar to that made for 2A5X1 was performed. However, because in this case there are only eight working hours per day (single shift), an overlap of two of these tasks occurs about once a week.[22] Given the low utilization rate, it is not obvious that the larger crew size (four) is justified. To examine this, we reduced the baseline sortie demand manning for 2A6S5 to a shift manning of three. There was no significant change in the mission or sortie production rates or in NMCS or percent operationally ready. However, the utilization rate for 2A6S5 increased from 24.5 percent to 50.7 percent. This increase is, of course, expected.

F-15C/D Results

The data for the F-15C/D indicate that the system is constrained: Attempts to increase the sortie demand result in a low response. Figure 3.7 indicates that only about 26 percent of the additional sortie demand is actually satisfied (note that the scale difference between the horizontal and vertical axes, which are necessary for readability, distorts the visual image). This compares with about 90 percent for the C-130, as sortie requirements increased by 30 percent. The result is that for the F-15C/D, the sortie accomplishment rate drops rapidly from its baseline value of 85 percent to 63 percent at 11,000 scheduled sorties. Changes in other measures, including NMCS and operationally ready rates, are consistent with this result.

It is not clear, however, that manpower is the binding constraint on the system. For the baseline case, the average M-UTE is only 32 percent, and no single AFSC has a utilization rate as large as 47 percent.

---

[22]Two hundred thirty-three two-man tasks were undertaken in a year for the nominal sortie demand case, with an average duration of 3.47 hours. Based on a seven-day eight-hour shift, a simplified calculation using eight hours per day indicates 1.24 overlaps per week, while a more detailed calculation gives 1.04 overlaps per week.

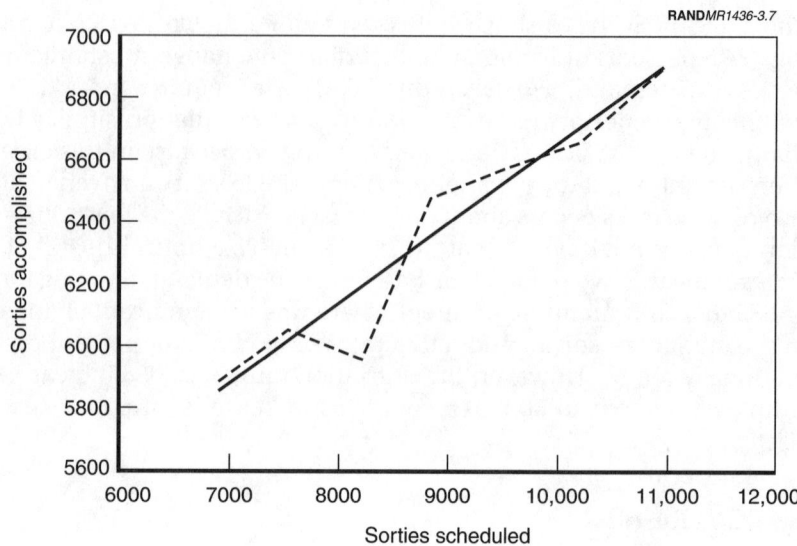

Figure 3.7—F-15C/D SGR Response to Increased Sortie Demand

Additionally, the shift manning levels for a number of AFSCs were well in excess of minimum crew-size requirements. However, one cannot rule out the possibility that manpower could still be a constraint owing to time-critical bottlenecks: It is possible that the M-UTE can be very high at certain critical but short time periods.

To check this hypothesis, we slightly lowered the staffing for several AFSCs (avoiding going below minimum crew size) and looked at the resulting sortie production. After five runs were conducted for both the baseline and low-manpower cases, it appeared that there was a small but marginally statistically significant degradation in the SGR (and in closely related statistics such as percentage of sorties accomplished). Table 3.5 shows that as maintenance manpower is lowered, the SGR decreases from 93.4 percent to 91.9 percent. This is a 1.91 σ effect, corresponding to a 5.6 percent chance occurrence. There is no significant change in NMCS, but the percent operationally ready rate decreases from 4.15 percent to 3.70 percent. This change is a 2.83 σ effect and thus is almost certainly significant (0.5 percent chance).

Table 3.5

Degradation of an 18-PMAI F-15C/D Squadron with a Six-Person
Maintenance Manpower Reduction[a]

Variable	Nominal Manpower		Lowered Manpower		Significance of Difference (standard deviations)
	Value	Standard Deviation	Value	Standard Deviation	
Percentage of scheduled missions accomplished	93.14%	0.34%	91.26%	0.47%	1.52
Percentage of scheduled sorties accomplished	84.94%	0.49%	83.56%	0.53%	1.91
NMCS rate	9.20%	0.29%	9.39%	0.18%	0.55
Percentage operationally ready	4.15%	0.12%	3.70%	0.10%	2.83
M-UTE	31.99%	0.20%	33.82%	0.11%	3.71
SGR	0.934	0.0054	0.919	0.0059	1.91

[a]PMAI = primary mission aircraft inventory.

Collectively, these results certainly appear to be statistically significant, although chance cannot be completely ruled out. Despite the fairly low average utilization rates, it therefore seems that manpower is in fact a binding constraint on the F-15C/D organization depicted in the ACC LCOM.[23] Compare this with the C-130 case, where, because minimum crew size determines so much of the shift manning, other network data play a lesser role in determining the manpower requirement. For the F-15C/D, more of the shift manning requirement will thus be determined by factors such as break rates, task durations, and business rule issues.

SUMMARY

In this chapter, we described how LCOM, a simulation model that uses Monte Carlo methodology, is used to estimate the requirement for maintenance man-hours. LCOM is driven by data on flying schedules required to support operational scenarios, break rates, re-

---

[23]As noted above, the lack of availability of the manpower matrix report in our version of the LCOM software prevented us from directly confirming which specific bottleneck constraints would explain the reported effects on the maintenance statistics in the presence of low average M-UTEs.

quirements for scheduled maintenance, descriptions of wing-level maintenance networks, fix times for maintenance actions, business rules reflecting policy decisions, and a representation of required resources other than manpower. We noted how analysts then translate the required man-hours into shift manning levels for each work center and occupational skill code. The result is a computation of the resources required to satisfy a desired output level. The most important element of the desired output is to meet the sortie requirements, but other goals, such as the avoidance of a steady decline in the pool of available aircraft or a continuously rising NMCS rate, also represent desired features of the final calibration of the model. Finally, we noted how important decisions are made by the analysts in charge of building and calibrating each model. Valid differences of professional opinion about networks or business rules, or about the relative importance of other output goals beyond SGRs, may have a degree of influence over the final estimates of maintenance man-hours and shift manning required by the model.

In our examination of the two working LCOMs provided by the Air Force, we found that in at least one such model, LCOM estimates of required shift manning are not determined primarily by the maintenance man-hours resulting from the simulation. Rather, inputs regarding the minimum crew size required to perform certain tasks largely determine the shift manning. As a result, some simulated M-UTEs are very low, varying from around 10 percent up to 45 or even 50 percent. Experienced LCOM modelers in ACC, AFSOC, AFMIA, and AMC have told us that this is a common feature of many LCOM mission design series (MDS) models.[24] On the other hand, this feature is not universal: For the F-15C/D model that we examined, minimum crew size was not the primary constraining factor for most AFSCs.

---

[24]An analyst in one command told us that one of their aircraft is a candidate for a new engine because the current engine is unreliable and consumes significant maintenance man-hours. The engine analysts asked how many manpower spaces would be saved in an LCOM run from a more reliable engine. The answer was essentially zero. The reason was that it will still take x number of engine specialists to raise and lower an engine on a swap-out, and there were other tasks with rules regarding crew size that would be completely unaffected by the purchase of a new engine.

Chapter Four

THE RED BOX: ASSESSMENT OF HOW LCOM IS APPLIED

INTRODUCTION

In this chapter, we examine some of the analytical questions that arise in the use of LCOM. We begin by discussing the role of the LCOM network representation and by outlining issues associated with its use of WUCs and appropriate levels of data detail. We then analyze the relationship between the networks and the available break-rate data. We also examine the quality of automated data and describe how these data are supplemented by field audits. Finally, we explore other key issues, including the application of spares constraints in the model; the role of minimum crew sizes in LCOM results; and the many challenges maintainers face that are not included in LCOM analyses.

WORK UNIT CODES AND THE COMPLEXITY OF THE LCOM NETWORKS

Since the network is such an integral element of the model, we provide a few illustrations to demonstrate the complexity of the LCOM approach. The first point to make is that the level of detail at which the network is described is a matter of analytical choice. The accompanying tables illustrate this point.

Table 4.1 gives the Air Force–designated name and assigned code number for the 32 major systems on all aircraft, designated as two-digit WUCs. Within each of these major systems there are major

Table 4.1

Air Force Two-Digit WUCs

Two-Digit Aircraft Systems[a]	Number of Three-Digit Subsystems in C-5	Number of Five-Digit WUCs in C-5
11 Airframe	23	4254
12 Crew Station	9	622
13 Landing Gear	17	752
14 Flight Controls	7	902
23 Engine	19	805
24 Auxiliary Power Plant	1	166
41 Environmental Control Systems	8	379
42 Electric Power System	7	224
44 Lighting System	3	284
45 Hydraulic and Pneumatic Systems	6	225
46 Fuel System	10	249
47 Oxygen System	2	89
49 Miscellaneous Utilities	3	207
51 Flight Instruments	6	176
52 Autopilot Instrumentation	7	358
55 Malfunction Analysis Recorder	3	476
59 Flight Management System/Global Positioning System	2	51
61 HF Communication System	13	115
62 VHF Communication System	5	72
63 UHF Communication System	3	84
64 Interphone System	3	80
65 Identification Friend or Foe (IFF) System	2	66
66 Emergency Communications	6	115
68 AFSATCOM	1	5
69 Miscellaneous Communications Equipment	1	20
71 Radio Navigation System	9	190
72 Radar Navigation System	4	168
74 Fire Control System	0	0
75 Weapon Delivery System	0	0
76 Penetration Aids and Electronic Countermeasures	2	28
91 Emergency Equipment	4	44
97 Explosive Devices and Components	1	5
Total	187	11,211

[a]HF = high frequency; VHF = very high frequency; UHF = ultrahigh frequency; AFSATCOM = Air Force satellite communications.

subsystems, and these become more specific to each aircraft type. In the Air Force classification system, subsystems embedded in the two-digit WUCs are designated as three-digit WUCs. There are 180 three-digit subsystems on the C-5 Galaxy transport aircraft.[1] Table 4.2 provides a listing of three-digit WUCs for the C-5 airframe.

While there is in principle a classification system at the four-digit level, LCOM analysts seem to bypass this level and instead go directly to the five-digit level. The five-digit WUC level generally represents a

Table 4.2

Three-Digit WUCs for the C-5 Galaxy Airframe (11)

WUC	System
11A	Windshield and Windows
11B	Visor Door System
11D	Forward Extension Ramp System
11E	Forward Cargo Loading System
11F	Aft Cargo Loading System
11G	Aft Loading Ramp System
11H	Aft Pressure Door System
11J	Aft Cargo Center Door System
11K	Aft Cargo Side Door System
11L	Doors, Fuselage
11M	Personnel/Emergency Exit Doors, Aft
11N	Service Relief Crew Compartment Door
11P	Service Door, Troop Compartment
11Q	Doors, Access and Inspection
11R	Hatches, Fuselage
11S	Structure Assembly, Fuselage, Complete
11T	Wing Structure Complete
11U	Empennage, Structure, Complete
111	SCM Moving Pressure Bulkhead System[a]
112	SCM Aft Cargo Door Instrumentation
113	SCM Pressure Door System
114	SCM Aft Ramp System
115	Internal and External Power, SCM Container

[a]SCM = space cargo modified.

---

[1]All the following information about the WUCs in the C-5B is taken from the C-5B technical order.

part on the aircraft that can be removed and replaced and that in many cases can also be repaired at the wing level. For illustrative purposes, Table 4.3 lists the five-digit WUCs for the C-5 airframe empennage. For wing-level maintenance, the five-digit level is a convenient stopping place: It represents parts on which unit personnel perform maintenance, especially servicing, testing, removal, replacement, and often repairs. Therefore, the five-digit level is in principle a natural order of detail to work toward in modeling Air Force aircraft maintenance as it represents discrete and recognizable maintenance actions undertaken by maintainers in sortie generation and maintenance squadrons.

The Appropriate Network Level of Detail

The WUCs represent critical decision variables in the design of a particular LCOM model for every aircraft. WUCs are particularly critical because they are the primary determinants of the workload that the model is designed to simulate. The more detailed the description of the aircraft—i.e., the finer the level of WUCs—the greater the fidelity in the simulation of actual workload (as long as attendant data on break rates are accurate). In principle, it would therefore be desirable to run the model at the five-digit WUC level.

There are two additional reasons one would prefer to base an LCOM on the five-digit level of codes. One is that maintenance personnel, as mentioned above, tend to think and perform their work at the five-digit level. This has practical implications for the data-gathering effort, which requires extensive interviews with people in the field. The other is that the automated data systems into which field maintainers routinely enter data on maintenance actions (e.g., Core Automated Maintenance System [CAMS] and GO-81) are designed to operate at the five-digit level. The examples in Table 4.3 are therefore the same codes that the specialist working on those parts of the aircraft is expected to enter into the data system at the end of the shift so that appropriate records of each maintenance action are kept. These computerized records are the basic source LCOM analysts use to estimate the workload that LCOM will simulate.

Table 4.3

**Five-Digit WUCs for the C-5 Galaxy Complete Empennage
Structure (11U)**

WUC	System
11UA0	Horizontal Stabilizer
11UAA	Horizontal Stabilizer Assembly
11UAB	Tip Assembly, Horizontal Stabilizer
11UAD	Frame
11UAE	Intercostal
11UAF	Box Beam Structure Assembly, Horizontal Stabilizer
11UAG	Access Panels, General
11UAH	Leading Edge Structure Assembly
11UAJ	Support, Hinge Fitting, Elevator
11UAL	Seal, Aerodynamic, Horizontal Stabilizer
11UAM	Bullet Assembly, Forward Section
11UAN	Cone, Long-Range Aid to Navigation (LORAN) Antenna, Forward Bullet Section
11UAR	Bullet Assembly, Center Section
11UAT	Shroud, Bullet Center Section
11UA9	Not Otherwise Coded (NOC)
11UC0	Vertical Stabilizer
11UCB	Frame
11UCC	Intercostal
11UCD	Box Beam Structure Assembly, Vertical Stabilizer
11UCE	Support, Rudder Hinge Fitting, No. 1
11UCF	Support, Rudder Hinge Fitting, No. 2
11UCG	Support, Rudder Hinge Fitting, No. 3
11UCH	Support, Rudder Hinge Fitting, No. 4
11UCJ	Support, Rudder Hinge Fitting, No. 5
11UCK	Support, Rudder Hinge Fitting, No. 6
11UCL	Support, Rudder Hinge Fitting, No. 7
11UCM	Support, Rudder Hinge Fitting, No. 8
11UCN	Leading Edge, Vertical Stabilizer
11UCP	Access Panels, General
11UCQ	Seal, Aerodynamic
11UCR	Pivot Assembly, Horizontal to Vertical Stabilizer
11UCS	Bearing Assembly, Pivot
11UCT	Ladder, Service, Empennage
11UCU	Fitting Assembly, Support, Rudder Actuator, Upper
11UCV	Fitting Assembly, Support, Rudder Actuator, Lower
11UCW	Seal, Side Bullet, Aft Bullet Section
11UCX	Seal, Shroud, Upper, Aft Bullet Section
11UCY	Seal, Aerodynamic, Skirt Fairing
11UCZ	Restraint Fitting, Personnel, Empannage
11UC9	NOC

FEEDING THE DRAGON: LCOM AS A DATA-INTENSIVE MODEL

Next, we discuss the implications of LCOM's data requirements; the requirements for accuracy that the use of the data implies; and whether the available data satisfy these requirements. Major subtopics deal with break data; the implications of time- and scenario-dependent break data for determining manpower requirements; and fix times (and the related issue of skill mix).

Break Data Requirements in LCOM

For LCOM to be an accurate simulation tool, the data must provide the best possible estimate of the removal rates caused by every sortie. In LCOM, break processes are represented as a mean X between failures, where X represents sorties, flying hours, or some combination of both. Even when working at the five-digit WUC level, LCOM analysts will often use failure clocks representing breaks at the two- or three-digit level. The network description then provides the probabilities of each more detailed (say, five-digit-level) failure, given that a failure somewhere in the system or subsystem has occurred. This is equivalent to specifying *mutually exclusive* five-digit failure rates. In particular, if the individual five-digit break rates for a system are given by r_i, then a single composite (three-digit) break rate given by $R = \Sigma r_i$ and mutually exclusive branch probabilities p_i given by r_i / R provide an equivalent model. This representation is illustrated diagrammatically in Figure 4.1.

Figure 4.1 illustrates a system failure clock that advances one tick every time an event (a sortie or a flying hour) occurs. On average, a failure in the illustrated system may occur, say, once every four events, but the random seed in LCOM allows for variation around this mean, and this sets the failure clock. After a given number of ticks, the clock triggers a failure of a three-digit-level system, labeled 11X00 in the figure. Once this system has failed, LCOM undertakes another random draw to determine which of the five-digit items has failed in accordance with appropriate conditional probabilities.

It is important to note that this practice assumes that the five-digit failures are mutually exclusive—that is, that only one subsystem at a time can fail. The obvious alternative formulation, where each five-

RANDMR1436-4.1

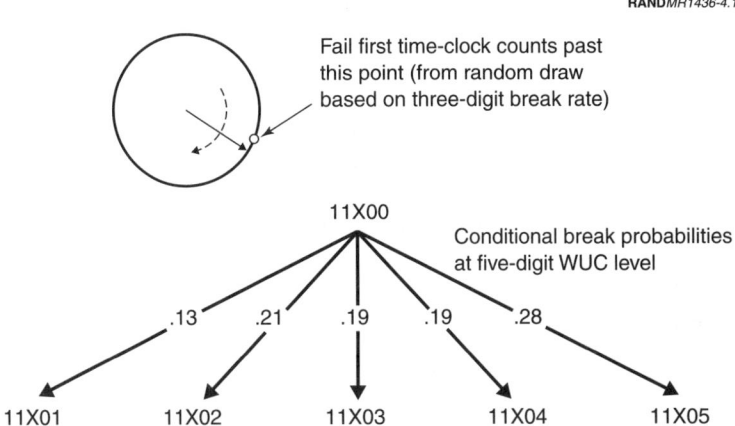

Fail first time-clock counts past
this point (from random draw
based on three-digit break rate)

11X00

Conditional break probabilities
at five-digit WUC level

.13   .21   .19   .19   .28

11X01   11X02   11X03   11X04   11X05

Figure 4.1—Break-Rate Representation in LCOM

digit subsystem ran on its own clock, would not have this mutually exclusive feature. Clearly, the real world must include simultaneous breaks, so it is not clear why the formulation in Figure 4.1 is used. In fact, one might expect that a common cause might actually correlate breaks so that more breaks would occur simultaneously than by chance. In fact, because it never allows simultaneous breaks, the method depicted in Figure 4.1 has perfect *negative* correlation, whereas running independent clocks at the five-digit level produces zero correlation. Neither method produces a positive correlation. It should be noted that it is not clear a priori whether break correlation will increase or decrease the stress on the system in a given case. Increased stress occurs to the extent that multiple repair demands arise together. Also, the diagnostic task might be more complex. On the other hand, there could be synergies, such as the effort required to access the broken subsystems.

While one could raise a theoretical objection to the LCOM process, in practice it is important to recognize that useful information on correlated failures is generally not available. However, the "least unrealistic" method seems to be one that leaves subsystem breaks independent of one another rather than perfectly negatively correlated.

The Quality of Break Data Available to LCOM

In summary, LCOM requires high-quality data on breaks at the three-digit level and potentially at the five-digit level as well. These data are drawn from field maintenance data systems such as CAMS and GO-81 and are archived in the Reliability and Maintainability Information System (REMIS). In order to make some assessment of the adequacy of automated maintenance records, we pulled all entries from REMIS for the C-5B[2] for an entire year, covering the period between July 1999 and June 2000. Table 4.4 shows the number of five-digit WUC entries by three-digit systems.

There may be three reasons a particular WUC is never entered into the automated data system. First, it may never break or require servicing at all; certain parts of the aircraft will never be replaced or repaired during the entire lifetime of the airframe. Second, work may be performed on a particular five-digit WUC but may then be recorded under another code—possibly an umbrella code that is used to describe a variety of maintenance actions. Third, some WUCs may be discontinued because they are rendered obsolete as modernizations are introduced, but the code will still exist in automated systems. Three WUCs listed in Table 4.5, account for 39 percent of all the entries in REMIS.

Can two doors on the auxiliary propulsion unit (APU) really be responsible for close to one-third of all the failures on the C-5Bs recorded in REMIS for an entire year? Conversations with an experienced 7-level C-5 maintenance technician revealed that both the left and the right doors to the APU are removed every time there is a scheduled inspection on the aircraft. The 11XPR and 11XJD codes may simply be used by technicians as general codes that indicate some kind of inspection involving many components on the aircraft other than just the APU. In a similar manner, the code 11TUE is typically used whenever work is done on any of the pylons on the wings, so it is equally likely that the 636 entries here represent work done on any one of the four pylons on the aircraft. The fourth-largest entry in REMIS was 11AA, with 240 entries for the year. This four-digit code stands for windshield, flight deck, and is typically used as a

---

[2] We would have liked to look at other weapon systems in addition to the C-5B but were unable to obtain electronic technical orders for any other system.

Table 4.4

Percentage of C-5B Five-Digit Codes Found in REMIS

	Two-Digit Aircraft Systems	Number of Five-digit WUCs in C-5	REMIS Entries	Share in REMIS (%)
11	Airframe	4254	2260	53.1
12	Crew Station	622	344	55.3
13	Landing Gear	752	548	72.9
14	Flight Controls	902	849	94.1
23	Engine	805	595	73.9
24	Auxiliary Power Plant	166	123	74.1
41	Environmental Control System	379	305	80.5
42	Electric Power System	224	148	66.1
44	Lighting System	284	246	86.6
45	Hydraulic and Pneumatic Systems	225	179	79.6
46	Fuel System	249	191	76.7
47	Oxygen System	89	70	78.7
49	Miscellaneous Utilities	207	150	72.5
51	Flight Instruments	176	110	62.5
52	Autopilot Instrumentation	358	131	36.6
55	Malfunction Analysis Recorder	476	144	30.3
59	Flight Management System/Global Positioning System	51	33	64.7
61	HF Communication System	115	36	31.3
62	VHF Communication System	72	35	48.6
63	UHF Communication System	84	29	34.5
64	Interphone System	80	42	52.5
65	Identification Friend or Foe (IFF) System	66	16	24.2
66	Emergency Communications	115	33	28.7
68	AFSATCOM	5	3	60.0
69	Miscellaneous Communications Equipment	20	13	65.0
71	Radio Navigation System	190	47	24.7
72	Radar Navigation System	168	76	45.2
74	Fire Control System	0	0	—
75	Weapon Delivery System	0	0	—
76	Penetration Aids and Electronic Countermeasures	28	28	100.0
91	Emergency Equipment	44	46	104.5
97	Explosive Devices and Components	5	7	140.0
	Total	11,211	6837	61.0

Table 4.5

Percentage of REMIS Entries for Top Three Five-Digit WUCs

WUC	Entries	Component
11XPR	1310	Auxiliary propulsion unit door, left
11XJD	737	Auxiliary propulsion unit door, right
11TUE	636	Wing structure assembly, pylon number 1
Total	2683	
REMIS entries	6837	
Percent	39.2	

"grab-bag" code for all work involving any of the windshields in the cockpit. Further interesting observations emerge from an examination of various service actions on the aircraft, a sample of which is offered in Table 4.6.

The single largest entry in the automated data system is code 03210, basic postflight inspection, which accounts for more than one-third of all entries of service codes in REMIS. If each postflight inspection corresponds to one sortie, as one would expect, this

Table 4.6

Sample of C-5 Service Codes from REMIS Entered During One Year

Service Code and Activity	Entries	Per Day	Share (%)
03210 Basic Postflight Inspection	17,595	48.2	35.7
03710 Major Inspection (Isochronal)	8557	23.4	17.3
03730 Home Station Check—Inspection	4832	13.2	9.8
03720 Minor Inspection	4369	12.0	8.9
04199 Not Otherwise Coded	2570	7.0	5.2
04170 Equipment Inventory	1922	5.3	3.9
03200 Throughflight Inspection	1473	4.0	3.0
09000 Shop Support General Codes	195	0.5	0.4
03100 Preflight Inspection	184	0.5	0.4
07000 Preparation and Maintenance of Records	66	0.2	0.1
04299 FO/FOD Inspection[a]	29	0.1	0.1
04620 Analysis of Oil Samples	10	0.0	0.0
0412B Auxiliary Power Plant	4	0.0	0.0
03109 Daily Walkaround Inspection on Alert	3	0.0	0.0
04150 Weight and Balance	3	0.0	0.0
02300 Cleaning (Vacuuming, Wiping, Polishing, etc.)	2	0.0	0.0
03750 Cannibalization	2	0.0	0.0

[a]FO/FOD = foreign object/foreign object damage.

would amount to 48.2 sorties per day for the little over 50-plus C-5Bs in the inventory. If true, this is a significant accomplishment for an airframe that has a reputation for having the poorest departure reliability of all weapon systems in the Air Force. With an average mission-capable (MC) rate of around 60 percent, this would average out to over 1.7 sorties per day per mission-capable aircraft. On the other hand, the data reveal only 184 entries for 03100, preflight inspection. It is true that for the C-5, a preflight inspection does not have to be made if one has been accomplished during the previous 48 hours. Nevertheless, there is too great a difference—about two orders of magnitude—for either of the two entries, pre- and postflight inspection, to be consistent. Similarly, code 03710, isochronal inspection, accounts for more than 23 entries per day. Yet it is not possible that 23 aircraft per day are undergoing isochronal inspections; the correct number is probably two to four. Therefore, this code probably represents a general code for many inspections done during isochronal inspection. At the bottom end, it is disappointing to see that code 03750, cannibalization, has only two entries for the entire year. For an aircraft that undergoes as much cannibalization as the C-5B, this represents a minuscule fraction of actual cannibalization actions.

Certainly, one cannot use examples from just one weapon system to infer fairly that all automated data systems in maintenance are inaccurate, incomplete, and misleading. Much analytical work would need to be done before such a conclusion could be substantiated. On the other hand, both CAMS and GO-81 have poor reputations for reliability, completeness, and accuracy.[3] Our conversations with various maintainers suggest that it is more likely that automated data systems reflect accurate entries for that subset of five-digit WUCs on which technicians work repeatedly. While a technician may be responsible for 100 or more WUCs, he will encounter many of these WUCs infrequently and perhaps not at all during an entire tour in the Air Force. Conversely, there is a subset that arises frequently, and the technician becomes intimately familiar with them. For these fre-

---

[3]It has been reported to us that studies of automated maintenance systems reveal an average discrepancy in the range of 15 to 20 percent. On the basis of our brief look at C-5B data, it seems obvious that this rate differs greatly between various WUCs. It may be accurate for some and off by a large magnitude for others. Thus, using an "average" adjustment factor is not appropriate.

quently encountered codes, it is likely that the system is more accurate.

Similarly, as indicated by the C-5B data, it is highly likely that infrequent and/or complex maintenance actions will be recorded by reliance on an umbrella code, a general code, or even a code called NOC, which stands for "not otherwise coded." Table 4.6 shows that this code is responsible for more than 5 percent of all entries, and Table 4.5 indicates that the top three five-digit WUCs in REMIS were all umbrella codes, representing more than 39 percent of all entries in the system. These are indications of a potential for severe problems in automated maintenance data systems.

A draft study by the Air Force Logistics Management Agency (AFLMA) analyzes the reasons aircraft in ACC are in a status of "non–mission capable due to maintenance" (NMCM). There is every reason to believe that the summary statement for this study, which addresses the accuracy of the CAMS data system used for fighters and bombers in ACC, also applies to the GO-81 data system used for the C-5B and probably to all weapon systems in the Air Force inventory as well:[4]

> The accuracy of TNMCM [total NMCM] data in REMIS is constrained by the lack of control of inputs into the CAMS computer system and lack of discipline in following information system instructions in the field. Required data is not always loaded correctly into CAMS and data can easily be erased or "backed out" of the system by field-level units. In addition, errors in entering data at field level and other computer system problems result in errors in loading data from CAMS to the REMIS system.

Since the uses of automated data in CAMS and GO-81 go well beyond LCOM, the problems cited here have relevance for many users of maintenance data. In view of the many problems in the supply system, it thus would appear beneficial to further explore the potential for using more easily entered and more accurate data on aircraft break rates at the five-digit level to assist supply managers. Such improved data could help these managers estimate optimal stockage

---

[4]See NMCM study (untitled), Maxwell Air Force Base, AL: Air Force Logistics Management Agency, p. iii.

rates and assess parts distribution among bases in peacetime. The benefit from more accurate break-rate data for both the manpower and the supply communities would likely be significant.

Another potentially important benefit from better automated maintenance data systems is the potential for the process of aging aircraft to be more effectively studied. To allow preventive measures to be identified ahead of time, break rates should be tracked by aircraft and system, including important parts, through making appropriate predictions regarding what systems are particularly prone to aging problems.

It would seem that the choice of running LCOM at the three- versus five-digit WUC level is an important and difficult choice to make. In fact, however, the issue is probably irrelevant. If the data are accurate at the five-digit level, there is no reason not to run the model at that level. Modern computing power is such that it does not really matter if the model requires simulating breaks and remove-replace actions over several thousand parts in an aircraft or just a few hundred. If the data exist or could be gathered with little effort, then working at the five-digit level is possible and may add some information by enabling the simulation to discover interactions that would otherwise be missed.

If, however, the data at the five-digit level are low quality, incorrect, or incomplete, it will not help to run the model at the three-digit level. Adequate representation at the three-digit level requires either that the underlying data at the five-digit level are correct or that there are random errors which can be canceled out by aggregation. Thus, the quality and statistical properties of the data at the five-digit level determine the accuracy of the simulation. Since the Air Force is well aware of the biases present in the CAMS/GO-81 five-digit-level data, we note that it is not sufficient to add a general error-correcting factor when aggregating to the three-digit level, as the systematic biases and shortcomings of the more detailed data are not eliminated or even reduced by this means. Moreover, no significant time or cost savings are to be gained from running the model at the three-digit level. Using five-digit-level data is simply a matter of providing computing power, which is not a constraining factor by today's standards. The implication of this reasoning is that the Air Force needs to pay a great deal of attention to obtaining high-quality data on break rates at the five-digit level. In order to get high-quality data on break rates, maintainers must be able to enter the data quickly and easily into machine-readable form, and various technologies exist to accomplish this goal.

The Break Process and Its Data Implications

LCOMs assume that the break process itself is *stationary*—i.e., that break rates, as a function of flying hours and sortie counts, do not vary over time or with the conditions associated with various operational scenarios. This is evidenced in the model by the use of the same break-rate parameters for all scenarios and time periods.[5] LCOM uses an exponential distribution of break intervals with a fixed MTBF parameter. Intervals are evaluated fleetwide, not for individual aircraft. This is mathematically equivalent to a Poisson distribution in the number of fleetwide breaks occurring in some fixed time interval. The validity of this assumption needs to be examined.

The Poisson distribution is characterized by a variance-to-mean (VTM) ratio of 1.0. It has been known for several decades, however, that this ratio generally exceeds 1.0 for any given system on an aircraft.[6] Physically, this can arise in several ways. First, the process can be nonstationary. That is to say, during any short time period the break intervals follow an exponential distribution, but the MTBF varies over time. Second, *compounding processes* that correlate breaks (across aircraft) give rise to a stationary non-Poisson distribution with a VTM > 1.0. Many Air Force models use this last approach. For example, in current work for the Air Force used in estimating spares requirements for the Aircraft Sustainability Model, the Logis-

---

[5]The parameters of the statistical distribution used in LCOM studies can change in two ways. First, insofar as recent data from CAMS or GO-81 show that the MTBF changes, this will provide additional data that may gradually change the distribution. Second, the relatively infrequent audits will provide potentially significant revisions of the database from which the distribution is calculated.

[6]See, for example, G. B. Crawford, *Variability in the Demands for Aircraft Spare Parts: Its Magnitude and Implications*, R-3318-AF, Santa Monica: RAND, 1988; F. M. Slay and C. C. Sherbrooke, *The Nature of the Aircraft Component Failure Process: A Working Note*, Report IR701R1, McLean, VA: Logistics Management Institute, 1988; and G. B. Crawford and M. Kamins, "The Effect of High Sortie Rates on F-16 Avionics," internal document, Santa Monica: RAND, 1989.

tics Management Institute (LMI) uses a VTM ratio of 4.0 or 5.0.[7] That is, the variance is assumed to be several times greater than the mean.

In contrast, the exponential distribution of break rates used in LCOM forces the VTM ratio to be exactly 1.0 (see Appendix B). This is a significant departure from the values reported by LMI for similar processes. However, using an exponential distribution where the MTBF parameter varies over time can also yield a distribution of breaks (over intervals that are short compared with the data collection period) with a VTM > 1.0.[8]

The implications for LCOM are significant. LCOM uses neither a distribution with a VTM > 1.0 nor an exponential distribution with a time-varying mean. Thus, it is inconsistent with what we know about break statistics.

How can this be corrected? First, note that the alternatives mentioned above are not equivalent. A stationary distribution with a VTM > 1.0 will exhibit a very short term bunching of breaks that stresses manpower and equipment. However, its impact on supply will be short term. On the other hand, a time-varying mean will, during periods of high break rate (small MTBF), tend to produce more stress on the overall supply capacity. RAND's analysis of Kosovo data, described in Appendix B, indicates that the time variance of break rates is an important real-world phenomenon. This is also consistent with common sense, since one would expect that for different scenarios, attributes of the sortie types (other than duration) and the physical environment will be different, leading to different MTBFs. Consistent with the philosophy of using "most stressful" scenarios, one would then want to run LCOM using the break rates characteristic of the highest-stress scenarios.

This has significant implications for the data collection process required to support LCOM. Essentially, it means that it is not sufficient to assemble, say, peacetime break data and then hope that such data will apply to the most stressful scenario in wartime. Instead, it be-

---

[7]See F. M. Slay, T. Bachman, R. Klein, T. J. O'Malley, F. Ichorn, and R. King, *Optimizing Spares: Support for the Aircraft Sustainability Model,* Report AF501MR1, McLean, VA: Logistics Management Institute, 1996.

[8]In this case, the MTBF refers to the long-term average.

comes critical to obtain an independent estimate of the average break rates associated with every possible operational scenario that each aircraft type may face and then select the most stressful one to be used in LCOM simulations. If the mean break rate is as unstable as the data suggest, then the current use in LCOM estimations of a fixed distribution based on peacetime data is likely to lead to a significant underrepresentation of the most stressful break rates—and therefore also engender an underrepresentation not only of the required maintenance man-hours but possibly of manpower positions as well.

It is, of course, possible that the compounding processes alluded to above are also important, in which case the best approximation to actual data does not follow a Poisson distribution at all but rather an entirely different one that would allow the variance to be much higher than the mean. This could be a negative binomial distribution, for example. To the extent that this contributes to the known high VTM ratios observed elsewhere, LCOM faces yet another problem: The model would be using the wrong distribution altogether and would have to substitute another one in future applications of the model.

These data issues are pivotal and are critical to establishing an acceptable confidence level in the simulated estimates of LCOM maintenance man-hours and manpower positions. Unfortunately, the issues are highly technical and are also difficult to resolve. A large data-gathering and analytical effort is required to establish the time-path properties of break rates and to test the data with statistical methods to gain a proper understanding of the mean-variance properties. It is possible that not all MDSs behave in the same way and that different subsystems on the aircraft have different statistical properties. We are of the opinion that the Air Force should begin to collect and analyze its break-rate data specifically to ascertain which distributions are appropriate for both spares requirements and LCOM manpower requirements. It is anomalous to have two such important but related requirements processes build on entirely different assumptions about aircraft break rates, as both cannot be correct. This issue, discussed further in Appendix B, demands resolution through further analysis.

Supplementing Automated Data with Audits

This brings us to the next data issue for LCOM analyses. As noted above, of the thousands of five-digit WUCs in a typical aircraft technical manual, only a subset will be found in CAMS/GO-81 data. Many of the "missing" WUCs probably represent parts that never break and thus are never worked on. Others, however, represent breaks and work performed that never made it into the automated databases. For the latter cases, various methods exist for finding supplemental data, such as the use of shop logs (for off-flight-line work) or Form 781A data directly off the aircraft, and these methods are used to varying degrees. What all LCOM database-building efforts have in common are the audits performed by LCOM analysts with field maintainers. These audits often represent the most important source of supplemental data and are sometimes the only source of data on certain WUCs. It is therefore important to discuss how the audits generate inputs into the model.

To study this issue, we accompanied a team of LCOM analysts from ACC as they performed an LCOM audit of F-117s at Holloman Air Force Base.

The audits were done at the five-digit level of the technical orders. This means that the LCOM analyst asked questions of interviewees (who had been selected by the field unit as skilled and competent maintainers) on the basis of the WUCs in the technical order. Each interviewee was asked whether he or she had performed work on this particular WUC, how often it was done, and how much time it usually took to perform that task. An example of such an interview is provided in Vignette 4.1.

In this particular type of interview, the LCOM analyst obtains information about the mean break rate as experienced by these three different interviewees; about the average time it takes each maintainer to undertake the repair; and about the variance between maintainers with regard to how long this repair action takes. In those cases where CAMS/GO-81 data exist for the particular WUCs examined in the interview, the audit questions serve to validate or provide corrective

Vignette 4.1

Typical Question from an LCOM Audit

Auditor: Look at WUC 11GH0—how often do you do it, and how long does it take?

Staff sergeant, 7-level, 2A6X1, squadron 1: I've done that maybe four times a month over the last six months; takes a crew size of two; a half hour to take it off; another half hour to put it back.

Staff sergeant, 7-level, 2A6X1, squadron 2: six times per month, crew size two, 45 minutes off, half hour back on.

Senior airman, 5-level, 2A6X1, squadron 1: twice a month, need two, half off, 45 minutes back on.

---

information to the recorded data. In some cases, however—it was not possible to ascertain how often—the audit question is the only source of information about break rates and fix times. In those cases where the CAMS/GO-81 data are considered unreliable, the audit interviews are the primary source of data.

In the typical question in Vignette 4.1, different individuals may give different estimates of fix times. When this occurs, all the variance in fix time is attributed to individuals—that is to say, certain maintainers are assumed to be more skilled and/or more experienced than others and can therefore accomplish a maintenance action in a shorter time. However, this is only one possible source of variance in fix times.

A second source of variance—idiosyncratic variations in equipment—may cause the same maintainer to take varying amounts of time to complete a particular action. For example, a bolt may be stuck or may break as it is taken off; a panel may come off easily or take a long time to remove; a particular short in an electrical system can be easy or hard to trace; or a leak in a fuel or hydraulic line can prove hard or easy to find. If variance in fix times is important in arriving at final manpower estimates for maintenance, then the causes for variance embedded in the equipment itself must not be over-looked.[9] Vignette 4.2 illustrates how this is done in an LCOM audit.

In the Holloman Air Force Base audit, most of the questions in the work centers we visited were of the type illustrated in Vignette 4.1 rather than that found in Vignette 4.2. There are likely two reasons for this. First, it would simply be prohibitive to establish equipment-caused variance for every one of the thousands of WUCs; the audits would take too much time to finish. Our investigation of LCOM indicates that variance in fix times has little or no impact on manpower requirements, and LCOM analysts are well aware of this fact—so the extra effort to obtain fix-time variance for every failing part is simply not warranted. Second, for many of the WUCs it is plausible that the equipment-caused variance is not of any great significance in any case.

Vignette 4.2

Finding Equipment-Caused Variance in an LCOM Audit

Auditor: How long does it take to do that action?

Respondent: That can vary a lot.

Auditor: OK, tell me how long is a short one?

Respondent: Well, maybe a half hour.

Auditor: And a long one?

Respondent: Oh, that can easily take three hours.

Auditor: How frequent are the short vs. the long?

Respondent: The short ones are maybe 60 percent and the long ones about 40 percent.

---

[9]As noted above, we have not, in our excursions in two LCOMs, found that variance in fix times is in practice of importance for estimating man-hours and manpower requirements. Thus, the issues discussed in the present context are of more academic than practical importance.

In some cases, a maintenance action consists of a series of complicated steps. In such situations, the LCOM auditor is faced with the specific challenge of trying to create a composite from several interviews that yields the best picture of what the action requires. Vignettes 4.3a–c illustrate such a case. These vignettes portray interviews with three engine specialists (2A6X1s) on the amount of time and the crew sizes required to complete each task in an engine swap-out. The three specialists are a 7-level engine specialist (2A671), a 7-level crew chief (2A373) working as a 2A671, and a 5-level engine specialist (2A651) waivered to work as a 7-level.

The estimates of the three individual specialists of their own time for engine removal and installation vary between about 10 and 15 hours depending on the interviewee, representing a 50 percent variation over the lowest estimate. The estimates for the total maintenance action, including all team members when additional personnel are

Vignette 4.3a

Engine Swap-Outs: Interview with an Engine Specialist (2A671)
During an F-117 Audit

Task	Hours	Crew Size	Total Hours
Access engine bay, check engine rack, turn off circuit breakers	0.500	1	0.50
Radar absorptive material (RAM) top half (paint removal for panel access)	0.700	1	0.70
Wheel well mount access	0.400	1	0.40
Remove doubler panels (stealth covers)	0.300	1	0.30
Remove engine bay panel	0.500	2	1.00
Disconnect hydraulics	2.000	3	6.00
Prepare jet trailer (unload, position)	0.500	2	1.00
Pump up trailer, lower engine	0.500	3	1.50
Transfer hard lines to new engine	1.500	1	1.50
Inspect new engine	0.500	1	0.50
QA inspection by specialists	0	0	0
Fixing QA write-ups	0.075	2	0.15
Position engine, attach to hang points	0.500	3	1.50
Reconnect hydraulics	2.300	3	6.90
Rig throttle (specialist)	0	0	0
Install environmental control system (ECS) pack (specialist)	0	0	0
Total	10.275		21.95

needed on a job, vary between 22 and 25 man-hours. This difference is much smaller, illustrating differences in judgment between the three interviewees regarding the appropriate crew size for various steps of the job. Thus, there are significant differences among the interviewees with regard to the time each step is estimated to take and the crew size that is judged to be required. Interestingly, all

Vignette 4.3b

Engine Swap-Outs: Interview with an Engine Specialist (2A373 working as a 2A671) During an F-117 Audit

Task	Hours	Crew Size	Total Hours
Preparatory: get tools, get lubes, etc., check forms	0	1	0
Preparatory work on aircraft	1.00	2	2.00
Access engine bay, engine rack	0.25	1	0.25
RAM top half, engine mounts	0.12	1	0.12
Remove engine bay panel	0.25	2	0.50
Prepare jet trailer	0.30	1	0.30
Disconnect throttle	0.25	1	0.25
Remove ECS panel	0	0	0
Hardware removal (fuel, electrical, hydraulics, etc.)	1.00	3	3.00
Move trailer into position	0.25	3	0.75
Pump up trailer, lower old engine	0.50	4	2.00
Transfer hardware	0.25	2	0.50
Inspect engine bay (insulation panels, etc.)	1.00	1	1.00
Inspect new engine	0.50	1	0.50
QA inspection of bay (specialist)	0	0	0
Position trailer	0.25	3	0.75
Install new engine	0.50	4	2.00
Reconnect hardware (fuel, electrical, hydraulics, etc.)	1.50	3	4.50
Initial servicing of engine	0.10	1	0.10
Engine run preparation	0.25	3	0.75
Engine checks in idle	0.25	3	0.75
Tow to trim pad (crew chiefs)	0	0	0
Trim pad preparation, stems	0.12	1	0.12
Run test	0.40	3	1.20
Tow back (crew chiefs)	0	0	0
Intake check	0.40	1	0.40
Intake and exhaust inspection prerun	0.30	1	0.30
Fill out forms	0.50	1	0.50
Close engine bay, engine panels	0.50	3	1.50
CAMS data entry	1.00	1	1.00
Total	11.74		25.04

three interviewees stated that each had at one time or another performed the removal and installation entirely by themselves—something they did not wish to repeat, as they considered it unsafe and
dangerous. In other words, for a complicated maintenance action
such as this, there will be variations in procedures depending on

Vignette 4.3c

**Engine Swap-Outs: Interview with an Engine Specialist (2A651 waivered
to work as 7-level) During an F-117 Audit**

Task	Hours	Crew Size	Total Hours
Center body inlet front fan	0.2	2	0.4
Access engine bay, inspect engine rack	0.2	2	0.4
Remove engine panel	0.3	2	0.6
Remove access panel mount	0.2	1	0.2
Remove ECS pack (electro-environmental specialist)	0	0	0
Remove power takeoff (PTO) shaft	0.3	1	0.3
Disconnect T-duct	0.4	2	0.8
Remove RAM and engine vent screen	0.3	1	0.3
Disconnect throttle	0.3	1	0.3
Disconnect fuel line	0.3	1	0.3
Engine quick disconnect, hydraulics	0.1	1	0.1
Position jet trailer	0.7	3	2.1
Disconnect thrust mount	0.3	2	0.6
In 50 percent of cases, aft mount pins OK	0.1	2	—
In 50 percent of cases, aft mount pins stuck	0.4	2	0.8
10 percent of cases find a fuel leak (fuel specialist)	0	0	0
If no leak, lower engine and roll back	0.4	4	1.6
Engine bay inspection (40 percent of cases, acceptance)	1.5	2	—
Engine bay inspection (60 percent of cases, no acceptance)	3	2	6.0
QA, no write-up 70 percent	0	0	0
QA, write-up 30 percent, fix	0.4	2	0.8
Prepare old engine	0.4	2	0.8
Tow new engine to aircraft	0.4	2	0.8
Prepare new engine	0.4	2	0.8
On-engine acceptance inspection	0.5	1	0.5
(reverse hardware removal actions, same time as above)	3.3	1	3.3
Rig throttle (aero-repair specialist)	0	0	0
Install ECS pack (e/e specialist)	0	0	0
QA no write-up 80 percent	0	0	0
QA write-up 20 percent, then fix	0.1	2	0.2
Trailer repositioning	0.3	1	0.3
Engine run at 80 percent throttle	0.4	3	1.2
Total	15.2		23.5

available personnel, and perhaps depending on the urgency of the action as well. It is one thing to work on a backup aircraft that is not on the flying schedule for the next few days, but entirely different pressures are present when an aircraft is on the next day's flying schedule.

It is interesting to note that while many of the steps given by the interviewees are identical, there are some significant differences. One of the interviewees specifically included the requirement to tow the aircraft to the trim pad for a full engine run; the others did not. One of them included one hour for CAMS data entry; the others did not. One of them forgot to include time to address the results of quality assurance (QA) write-ups. This variance in responses means that LCOM analysts must not only decide which combination of the three interviews best represents the entire engine remove-install action but also make an informed judgment about time estimates and minimum crew sizes. The three interviewees all agree that the step in the process which requires the largest crew size involves lowering the old engine onto the trailer (for which three or four people are required) and raising and installing the new engine (for which four people are required, according to all three). In an actual engine remove-install action, the additional people would be pulled from wherever they are available and would most likely be crew chiefs or specialists from the SGF in the fighter squadron, but anyone else who is handy and available could be asked to help out. How this minimum crew size is handled in the model will then be left to the LCOM analyst. Does he or she add enough people to make up the minimum crew, meaning that these people stand idle and wait to be called, or are they pulled from other AFSCs that may be available because of low M-UTEs? Different analysts may make different judgments on such issues, and it is quite probable that these judgments will differ among different user groups around the MAJCOMs that rely on the model.

While the data collection methods described above may strike readers as seriously wanting because they seem impressionistic and subjective, it is important to consider the available alternatives. The intent of CAMS/GO-81 is to provide complete data on all maintenance actions at the five-digit WUC level so that proper records can be kept over time of failures by aircraft, failure type, failure reason, length of sortie, and the like. If such data were of high quality and available for long time periods, LCOM would be able to rely on them. The data from these systems are not completely reliable, however, so the audits are both a second-best option and necessary. Naturally, the audits cannot be expected to completely replace the inadequate automated records. Interviews with a few technicians can undoubtedly yield important information that proves highly useful, particularly in constructing the networks that represent wing-level maintenance practices. Automated data are useful for constructing networks, but interviews with technicians regarding which portions of the technical order they are responsible for in practice and exactly how they apply specific work rules are likely to be much more accurate. With regard to break rates and average fix times, the audits certainly do not provide statistically valid data that can be used to estimate the mean and variance of these variables—*but at the present time there is no better method available.* If the interviewees are experts in their field and respond as honestly as they can, there is no reason to believe that the results will be biased—at least with respect to the means of break rates and fix times, the two most critical inputs into LCOM. Finally, with respect to the minimum crew sizes required for various maintenance actions, there is probably no better source than field interviews, as this information will not be available either from technical orders or automated systems. For all these issues regarding data accuracy, close cooperation between maintainers with current field experience and LCOM analysts—many of whom have maintenance backgrounds themselves—is crucial.

There is one area in which it appears that the current audit method could be complemented and improved. The purpose of LCOM data collection is to provide estimates that are as pure as possible of the time it takes to perform direct maintenance and servicing tasks on aircraft. However, no productive task in any occupation can be performed with 100 percent efficiency. It takes time to move between work stations, to wait for a prior task performed by others to be completed, to wait for all members of a team to arrive, to get tools, to put on protective clothing, and to perform all the chores that are incidental to undertaking the maintenance action that is at the heart of LCOM estimates. Moreover, there is variance in all these times as a result of factos such as weather, manning, yesterday's flying schedule, the availability of backup aircraft, and the like. These incidental tasks are real and are important to the performance of maintenance actions—yet there would appear to be no attempt made to collect relevant data during audits or to include such estimates in LCOM analyses. It seems likely that this is one of the reasons LCOM manpower utilization factors are generally low. If all the inefficient but unavoidable incidentals were included, the actual time maintainers spent performing not just direct maintenance but maintenance-related tasks would be higher. Data collection on incidentals might require that time diaries be kept by maintenance technicians or that time-in-motion studies be conducted that followed a sample of maintainers with various AFSCs for a period of time. In the meantime, it is unclear what role, if any, these inefficiencies play in LCOM audit estimates of expended man-hours.

SPARES CONSTRAINTS DURING LCOM "MANUAL OPTIMIZATION"

At this point, it is appropriate to discuss a number of issues associated with LCOM analysis. The first involves the way in which spares constraints are applied.

Chapter Three described the manual optimization process that uses LCOM to determine shift manning. One step in this process applies constraints on spares until a specific target NMCS rate, generally set at a "policy" level of x percent, is obtained—where the number x varies by aircraft type as determined by each MAJCOM. A recurring point made above is that when maintenance manpower requirements are determined, they should be based on the most stressing realistic scenarios. Suffice it to note here that LCOM's use of a policy level rather than the higher levels more typically encountered in practice stands in violation of this principle.

Yet another issue relates to the fact that the target NMCS rate can be reached in many ways. That is to say, the same overall NMCS rate can be obtained by "shorting" either different parts or different mixes of parts. This iterative adjusting is done manually using analysts' judgment to arrive at a realistic spares situation. Presumably, the shortages are spread out in a way that equalizes the impact of particular parts rather than having a small number of parts serve as the dominant sources of the global NMCS rate. However, the criteria used do not appear to be formalized or even clearly reported in published LCOM studies. ACC, for example, "tries to make for even shortages." It is doubtful, however, that this claim can be taken literally, since it would mean that if an aircraft is NMCS, the probability that a particular part is back-ordered is the same for all parts. This is clearly not representative of either actual or best policy. In reality, parts inventories are determined with careful attention to unit costs, which differ vastly between parts.[10] A more "rational" policy for LCOM to contemplate would be to directly consider the cost of adding an additional spare to the inventory, as well as the marginal contribution of each added part to increasing the probability that an aircraft will be returned to the pool of ready and available aircraft.[11] Quantitative approaches of this type do not appear to be used during the usual LCOM process of limiting spares, but there is no evidence to the effect that this is an important issue from the perspective of manpower determination.[12]

THE VALUE OF LCOM IN THE PRESENCE OF MINIMUM CREW-SIZE ISSUES

Chapter Three noted that LCOM shift manning requirements are often determined by minimum crew-size requirements. We found, for example, that this is the case for many C-130 AFSCs. If predetermined minimum crew sizes in many cases set required shift manning, the question immediately arises as to why LCOM should be run at all. While there are good reasons for running LCOM even in situations where minimum crew-size issues are known to be important, there are valid arguments on both sides.

---

[10]Both the DO-41 inventory requirement models, including analyses of aircraft availability and aircraft sustainability, and the DynaMetric family of models include replacement and, in some cases, repair costs for parts. Thus, both peacetime and wartime spares inventories are partially determined by costs and are not solely determined by the break rates associated with sorties.

[11]There is an actual model, called EXPRESS, that does exactly this for inventory requirement determinations and allocations of work flows. This model is now actively used in some Air Force logistics centers.

[12]ACC/XPMP personnel indicate that they try for "even" shortages but have also used real data. They state that "the result is no difference." AFMIA makes similar statements to the effect that they avoid having any particular part dominate the NMCS rate.

Some observers would argue that LCOM should *not* be run in these cases, as the time and effort it takes to gather the data and calibrate the model may be prohibitive. Furthermore, since few outside a small LCOM/manpower professional community really understand the critical role minimum crew sizes play, the simulation lends an aura of analytical rigor to what is essentially a mundane act of putting a requirement for a minimum crew size into the model. That is to say, if the logistics community is responsible for the work rules that determine minimum crew size, then that is where their efforts should be concentrated—in supporting a proper determination of maintenance manpower requirements. The highly technical and even obscure features of LCOM militate against such an effort because they hide the importance of simple assumptions but stress the technical nature of the simulation.

These points being granted, we argue that LCOM models should continue to be used and calibrated even when minimum crew size is a dominant factor in determining shift manning. The reasons include the following:

While restrictions on minimum crew size may be a determinant for many and perhaps most work centers, there will be some for which this is not the case. In addition, it may not be known, before LCOM is run and constraints are applied, whether minimum crew size is really the constraining factor. It takes a full calibration of the model to find the binding constraint.

The simulation and the attendant sensitivity analyses to which the model is subjected in calibration are really the only method available to identify when a threshold set by a minimum crew-size requirement has been crossed—and hence to determine when it is time to add personnel above the minimum level. An example of the importance of this argument can be taken from the current and ongoing estimation of the CV-22 LCOM model. For the typical mission, a CV-22 unit will require two weapon loaders. At home station, two weapon loaders can service a squadron of 12 aircraft. However, the operational requirement for CV-22s will seldom be in deployable units of 12 aircraft but will instead be in small unit type codes (UTCs) of two and sometimes four ships. Therefore, the simulation, expressly modeling operational scenarios of smaller UTCs, will identify the constraint and provide a demand for weapon loaders that otherwise could easily be missed.[13]

LCOM offers a critical advantage that nonanalytical approaches cannot. Simulation practitioners have found that the very act of building and running a model promotes the identification of synergies and relationships that would otherwise remain hidden from view. For example, using business rules regarding minimum crew sizes may in most cases provide enough maintenance manpower to support a given sortie requirement scenario. However, only a strict simulation can reveal whether other important goals, such as maintaining the health of the pool of aircraft or staying below a critical NMCS threshold, have also been met.

LCOM offers a mechanism for understanding the impact of many detailed rules on overall manpower requirements. This additional advantage seems virtually unexploited in the current division of labor between the manpower and maintenance communities. Exploring proposed changes to these rules in this way permits a quick assessment of the proposals. Potential problems can be identified before actual maintenance organizations are subjected to the changes, and in many cases the simulation will also point to solutions to those problems.

For example, some minimum crew-size requirements appear to be good candidates for reduction if accompanied by appropriate rule changes and cross-training. The rules and regulations regarding both minimum crew sizes and the business rules that determine the interaction between work centers and the assignment of tasks to particular AFSCs can and should be modeled by the functional community. Such LCOM-based analyses have a high potential to reduce minimum crew sizes in many areas.

---

[13]In their determination of CV-22 maintenance manpower requirements, the Marine Corps, lacking access to a model like LCOM, simply determined by assumption that no more manpower would be required than for the CH-46 and the CH-53 that are to be replaced. That is the ultimate, it seems, in using minimum crew size as a constraining factor: manpower first, maintenance second. LCOM affords the Air Force an opportunity to check the validity of such a procedure, and that is an important advantage.

LCOM ANALYSES OMIT CRITICAL CHALLENGES FACING MAINTAINERS

Finally, there are important challenges maintainers face in the field that LCOM analyses do not adequately address. First, the scenarios that feed LCOM do not adequately represent the current environment under which maintainers must operate. In particular, there were major increases in operational tempo (OPTEMPO) in the 1990s, especially in the fighter world. Rotational deployments became more prevalent and levied stressful demands on the maintenance force.

In the fighter world, the most stressful demands seem to relate to preparation for, workload during, and recovery from split operations (split ops)—yet this is not reflected in official Air Force manpower estimates. Split ops usually refer to overseas deployments in which a squadron is required to deploy only a portion of its aircraft, pilots, and maintainers. The deploying part of the squadron naturally takes the best equipment and more experienced people to minimize any risks inherent in an operational environment. The nondeploying part of the squadron remains at home station and continues normal peacetime operations, but it does so with the less reliable aircraft and less experienced technicians who need training while continuing to meet a flying schedule for the pilots who stay behind. Training at home station usually suffers as a result.

Second, LCOM analyses do not explicitly and systematically account for the man-hours that senior technicians (trainers) and junior personnel (trainees) dedicate to OJT. OJT is a crucial activity for sustaining the long-term health of the Air Force's personnel inventory, particularly in such technically demanding fields as maintenance. OJT constitutes an important part of the duty day for junior maintainers as well as for the senior maintainers who must train them. Opportunities for OJT are driven by break rates, which should in turn drive a time requirement for both trainers and trainees.

Third, LCOM analysis does not explicitly address experience mix. Changes in experience mix (the ratio of senior to junior technicians in a unit) affect the productivity of a unit as well as the ratio of trainees to teachers and the resulting ability to conduct OJT. Such changes can be caused by problems with retention or recruiting, and because of selective calls on high skill levels to go on deployments, when a less experienced mix may be left at home station. Current models do not incorporate the concept of performing tasks with alternative experience mixes; as far as standard LCOM practice goes, an AFSC is a homogeneous category across all skill levels.

Mean fix times (as opposed to variances) can increase when the average experience level of the work force declines. LCOM auditors indicate that their interviews aim to determine task times using an average experience mix, and it might seem that this is all that is necessary given that the variance in fix times is relatively unimportant. Even so, the lack of information on the impact of experience mix on average fix times precludes the simple adjustment of LCOM data as the experience mix changes over time. A new audit would be necessary to obtain the new average. This also begs the question of whether it is appropriate to base manpower requirements on the current experience mix.[14] Additionally, it is questionable whether the auditing methodology actually extracts task times averaged across experience mixes. The issue of *whose* task time is being elicited—that of the interviewee or an average for his AFSC—may at best be ambiguous and subject to misinterpretation by the interviewee. Finally, there is the added complication that 3-levels are not cleared to complete all tasks independently. Thus, the greater the percentage of 3-levels in the force, the more misleading may be the results that merely average fix times across all skill levels.

Were LCOM to incorporate the important effects of OJT, split ops, and falling experience, it would mean an increase in the manpower requirement. In the real world, senior maintainers compensate for shortfalls by working longer hours or by delaying the completion of lower-priority tasks.

---

[14]There is a parallel here to the discussion above regarding modeling policy versus reality. In principle, one could estimate LCOM maintenance man-hour requirements using data on desired skill mix and then compare these estimates using data on current actual skill mixes. This would require data on productivity differentials and mean fix times for various skill levels as well as knowledge about how many additional trainers are required to support a lower skill mix. The next logical step would then be to authorize manpower spaces against a "bad-luck" scenario of low skill mix, in keeping with the LCOM philosophy of picking the most demanding sortie scenarios and relying on the Monte Carlo approach to find, probabilistically, the most stressful break-rate sequences.

SUMMARY

The main purpose of this chapter has been to show how difficult it is, in practice, to provide the data needed to support the ambitious simulations that are at the heart of LCOM. Absent good data on break rates and average fix times, the model will continue to provide manpower requirement estimates that raise important questions regarding the most demanding break-rate scenarios. Absent a clear expression of how minimum crew sizes are handled in LCOM analyses, the model will also continue to be highly opaque to outsiders.

From a technical data standpoint, the statistical nonstationarity of the break rates during peak sortie scenarios is a potentially important point. The variability in actual break rates also remains an issue that available data do not illuminate. In principle, it is important to estimate the variance for all five-digit-level WUCs and thus go beyond the simplistic use of a single distribution to represent all breaks. In addition, the effect of changes in average sortie duration (ASD) must be estimated empirically on actual break-rate data, as it appears that the values that current policy assigns to this effect are much too small. Preliminary RAND research on Kosovo shows that these issues also have important implications for the estimation of maintenance man-hours in the simulations. There are at present substantial data shortcomings in LCOM that must cast considerable suspicion on its maintenance man-hour estimates and hence on its M-UTEs as well. Whether this also affects estimates of manpower requirements will remain uncertain until the detailed data mining suggested here has actually been completed.

In sum, there are two central advantages to LCOM: its Monte Carlo simulation approach and its description of wing-level maintenance organizations and work centers with appropriate AFSCs (along with other resources). These are important advantages, but their potential can be realized only at considerable expense. Most critically, LCOM demands a high-quality database to provide inputs on break rates and maintenance man-hours. In the absence of such a database, LCOM cannot be expected to provide precise estimates of the maintenance man-hours and shift manning required to support any given sortie generation scenario.

An important aspect of Air Force LCOM simulations is that shift manning can be heavily dependent on minimum crew sizes. This feature of the model implies that it is incumbent on manpower and maintenance analysts to justify as clearly as possible each requirement for a minimum crew as well as to find methods for minimizing required manning. This can be done only by analyzing, on a case-by-case basis, the particular mix of occupational skills that must be present for each task and then asking if there are ways—perhaps through partial task training—to assign supporting tasks to alternative occupational skills where large crew sizes are required. The key to ensuring that LCOM has yielded a required but not excessive number of authorizations is to analyze in detail the composition of the crews that set the minimum crew size, as these often become the drivers for setting manpower requirements.

Another important aspect of the simulation approach is that the nature of the data is subject to continuous scrutiny and analysis. This is a specific reference to the questions regarding the nonstationarity of the mean and the effect of longer average sortie durations on break rates and therefore on maintenance man-hours. There are strong indications that available data in these areas are inadequate.

Finally, systematic assessments of the effects of declining experience, rotational deployments, and OJT—and their interrelationships—are critical to estimating the true requirements for maintenance manpower. These assessments are absent from LCOM analyses, yet they present challenges that maintainers in the field face every day.

Chapter Five

THE BLUE BOX: BOUNDING WORKING HOURS

INTRODUCTION

In this chapter, we first describe how LCOM-simulated shift manning is translated into total manpower required. We then discuss how this method suggests that a large block of time remains available for other tasks that are required of maintainers in addition to servicing and repairing aircraft to support a sortie generation requirement. This raises the question of whether a sufficient amount of time is allotted during an average duty day, under the budgetary and operational conditions facing today's Air Force, to perform the non-maintenance-related duties that are demanded of maintenance personnel—an issue taken up in Chapter Six.

FROM LCOM MAN-HOURS AND SHIFT MANNING TO MANPOWER REQUIREMENTS

The preceding chapters describe how LCOM, using the networks and the Monte Carlo simulation method, arrives at maintenance man-hours and then constructs manning by shift. LCOM analysts successively reduce the manpower allotted to the work centers by shift until either some minimum crew-size rule or a sortie generation constraint indicates that a stopping point has been reached. The LCOM analytical process then arrives at manpower by occupation (AFSC) and by work center.

The next step is to translate shift manning into total manpower required. The number of manpower slots required to meet a certain level of shift manning differs in peacetime and wartime for two reasons. First, wartime is a 24-hour-per-day, seven-day-per-week affair.[1]   Second, Air Force work rules state the number of hours that a person is expected to work during various kinds of operational conditions. This is shown in Table 5.1, which contains the relevant portions of an instruction issued by the Directorate of Manpower in the Office of the Deputy Chief of Staff for Plans and Programs on the Air Staff (AF/XPM).[2]

Table 5.1

Standard Air Force Work Weeks and Man-Hour Availability Factors

Standard Work Week	Normal	Wartime	Surge
Computation of assigned hours	5 days, 8 hrs/day	6 days, 10 hrs/day	6 days, 12 hrs/day
Calendar days per month	30.4	30.4	30.4
Less:			
Holidays/month	−0.8	−0	−0
Weekend days/month	−8.7	−4.3	−4.3
Assigned days/month	= 20.9	= 26.1	= 26.1
Hours/day	× 8.0	× 10.0	× 12.0
Monthly assigned hours	167.3	260.9	313.1
Nonavailable categories:			
Leave	9.3	5.8	0
PCS related[a]	1.2	1.4	0
Medical (sick leave)	1.9	2.4	2.3
Organizational duties	0.5	3.7	1.1
Education and training	2.9	0.5	0
Social actions	0	0.1	0
Miscellaneous	0	0.3	0.5
Total nonavailable hours	−15.8	−14.2	−3.9
Monthly hours available to primary duty	151.5	246.7	309.1
Overload factor (%)	7.7	1.2	0.0
Monthly hours available with overtime	163.2	249.7	309.1
Daily assigned hours with overtime	8.6	10.1	12.0

[a]PCS = permanent change of station.

---

[1]That is, for the major combat commands in ACC, the Pacific Air Forces (PACAF), the United States Air Forces in Europe (USAFE), and AFSOC. AMC already operates tankers and strategic transports around the clock in peacetime as well as in wartime.

[2]See U.S. Department of the Air Force, *Determining Manpower Requirements*, AFI 38-201, Washington, D.C., Table A2.1.

As noted in the top row of Table 5.1, the standard work week used in programming manpower is 40 hours in normal peacetime operations, 60 hours during sustained war, and 72 hours during surge operations. Including overtime, which varies by peace and war (see the overload factor on the third line from the bottom), this implies daily working hours of 8.6, 10.1, and 12.0 for the three categories of operating conditions. Looking at the wartime scenario, personnel are required to work ten-hour shifts six days a week, which translates into 261 available working hours per month. From these hours are deducted various factors representing nonavailable hours as specified by the instruction. Accordingly, the man-hour availability factor (MAF)—the monthly hours per person available for "primary duties" under sustained wartime conditions—is 246.7 hours. Adding an "overload" (or overtime) factor of 1.2 percent, the total is 249.7 hours.

However, each shift must be manned 12 hours per day every day of the month, not just the 10 hours for 26 days each person is available. To attain full 24/7 manning, each shift manpower position must therefore be multiplied by an augmentation factor equal to 1.479 (30.4 x 12/246.7, where 30.4 is the average number of days per month [365.25/12]). Using this methodology, LCOM studies translate simulated shift manning requirements into actual manpower positions for programming purposes. Air Force manpower-planning instructions and MAJCOM LCOM studies are not specific in how actual manning is to be divided between the shifts during wartime, implicitly leaving this to the responsible commanders' discretion.

For peacetime, the denominator in the equation, which represents available hours, would be $151.5 \times 1.077 = 163.2$ to include the permissible overtime of 7.7 percent. In peacetime, some work centers may be manned three shifts seven days a week, whereas others may be manned only two or even one shift. Table 5.2 gives the values for the augmentation factor to be used in each case.

As an example, for AMC, which in peacetime operates 24/7, a peacetime work center that must be manned by two people per shift for three shifts per day requires $2 \times 4.47 = 8.94 \rightarrow 9$ manpower spaces. For work centers that need to stay open for only two shifts, a two-person shift manning requires six manpower slots, and a one-shift work center would need three.

Table 5.2

Factors for Translating Shift Requirements to Manpower

Number of Shifts	Formula	Augmentation Factor
Three	$30.4 \times 24/163.2$	4.47
Two	$30.4 \times 16/163.2$	2.98
One	$30.4 \times 8/163.2$	1.49

MANPOWER REQUIREMENTS AND MANPOWER UTILIZATION RATES

Next, we compare proposed manpower requirements with actual M-UTEs. Figure 5.1 illustrates this as it might be computed by an LCOM simulation. The number of days, shown on the horizontal axis, is 180 in this example. The straight horizontal line on the top of this figure represents the total primary duty hours available from the authorized

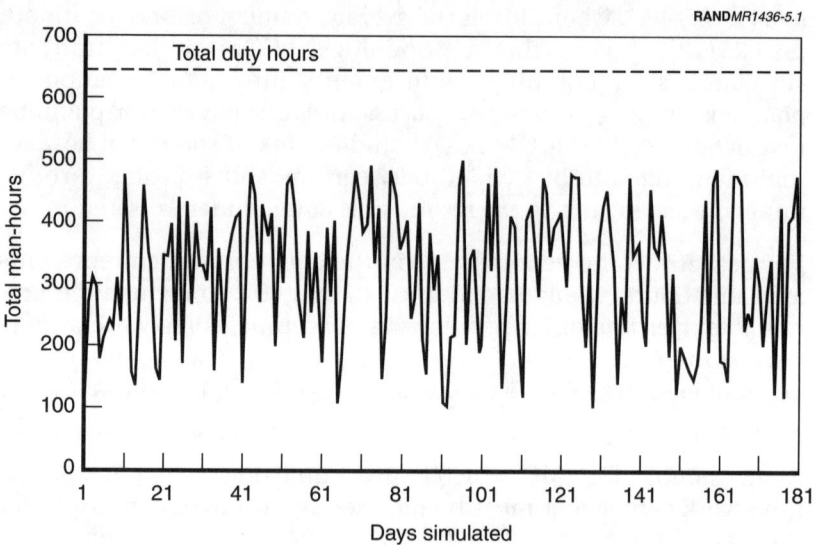

Figure 5.1—Simulated Man-Hours, Minimum Crew Size, and Available Time

manpower positions. The lower, random line illustrates direct maintenance hours used by day. The randomness is primarily a consequence of the random break process associated with aircraft flying sorties and is computed using the LCOM Monte Carlo approach by draws from an exponential distribution, as described in the previous chapters. The upper, dashed line represents the man-hours available from determining a minimum crew size for this work center, including requirements for supervisors. Overall, the M-UTE—i.e., the percentage of total available time spent on direct maintenance and servicing of aircraft—is quite low.[3] In other words, the LCOM simulation, by manning to a minimum crew size that provides man-hours significantly greater than the average daily workload, seems to provide a significant amount of time over and above maintenance requirements. In Figure 5.1, it seems that it would be possible to raise M-UTEs considerably without confronting minimum crew-size constraints.

INDIRECT LABOR TASKS

The Air Force makes a distinction between direct and indirect labor. Direct labor is time spent on maintenance tasks. Indirect labor represents a series of activities, the most important of which are the following:

1. Indoctrination, performance evaluation, performance feedback, and counseling;

2. Reenlistments, awards, and ceremonies;

3. Oversight and personnel management;

4. Development of training standards and training materials;

5. Administrative support and documentation management;

6. Maintenance of personnel records;

7. Attendance at meetings;

---

[3]That is, it is low at least in absolute terms. Although we have attempted to find data on direct M-UTEs in commercial activities, we have been unable to do so. Thus, if anecdotal evidence is relevant, it is at least possible that the utilization rates in private industry are also quite low.

8. Administrative supply management and administrative training;

9. Cleanup of work areas;

10. Maintenance of assigned tool kits;

11. Maintenance of assigned vehicles; and

12. Maintenance of test equipment.

As can be seen, these functions will differ considerably between different occupations and different grades. Senior noncommissioned officers (NCOs) will use most of their time on the first eight items. All personnel assigned to direct maintenance will be involved in item 5 (entering their activities into automated data systems such as CAMS and GO-81), item 7 (attending stand-ups and other meetings), and items 9 to 12 (cleaning up and maintaining tools, vehicles, and test equipment).

The Air Force has never formally issued a regulation on how much time should be set aside for indirect labor. However, an AFMIA draft regulation from May 1, 1989, states that "in the absence of certified MAJCOM maximum utilization factors, use the following AFMIA-approved factors to establish upper simulation constraining limits." The draft regulation then proposes a factor of 77.8 percent for direct labor for almost all maintenance work centers. Since the regulation was never made official, the controlling words in the document are "in the absence of certified MAJCOM maximum utilization factors." Each MAJCOM is therefore empowered to set its own factors. In its simulations, ACC currently uses the AFMIA-proposed standard of 78 percent direct labor as an upper bound, but AMC has determined that the appropriate maximum for its aircraft should be 60 percent. Neither of these two figures is particularly significant for the LCOM simulations, as the manpower utilization factors are almost invariably less than the maximum set in each of the two MAJCOMs. However, they are important for estimating how much time is really available for non-maintenance-related activities, as discussed below.

DERIVING NONSIMULATED WORKING HOURS

The following discussion illustrates how simulated direct labor hours are combined with man-hour availability and indirect labor rules to derive nonsimulated working hours—which are the residual hours that make up the white box. Table 5.3 shows M-UTEs by work center and AFSC resulting from the simulations reported in ACC's official F-16 LCOM study.[4] The first column in Table 5.3 indicates the work center, with CRS being the component repair squadron, EMS the equipment maintenance squadron, SGF the sortie generation flight, and SSF the sortie support flight. In LCOM studies, the AFSC designations are altered from the standard Air Force coding, with the fourth letter indicating the work center or specialty to which a particular person is assigned. Thus, 2A3A2, 2A3B2, and 2A3C2 are all avionics specialists, but each fourth letter here designates a distinct subspecialty within avionics for which there is a simulated maintenance man-hour requirement. Also, 2A3X3 is the general designation for a crew chief, and 2A3P3 in the table stands for crew chiefs assigned to the phase dock.

The third column in Table 5.3 shows the simulated maintenance man-hours, as a total over the entire simulation, which is 180 days in this example. The column labeled "manpower" presents the resultant manning required in that center. It is arrived at by first going through the LCOM constraining process to determine shift mannings and then applying the wartime sustained factor of 1.479, discussed earlier, to convert the shift mannings to manpower requirements. The column labeled "M-UTE" represents the percentage of total available man-hours (hours making up direct *and* indirect labor) that were actually spent on direct maintenance actions.

Table 5.4 shows that the M-UTEs differ considerably across work centers. The average for the flying squadron (indicated in Table 5.4 as FS) is much higher than those for the CRS and EMS even in wartime, when everyone works long hours. This raises the question of whether it is possible to find methods for bringing about a more equal distribution of working hours across AFSCs and work centers. It would in principle be possible to use the LCOM simulation to perform this analysis. As noted above, a manpower position in LCOM is just a resource that performs work on a set of specified WUCs. LCOM simulations take the WUCs assigned to a particular

---

[4]The data are compiled from a report by HQ ACC/XP-SAS entitled *F-16C/D Block 40 Final Report,* Langley Air Force Base, VA, February 1998.

Table 5.3

M-UTEs by Work Center and AFSC[a]

Work Center	AFSC	Maintenance Hours	Manpower	Assigned Hours	Direct Labor Hours	M-UTE (%)
CRS	2A0B1	4926	9	14,025	10,939	35.1
CRS	2A1S1	5209	15	23,374	18,232	22.3
CRS	2A1S7	1733	6	9350	7293	18.5
CRS	2A6S1	7274	15	23,374	18,232	31.1
CRS	2A6S3	3876	12	18,699	14,586	20.7
CRS	2A6S4	4241	15	23,374	18,232	18.1
CRS	2A6S5	513	3	4675	3646	11.0
CRS	2A6S6	3546	8	12,466	9724	28.4
CRS	2A6T1	877	6	9350	7293	9.4
EMS	2A3W3	2155	6	9350	7293	23.0
EMS	2A7C3	3852	8	12,466	9724	30.9
EMS	2A7S1	1484	6	9350	7293	15.9
EMS	2A7S2	2800	6	9350	7293	29.9
EMS	2A7S3	1372	8	12,466	9724	11.0
EMS	2A7S4	1292	3	4675	3646	27.6
EMS	2W1S1	4827	14	21,816	17,016	22.1
SGF	2A3A2	9922	21	32,724	25,525	30.3
SGF	2A3B2	2448	8	12,466	9724	19.6
SGF	2A3C2	9848	21	32,724	25,525	30.1
SGF	2A3X3	34,258	42	65,448	51,049	52.3
SGF	2A6X1	6560	15	23,374	18,232	28.1
SGF	2A6X6	3803	9	14,025	10,939	27.1
SGF	2A1L1	16,615	42	65,448	51,049	25.4
SGF	2A1X1	7755	24	37,399	29,171	20.7
SSF	2A3P3	6781	15	23,374	18,232	29.0

[a]Assumes 10.1 hours per day, six days per week, indirect labor factor = 0.78.

Table 5.4

M-UTEs by Squadron[a]

Work Center	Maintenance Hours	Manpower	Assigned Hours	Direct Labor Hours	Average M-UTE (%)
CRS	32,195	89	138,687	108,176	23.2
EMS	17,782	51	79,473	61,989	22.4
FS	97,990	197	306,982	239,446	31.9

[a]Assumes 10.1 hours per day, six days per week, indirect labor factor = 0.78.

AFSC as given and do not ask whether it is possible to further reduce manpower requirements through a different assignment of WUCs to each AFSC. It is not possible to randomly assign WUCs to various AFSCs to arrive at a common M-UTE, so that everyone works the same hours. Given their training and basic knowledge, each AFSC is adapted to maintain certain systems on an aircraft. Thus, while it may be possible to further reduce manpower requirements by reassigning WUCs across AFSCs, this is not something that can be done by anyone who is not intimately familiar with the maintenance skill requirements on each specific aircraft design series.

This leads to the following consideration: If under the most stressful scenarios available—typically wartime, according to most LCOM analyses, but whatever it may be—only a fraction of available time is actually required to perform aircraft maintenance, then there should be a significant amount of time left over during duty days in much less stressful times to do all the other things required of a member of the Air Force. This follows immediately from Figure 5.1 and Table 5.3, but the argument can be further illustrated in Figure 5.2.

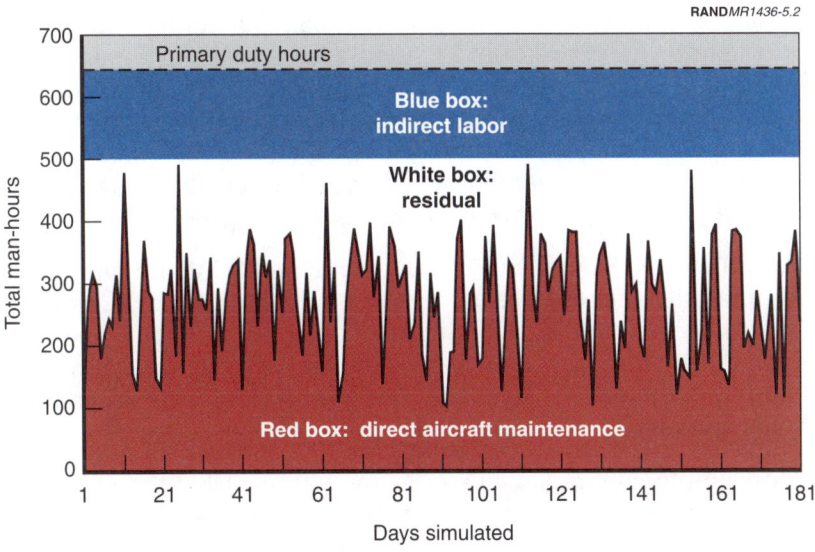

Figure 5.2—Maintenance Hours and Total Available Time

It follows from an inspection of Table 5.3 that since manpower utilization factors vary significantly across work centers, the size of the red box labeled "direct aircraft maintenance" in Figure 5.2 will also vary across work centers and Air Force skill classifications. A basic point illustrated in Figure 5.2 is that the man-hour rules in Table 5.3 are critical for setting the upper bound on the area between the random line and the daily available working hours in that these rules determine the size of the blue box. Another point brought out by Figure 5.2 is that programming rests on the clear assumption that all activities represented by the white and blue boxes can be moved across days. If direct maintenance man-hours are so high on certain days that the red line cuts into the blue box, then there is no time left to perform non–direct maintenance tasks. Hence, they must be assumed to be movable to days when there are lower demands for direct maintenance.

It stands to reason that peacetime maintenance man-hours will be significantly shorter than those for wartime for at least two reasons. First, the required SGR in peacetime is programmed lower than the wartime sortie rate in the war plans. Second, the ASD in peacetime is, for most MDSs, considerably shorter than that during war. On the other hand, there are only 21 maintenance days in a peacetime month and 163.2 available hours (see Table 5.1). On the whole, it is likely that the former outweighs the latter, so that the average M-UTE during peacetime is considerably lower than it would have to be to sustain the more demanding wartime flying schedule. Again, this will vary considerably by work center, as indicated in Table 5.3.

Nevertheless, it is implicitly concluded in the LCOM and manpower communities that the size of the white box provides ample time for maintainers to perform a multitude of other relevant Air Force tasks during their duty day. With the blue box setting the ceiling, the manpower utilization "floor" that LCOM provides leaves a number of hours available for other activities.

For example, Figure 5.3 illustrates the net available time for non-maintenance activities for an F-16 engine specialist (2A6X1) on the flight line. According to LCOM (Table 5.3), his M-UTE is 28 percent. Given the 22 percent of his duty hours set aside for indirect labor activities, half of his day is available for other Air Force tasks. In a 10.1-hour wartime working day, no fewer than 7.2 hours, on average,

RAND*MR1436-5.3*

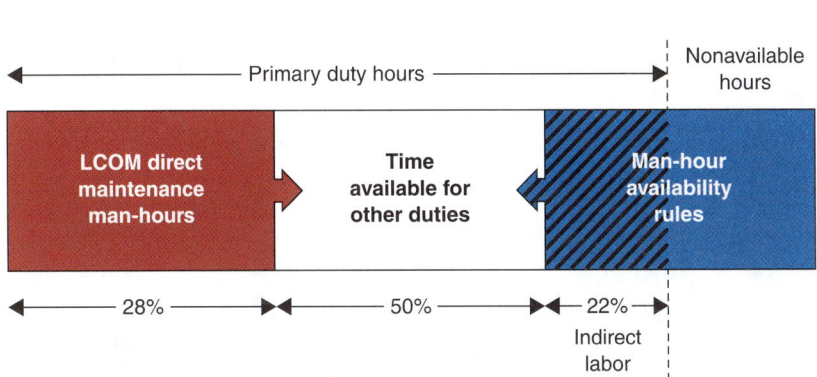

Figure 5.3—Illustration of How to Compute Time Available for Nonmaintenance Activities

should be available for engine troops to accomplish their indirect duties and all other tasks that may be assigned to them. This provides the basis for why LCOM simulations are simply not concerned with non–direct maintenance tasks. Since the most critical activity, after much data gathering and intense analysis, seems to have been amply funded to the most demanding scenarios and there is so much time left over, there has never been any reason to proceed further with data and analysis. However, the assumed conclusion that there is ample time left for duties outside direct maintenance has not been empirically validated by the Air Force. We address the realism of this methodology in Chapter Six. Suffice it to say here that the issue of whether there really is enough time to accomplish all tasks during the duty day turns out to be a critical issue that is worthy of further examination.

SUMMARY AND ISSUES FOR CONSIDERATION

The discussion in this chapter points to several anomalies in the manner in which manpower authorizations are determined. At the present time, the Air Force needs to take a fresh look at the blue box and at its role in determining manpower requirements.

Let us first examine the MAF as reported in Table 5.1. There are several questions that arise upon examination of the assumptions underlying the calculation of nonavailable categories. For reference, we show these factors in Table 5.5.

The first item to note about Table 5.5 is that it is, by regulation, *assumed to be valid for all occupations* in the uniformed Air Force, independent of grade. This may be a perfectly valid assumption for the first three categories—leave, permanent change of station (PCS), and medical. Since the values in the table are statistical averages, they are clearly not intended to be used to account for any particular individual's time or even for the actual use of time among fairly small groups. Instead, they are designed as planning factors to be used only for setting manpower requirements at the Air Force and MAJ-COM levels. It seems clear, however, that there are instances in which these planning factors can lead the organization astray.

To begin with, the category labeled "education and training" refers to formal training, be it in civilian institutions, correspondence courses, educational institutions run by the Air Force (e.g., the NCO academy or Air Education and Training Command (AETC)-managed specialized courses), or local classroom training offered by specialists from AETC. There are significant variations across various skill categories with regard to the availability of and requirements for formal training depending on the level of technical complexity of the tasks appropriate for each AFSC. Also, the amount of education and training appropriate for the force varies with the experience level of the personnel inventory: The younger the force, the greater the demand for formal education and training. This appears to be an area that is ripe

Table 5.5

Nonavailable Categories, Hours per Month

Category	Peacetime Hours per Month
Leave	9.31
PCS	1.20
Medical	1.93
Organizational duties	0.46
Education and training	2.85
Social actions	0

for close investigation. It is unclear how sensitive this particular planning factor is to variations across AFSCs and the experience level of the maintenance personnel inventory.

With regard to the category designated "organizational duties," it seems appropriate to use an average planning factor for the high-level determination of manpower requirements—yet the amount of actual time spent in the field on the tasks assumed under this category is probably invariant with the size of the force. As the force has shrunk, however, many overhead positions on the staff of various field units have decreased as well. As a consequence, the actual time per person spent on organizational duties is likely to have increased. Reports of the migration of field maintainers to various organizational duty positions are a clear indication of this phenomenon. It is time for the Air Force to assess the concept of organizational duties and to determine how much time is actually used in present field units.

There is a basic asymmetry in LCOM-based manpower programming practices. On one hand, LCOM uses detailed data on work-center-associated AFSCs and the particular tasks assigned to specific occupations. As noted, LCOM even allows one to compute the precise number of hours a maintainer can be expected to perform the direct maintenance and servicing of aircraft over a long simulation period. On the other hand, the final estimates of manpower requirements are based on broad programming factors that encompass all occupations and all activities across the Air Force. While the use of such broad parameters may be appropriate at highly aggregated levels of planning such as that performed on the Air Staff in building programmatic estimates consistent with a given top line, they are not consistent with the details of the rest of the LCOM simulations for each work center and for every MDS. At the very least, one would expect that more precise data would be gathered within each of the MAJCOMs that rely on LCOM so that the blue box is sized using the same class of data as the red box. Although this would require further data collection, it seems eminently feasible given the overall effort devoted by the Air Force to setting maintenance manpower requirements.

Further, current practices allow each MAJCOM to set its own levels for indirect labor. Since ACC uses a factor of 78 percent and AMC one of 60 percent, the size of the blue box is very different in the two commands. This means that there is a different threshold in the simulations for when manpower is added by analysts to meet peak demands. However, the difference between the two commands also affects the size of the residual—i.e., the size of the white box, or the time remaining after indirect labor and direct maintenance tasks have been accounted for. In its assumptions in setting the indirect labor factor, ACC arrives at a statement which implies that considerably more time remains for other, non–direct maintenance tasks than does AMC. Since there are no obvious reasons the activities covered under the indirect labor category should be different between the two commands, this too is an area worthy of further investigation.

Finally, foreshadowing a discussion reserved for Chapter Six, there is nothing stated in either the man-hour availability factors or the descriptions of indirect labor activities that accounts for time needed for OJT. Since this is both a time-consuming and a functionally critical activity at the unit level, it should be included in manpower requirement determinations. This will not happen until OJT is formally included in the appropriate manpower instructions.

Chapter Six

THE WHITE BOX: AMPLE TIME FOR "EVERYTHING ELSE"?

After LCOM determines shift manning and the man-hour rules are applied as appropriate, residual time remains for maintainers to carry out any other duties that might be required of them. The duty hours that maintainers in the field currently log are quite long, the reasons for which may include both a dismal fill rate and potential shortfalls in authorizations. Our research suggests that a primary source of these problems is a white box that is "bursting at the seams." More pointedly, a loss of focused oversight over the direction of a significant part of the maintainer's duty day is leading to a form of "mission creep"—as well as to an overtasked workforce, especially among midlevel and senior technicians. This lack of oversight is the reason we identify a white box in the first place; in fact, there would be *no white box at all* (i.e., what we have designated as the white box would be a known entity) if all duties were accounted for in planning and programming.

Since the Air Force does not routinely track the level of effort maintainers exert to carry out duties associated with the white box, we surveyed maintainers at three bases—one fighter base and two mobility bases—in the context of separate research on Air Force readiness.[1] As in the LCOM audits described in Chapter Four, we asked maintainers in the field how they spend their time under various conditions, how many hours they work per week, and what their

---

[1]See, for example, Carl J. Dahlman and David E. Thaler, *Assessing Unit Readiness: Case Study of an Air Force Fighter Wing*, DB-296-AF, Santa Monica: RAND, 2000.

manpower needs are on the basis of the requirements to produce sorties and to conduct OJT. For the same reasons LCOM audit data are preferable to no data at all, the results of the surveys have value in that they quantify important issues for which existing data are incomplete or nonexistent. There is a dire need to lay an empirical foundation for decisionmaking relevant to white-box activities.[2]

In this chapter, we first describe white-box activities in detail and, where possible, attempt to quantify some of the level of effort maintainers are exerting on these tasks. We then explore the adequacy of the size of the white box under alternative assumptions.

WHITE-BOX ACTIVITIES

We identify at least four classes of duties maintainers must perform that are not adequately covered in processes for determining maintenance manpower requirements. These are as follows:

- OJT;
- Changes in duty emphasis that accompany high-OPTEMPO demands;
- Additional duties involving direct maintenance; and
- Out-of-hide activities.

We address each of these white-box activities in turn.

On-the-Job Training

High-level maintenance skills can be acquired only through hands-on training. Maintainers learn by observing senior people performing the tasks and then by taking their turn at the same tasks with adequate supervision. Mastery is attained through repetition, and a trainee can then progress to more complex tasks and to higher levels of experience. This training requires two essential elements. First, there must be something to maintain or repair—i.e., some part on the aircraft that requires diagnosis, removal, repair when appropri-

---

[2]For more on these questionnaires, see Appendix C.

ate, and replacement. In other words, most maintenance training requires equipment to break; otherwise there is nothing to repair and no teaching or learning opportunity. Second, the trainer must have time to teach and the trainee time to learn. That is, maintenance man-hours must include time for the OJT that is such an essential element of maintenance. The more time there is to train, the more systematic the training can be, and the more a sound maintenance philosophy can be imparted to the trainee.

Figure 6.1 illustrates the OJT process and shows that pilot training—in the case of this figure, fighter pilot training—is at heart nothing but OJT. Senior pilots train junior pilots inside the unit. New pilots enter their first operational assignment from undergraduate pilot training (UPT) and progress through mission qualification training (MQT) to become combat mission ready inexperienced (CMR-N, entailing fewer than 500 hours in the weapon system). They then attain the level of combat mission ready experienced (CMR-E), and after more training and experience they graduate to flight lead, instructor pilot, and eventually mission commander (FL, IP, and MC).[3] Squadrons lose pilots when they are reassigned or leave the Air Force for civilian jobs.

The lower half of Figure 6.1 depicts exactly the same process for maintainers. They come out of tech school as mission ready technicians (MRTs) and start as 3-level apprentices in their occupations. After some time, which varies with each occupation, they progress to 5-level journeymen and, after several years, to 7-level craftsmen. As senior 5-levels and 7-levels, they often perform supervisory duties. The more experienced 5- and 7-levels serve as OJT trainers for the less experienced technicians. As with pilots, units lose maintainers to other assignments and to civilian life. Maintenance training must be accomplished at the same time the maintainers are supporting the generation of sorties for pilot training and performing life-cycle maintenance on the aircraft. The unit must also accomplish all of these things while preparing for and meeting high-OPTEMPO demands (e.g., contingency or rotational deployments, inspections, and surges).

---

[3]In large aircraft such as airlifters and tankers, the corresponding terms are pilot initial qualification (PIQ), copilot, first pilot, aircraft commander, instructor pilot, and flight examiner.

Figure 6.1 conveys a message not only of rapid flow-through of personnel, which necessitates constant OJT for continuation and upgrade, but also of the sensitive balancing act that is required between production and training. Pilots have a requirement for continuation and upgrade training that can be met only by generating sorties from the relevant aircraft; the maintenance side is constantly under pressure to meet these sortie requirements. If the demand for sorties increases beyond what maintenance personnel can reasonably produce during regular working hours, they will be asked to work overtime. If the imbalance between sortie demands and maintenance resources persists, overtime will then become expected and normal. This is especially true during periods of high OPTEMPO.

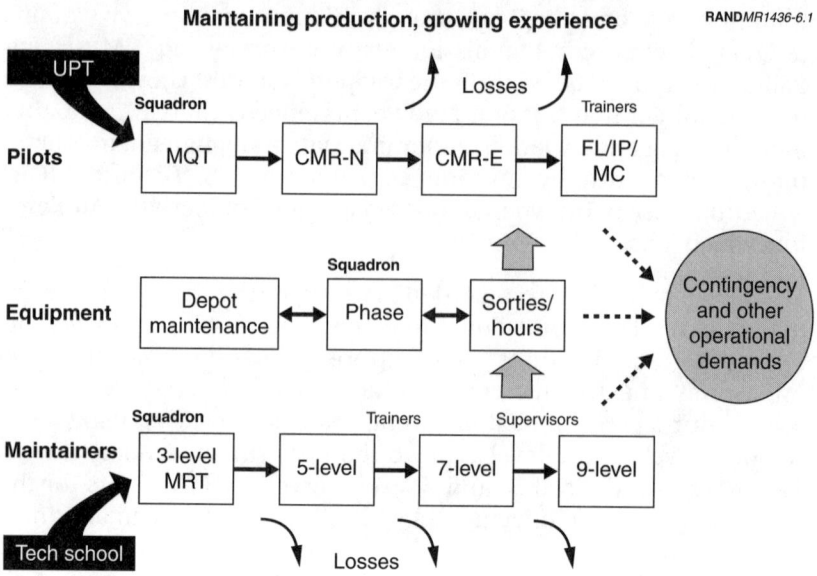

Figure 6.1—Striking a Delicate Balance in Flying Squadrons

Furthermore, there must also be a balance between senior and junior personnel among both pilots and maintainers.[4] Junior personnel are

---

[4]Our colleague Bill Taylor has developed a linear programming model that makes it possible to estimate the flying hours required to support training requirements when

required to replace senior personnel who leave the unit, and senior personnel are required for supervision and training. Our research indicates that during the last few years, both the balance between senior and junior personnel and that between production and training have been upset. The results have manifested themselves in longer working hours, lower productivity, and, potentially, lower-quality training—at a time when several factors have caused an increased demand on maintainers.

Receiving OJT as a learner and providing OJT as a teacher together comprise significant blocks of time in the duty days of maintenance technicians. Figure 6.2 illustrates the percentage of their duty days maintainers say they spend on producing (including supervision of production) and on teaching and learning via OJT.[5] In both the fighter wings (FWs) and air mobility wings (AMWs), 5- and 7-levels responded that they spend more than half their time on generating sorties and repairing aircraft or on supervising these activities. Another 15 to 20 percent of their time is devoted to training junior personnel and upgrading themselves—representing a significant amount of time that is not adequately captured in programming. In the AMWs, 3-levels spend between one-quarter and one-third of their time learning.[6] Notably, 3-levels said they spend about 4 percent of their duty days *teaching* OJT. This is certainly a sign that pressures associated with the supply of—and demands on—

---

pilot experience mix changes. See William Taylor et al., *The Air Force Pilot Shortage: A Crisis for Operational Units?* MR-1204-AF, Santa Monica: RAND, 2000. While it is, at present, impossible to build a parallel linear programming model for maintainers, exactly the same logic applies to maintenance technicians: that as experience mix declines, the requirement for training increases disproportionately.

[5]Although OJT is often accomplished while producing, we asked respondents to separate the two activities. We are mindful of the fact that for many maintainers, this may not be a straightforward separation. However, we did not get huge response ranges, indicating that respondents were able to differentiate.

[6]Our survey of maintainers at the 388th FW focused only on 5- and 7-levels. Subsequent surveys at the 60th and 305th AMWs included questionnaires tailored to 3-levels as well. Our efforts to define questions and gather information evolved after our initial effort at the 388th FW.

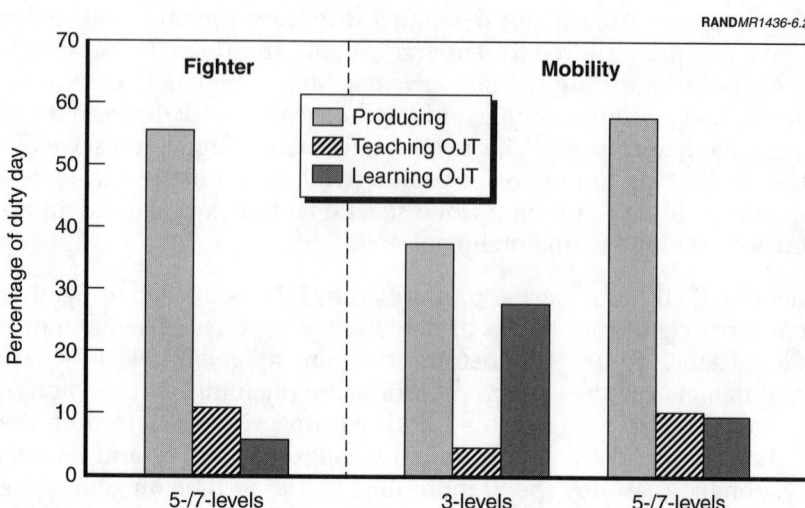

**Figure 6.2—Time Spent on Production and OJT as a Percentage of
Total Duty Day (normal OPTEMPO)**

maintainers are pushing some responsibilities down to more junior technicians.

Figure 6.3 shows 5-levels' and 7-levels' perceptions of the number of hours per week they spent producing, teaching OJT, and learning OJT at mid-decade compared with today. We calculated these hours by multiplying total duty hours (which also include administrative and other duties not depicted here) by the percentage of duty hours maintainers say they spend on each activity. Maintainers in the FW said they worked a total of 53 hours per week at the end of the 1990s, up from 50 hours at mid-decade. The duty week for AMW maintainers increased from about 41 to 45 hours during that time.

Changes in operational demands and manning seem to have had different effects on the FW and AMW. By 2000, as production hours increased by one-third in the FW, both teaching and learning declined to just over half the level of effort applied in the mid-1990s. Time on administrative tasks climbed by 20 percent to 11 hours per week, while other tasks (including out-of-hide activities) increased by one-third to about four hours per week.

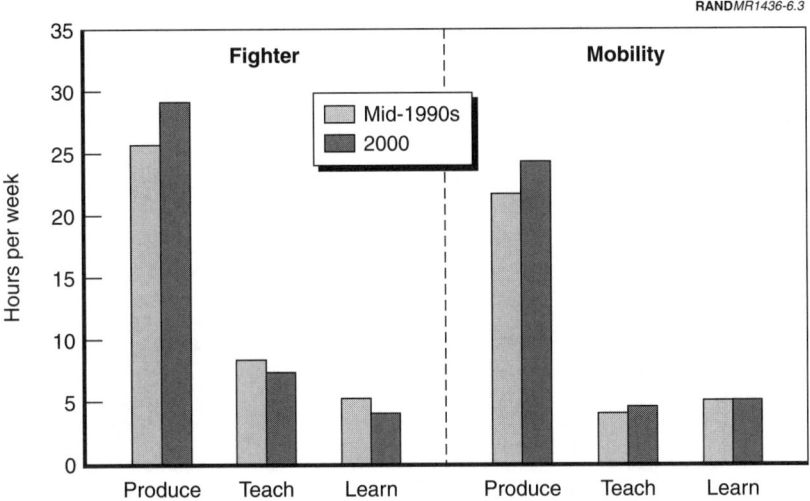

Figure 6.3—Hours per Week Spent by 5- and 7-Levels on Producing, Teaching OJT, and Learning OJT, Mid-1990s vs. 2000 (normal OPTEMPO)

The 5- and 7-level maintainers in the AMW also increased their hours dedicated to production, but only by about 12 percent. In addition, they were able to maintain a relatively constant level of effort on teaching OJT, despite reduced manning, by slightly increasing the hours they each spent on this activity. The more junior 5-levels had the largest percentage increase in time on teaching. Conversely, the senior 5-levels and the 7-levels reduced the time they devoted to upgrading themselves, with the latter diminishing by 23 percent to about 2.8 hours per week.

Figure 6.4 compares the mid-1990s and 2000 OJT training capacity of the FW and AMW, depicting this capacity as a function of the number of 3-levels per "trainer equivalent." This measure is important in that the more 3-levels a trainer must teach, the less focused that training is and the more time a trainee may take to gain experience. We define a trainer equivalent as the product of a 5- or 7-level's relative teaching effectiveness and the amount of time he spends teaching OJT. In our calculations, there are two types of 5-levels: junior 5-levels holding the grade of airman first class, or A1C (E-3), and senior

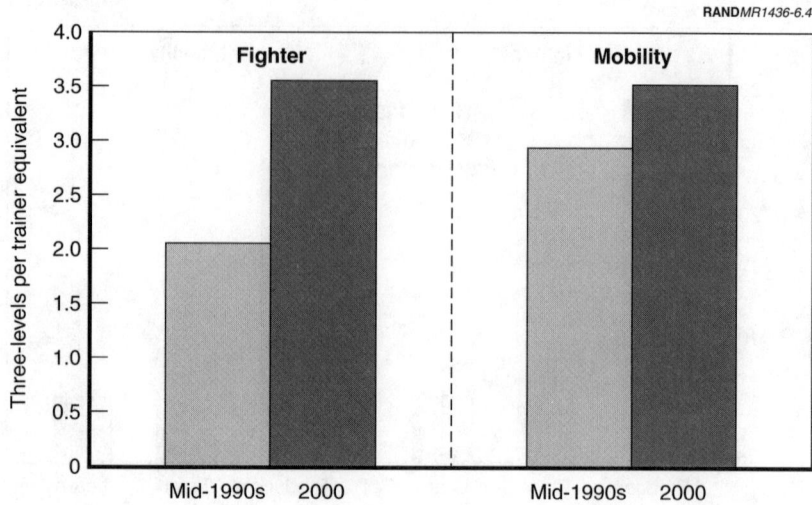

Figure 6.4—Three-Levels per Trainer Equivalent in Fighter and Mobility Wings, Mid-1990s and 2000 (normal OPTEMPO)

5-levels holding the grade of senior airman, or SrA (E-4), and above (SrA+). Teaching effectiveness is measured in relation to a 7-level at 1.0; the teaching effectiveness of senior and junior 5-levels is 0.91 and 0.56, respectively. These assumptions are based on our field surveys.[7]

The number of 3-levels per trainer equivalent in the FW has risen 71 percent since mid-decade from about 2.0 to roughly 3.5. In part, this reflects a deterioration in the experience mix: an increase in the proportion of trainees from 25 to 31 percent and an increase in the proportion of junior 5-levels (who are less effective teachers) from 11 percent to 19 percent of total assigned 5-levels. The number of trainer equivalents has fallen precipitously in the FW from about 140 to 95 trainer equivalents. The AMW wing has had similar, albeit less pronounced, changes in its training capacity, which has declined by 19 percent. The AMW trainee-to-trainer ratio began in the mid-

---

[7]We asked maintainers to assess the relative productivity of 3-levels, junior 5-levels, senior 5-levels, and 7-levels. We assumed the same values for teaching effectiveness.

1990s somewhat higher than in the FW, at nearly three 3-levels per trainer equivalent.   For the most part, this resulted from FW maintainers' perception that they spent more time teaching in the mid-1990s than was the case with maintainers in the AMW.[8]   Still, the percentage of primary 3-levels assigned to the AMW rose from 23 to 26 percent during the period, and this accounts for much of the change in the trainee-to-trainer ratio.[9]

In sum, all three wings we surveyed gave similar qualitative responses—that OJT is a relatively time-consuming component of maintainers' working hours.   Yet teaching and learning OJT are not systematically accounted for in either man-hour rules (the blue box) or LCOM (the red box).   In the determination of manpower requirements, OJT seems to be taken simply as a cost of doing business. Given its importance in the maintenance field, however, OJT should be seen as a separable and variable requirement.

Unfortunately, OJT is also a volatile component of a duty day.   It shows signs of constituting a "bill payer" when units respond to stress induced by manning shortfalls.   This effect is more pronounced in the fighter wing, especially during periods of high OPTEMPO—a second white-box issue to which we now turn.

Meeting High-OPTEMPO Demands

Duty hours increase substantially when maintainers are challenged to meet operational demands such as deployments, inspections, surges, and exercises.   These periods can total about five to six months annually for fighter units and somewhat less for mobility units.   In the fighter world, the most stressful demands seem to relate to preparation for, workload during, and recovery from split ops. Split ops usually refer to overseas deployments that require a

---

[8]In part, this could be due to the formal training regimen at the AMW, whereby newly assigned 3-levels spend their first three to six months on base in a "logistics university" that provides hands-on training to lessen the OJT burden on experienced flight-line maintainers.

[9]Since some 5-levels also receive OJT, the method in the text and displayed on the chart is actually an undercount, as all 5-levels are treated there as instructors and only 3-levels make up the students.   The real decline in trainer equivalents is therefore even deeper than the chart shows.

squadron to deploy only a portion of its aircraft, pilots, and maintainers. The nondeploying part of the squadron remains at home station and continues to generate sorties for pilot training and to conduct OJT for maintainers. Naturally, commanders leading their units on a deployment choose to bring along their best equipment and more experienced people to minimize any risks inherent in an operational environment. In preparation, wings focus on readying the deploying jets and on completing required training for deploying maintainers; this often involves aid from the wing's other squadrons, thereby increasing demand on them as well. The less reliable aircraft are left at home station to be maintained and generated by less experienced, less productive technicians who need training while continuing to meet a flying schedule for the pilots who stay behind.

Figure 6.5 shows how manning at home station changed when the 34th Fighter Squadron (one of the three F-16 Block 40 squadrons in the 388th FW at Hill Air Force Base) deployed 10 of its 18 jets to al-Jaber in Kuwait from November 1998 through January 1999.[10] Of the 202 3-, 5-, and 7-levels assigned to the squadron, only about 35 percent deployed (see the striped bar to the left in Figure 6.5). However, almost all those who deployed were primary-assigned 5- and 7-levels, leaving only half of the more experienced personnel at home station (the dark gray third bar from the left). As a result, 3-levels made up 47 percent of the home station maintenance force in the 34th during split ops (second bar from the right)—much worse than the 32 percent assigned to the entire unit.[11]

For the nearly three months of split ops, then, the experience mix at home station was much less favorable than the assigned mix for the entire unit. Certainly, the resulting productivity at the deployed location was high, as it should be in an operational environment. However, split ops negatively affected productivity at home station at a time when pilots still needed sorties for training. The TNMCM rate hovered between 30 and 35 percent, about twice the usual rate.

_____

[10]During this deployment, the 34th participated in Operation Desert Fox against Iraq.

[11]Using primary AFSCs. With control AFSCs, the experience mix would look much worse.

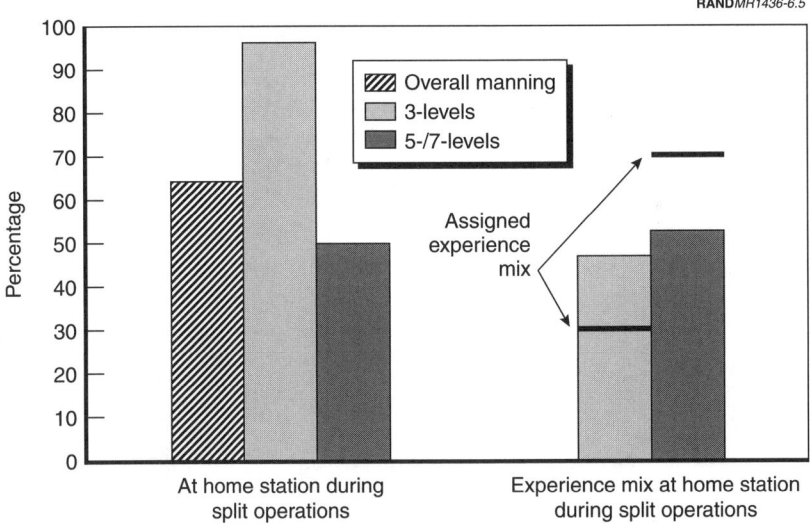

Figure 6.5—Maintenance Manning at Home Station During Split Ops,
34th Fighter Squadron, November 1998 to January 1999

Pilots at home were able to fly fewer than half of planned sorties in December, thereby delaying upgrade schedules.

OJT suffered greatly under these circumstances. Maintainers in the 34th reported that OJT and upgrade training at home station were virtually nonexistent during split ops. The senior technicians who remained at home were heavily engaged in generating and repairing the unit's more problem-plagued jets, and 3-levels were producing much more than they normally would in lieu of training. Maintenance training was postponed until after the deployed portion of the squadron returned, and then OJT was competing with the need to provide sorties for pilots who were trying to "catch up" as well. From the maintainer's standpoint, therefore, the recovery from split ops was nearly as stressful as the split-ops period itself.

Figure 6.6 shows how 5- and 7-level maintainers perceive that their duty days change during high-OPTEMPO periods. According to this figure, total duty hours rise by about 15 percent in both the FW and the AMW (in this case, the 305th AMW at McGuire Air Force Base).

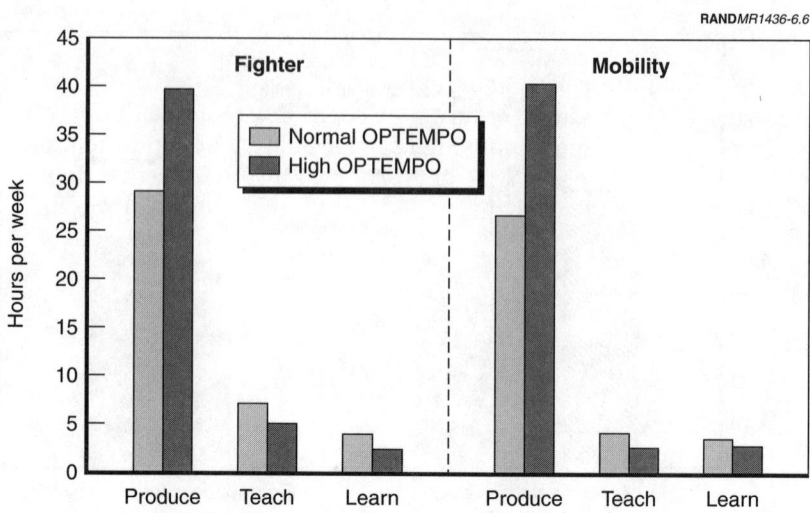

Figure 6.6—Percentage of 5- and 7-Level Time Spent on Activities,
Normal vs. High OPTEMPO

The percentage of time spent on production and supervision—i.e., sortie generation and associated maintenance activities—also increases. Moreover, technicians in both wings reduce the portion of their duty days spent on training others and upgrading themselves. The data from the 388th FW on the left show that high-OPTEMPO periods cause an increase in production hours of about 36 percent, particularly during exercises, inspections, and preparation for no-notice contingencies. A key bill payer is training, which declines by roughly 28 and 36 percent for teaching and learning, respectively.

The right side of Figure 6.6 illustrates a similar situation for 5- and 7-levels in the 305th AMW, where production time shares increase by 50 percent during surges, dispatch of maintenance repair teams, deployments, and exercises. The 37 percent decline in teaching activities is as dramatic here as in the FW. The reduction in learning time is much less pronounced, however, with a decrease of only 19 percent. Notably, 3-levels in the AMW actually *teach others OJT* about 4 percent of their time during normal operations, and this goes up considerably (to about 12 percent in the extreme) during high-OPTEMPO periods.

The message from these wings is that high OPTEMPO can reduce training opportunities. This has, of course, been known anecdotally before—it is hardly news to maintainers that higher OPTEMPO raises production and reduces training. The more frequent the deployments and other factors causing high OPTEMPO are and the longer their duration, the deeper the effect on training. A force that deploys or faces other high-OPTEMPO situations much of the time has a higher manpower requirement than one that deploys only to (presumably infrequent) major wars. That is, air expeditionary forces used for a series of frequent contingency deployments must be made more robust through higher manpower authorizations and personnel fill rates than a garrison force that deploys only rarely.

The question then arises whether peacetime can be more stressful on maintenance personnel than wartime. Taking LCOM at face value, the answer is an emphatic yes. Even under wartime conditions, the most stressful scenarios possible, LCOM finds that M-UTEs are at most in the 40 to 50 percent range, with many occupations and work centers considerably below that. Additionally, some of the white-box tasks discussed in this chapter may simply go away in wartime (although other tasks may replace them). Most training is assumed to be held in abeyance until the war is over, and fill rates are often increased in fighting units by borrowing experienced personnel from nonfighting units. Many of the tasks assumed under nonavailable and indirect labor categories in the manpower rules also decline significantly in warfighting units. In other words, while direct maintenance tasks may increase during war as a result of higher sortie rates and longer sortie durations, many other tasks simply get put off until the war is over. During high-OPTEMPO periods in peacetime, maintainers must continue to accomplish all of these tasks. Thus, peacetime, especially when combined with the requirement to support contingencies and other external demands, can be more stressful than war for maintainers.

Performing Additional Maintenance Duties

Several direct maintenance duties are not captured in LCOM's red box. As discussed in Chapters Three and Four, certain inputs to LCOM analysis are based on policy goals that may not reflect actual observations in the field. In the current climate, actual experience often fails to achieve the goals set by the Air Force. Thus, any added duties created by differences between policy and reality are left to maintainers to perform in the context of the white box.

One example of this can be found in cannibalization rates, which are much higher in the field than in Air Force standards and thus provide a source of added workload. When parts are unavailable and sorties need to be flown, maintainers often cannibalize parts from other aircraft. Certain aircraft may be designated as "cann birds" when they are under repair and unavailable for the flight line. Sometimes, when specific components break frequently and supplies of those components are continually low, maintainers must also cannibalize parts from aircraft that are undergoing scheduled maintenance, from "hard broke" aircraft, or, in extreme cases, from a second cann bird.[12]

Cannibalizations are poorly recorded in automated maintenance databases such as CAMS and GO-81. Because the Air Force cannot afford to stock parts inventories to meet its total non–mission capable due to supply (TNMCS) goals, parts are often cannibalized from one aircraft to another, typically at significant manpower cost. LCOM estimates include policy-sanctioned cannibalizations, but the fact that the latter do not reflect current reality can have a significant effect on the time it takes to complete a maintenance action owing to the extra removal and replacement involved.

Cannibalization actions can be highly time-consuming activities. Ideally, a technician identifies a bad part, removes it, orders and retrieves a replacement part from the on-base supply shop, and then places the new part in the aircraft. Frequently, however, when the on-base supply shop reports the part out of stock, the maintainer must go to the cann bird to acquire the needed part. This can involve removing incidentals such as panels and other components in order to reach the part to be canned. Once the part is removed from the cann bird, the technician may need to perform other tasks such as cleaning up the work area and checking the operation of the part ("ops checks"). Moreover, the technician must often complete additional paperwork to enable tracking of the cann action and of all

---

[12]A hard-broke aircraft is one that is non–mission capable and requires substantial work to return it to mission-capable status. This is a term of art.

parts that have been canned from the cann bird. He must then replace the part in the jet he was initially repairing.

Efforts to return cann birds to a flyable condition are manpower intensive as well. At the 60th AMW at Travis Air Force Base, the length of time during which a specific C-5 is designated a cann bird is about 90 days, after which it is returned to operational status and replaced by a new cann bird. The 60th Aircraft Generation Squadron (AGS) reports that a team of seven recovery personnel plus two to four specialists work 12 days in 12-hour shifts to bring the cann bird to a status where it can be towed. The team then tows it to a parking spot and spends another 12 days on eight-hour shifts to complete the recovery.

In sum, a significant amount of time is consumed performing cannibalization-related activities. When there are shortages of parts in the supply system, canning can add substantial amounts of time to direct maintenance actions captured in LCOM. Even the administrative duties required to track cannibalizations consume man-hours, especially for large aircraft with many thousands of parts. At Travis Air Force Base, for example, three experienced technicians (two 7-levels and one 5-level) manage the C-5 cann bird *full time*. About 60 other 7-levels responding to our survey report that they spend an average of ten hours per week tracking cann actions. Thus, at least 15 percent of total primary-assigned 7-levels at Travis average two hours per day just on cann administration.

Another issue affects certain aircraft more than others, but all to some degree: the increased frequency of time-change technical orders (TCTOs). TCTOs are mandates from system program offices for certain upgrades or changes to aircraft systems that must be completed before a certain date, sometimes as a result of safety considerations but usually for improved performance. Many TCTOs are assigned to the depots, but some are the responsibility of the wings. Air Force guidance states that TCTOs requiring more than 25 working hours should be transferred to the depot; this limit is not infrequently exceeded.[13] LCOM audits capture the recent history of

---

[13]See Dahlman and Thaler, DB-296-AF, RAND, 2000, pp. 29–30.

TCTO maintenance hours but not the growth that occurs between audits.

The requirement to meet high standards for MC rates can add workload if these standards are higher than what is needed to generate required sorties—the metric driving LCOM calculations and, therefore, maintenance manpower. The Air Force calculates MC rates by dividing the total hours in a month aircraft are possessed by the total hours in a month the aircraft are mission capable. Nominally, for an 18-aircraft squadron, this is 18×24 hours a day $\times 30.44$ average days a month, or 13,150 hours. A squadron of 18 F-16s for which the Air Force goal is an MC rate of 83 percent should attain 10,915 mission-capable hours.

To illustrate how the standard MC rate can exceed the SGR, let us assume that an aircraft must be ready at least one hour before takeoff. If it flies an average of two sorties per flying day with an ASD of four hours, it needs to be mission capable a minimum of ten hours per day (including the two preflight hours). On a monthly basis, assuming a seven-day flying schedule in wartime, this equates to an MC rate of only $18 \times 10 \times 30.44$, or 5479 mission-capable hours; dividing by 13,150 hours yields an MC rate of only 42 percent, or about half the Air Force standard. While this illustration is extreme, efforts to improve MC rates have little or no impact on the SGR in LCOM and may represent an unfunded increase in workload for maintainers. A number of maintainers cite the practice of weekend and Friday-evening repairs of aircraft even if the repairs could be performed on Monday without restricting scheduled sorties.

There are other examples of direct maintenance duties that are not captured in LCOM. Some of these may result from problems associated with aging aircraft, the disappearance of key vendors who manufacture aircraft parts, and a breakdown in two-level-maintenance (2LM) policies. Under three-level maintenance (3LM), the wing accomplished both minor and intermediate maintenance activities on base; for major maintenance, the wing would send aircraft to the depot. The 2LM concept, instituted in the early 1990s, was designed to move intermediate-level maintenance—and the associated workload—from the wing to the depot. Accordingly, manpower was reduced in wing back shops. Unfortunately, many wings are experiencing a growing need to perform intermediate maintenance such that 3LM exists de facto. Feeding this return to 3LM is a concern on the part of squadron and wing commanders that the aircraft they send to the depot will be away and unavailable to fly for too long. Thus, the commanders turn to their own back shops for intermediate maintenance actions. At Travis, for example, the back shops are actually manufacturing their own parts because these parts are no longer produced by outside vendors. Yet the manpower has not increased along with the added workload.

Finally, some added maintenance duty may arise from the policy of programming manpower based on primary mission aircraft inventories (PMAIs). Squadrons do not earn manpower slots for backup aircraft inventories (BAIs) or attrition reserve (A/R) aircraft, yet squadrons are expected to maintain them. For example, in addition to the 949 PMAI fighter aircraft in the FY 2000 inventory, there were 149 BAI and A/R aircraft. Thus, maintainers in FWs earn manpower for over 13 percent fewer aircraft than they are actually expected to maintain. This does not directly translate linearly into manpower because these aircraft are often used to replace PMAI aircraft that have been sent to the depot for major maintenance. In some circumstances (such as high OPTEMPO), however, these additional aircraft can add to maintainers' duties.

Manning Out-of-Hide Positions

The requirement to man out-of-hide positions is a "hot-button" issue for maintainers in the field, as it can be an important drain on maintenance manpower. Although these positions largely involve tasks that must be accomplished to ensure the smooth operation of the wing, group, squadron, or flight, they are not funded in programming. To fill these positions, personnel are moved from their primary occupations. The "losing" organization (e.g., an SGF) retains these personnel in its manning document, but they may show up for work elsewhere—i.e., they are taken "out of hide" and are not replaced. In some cases, personnel may stay in the same organization but work in an unfunded position that is different from their primary occupation. Although personnel in out-of-hide positions in operational units may be from any career field, maintainers often bear the lion's share of the burden. They are usually the largest occupational group in the wing.

Table 6.1 gives a list of out-of-hide positions at Travis Air Force Base that were filled with maintainers as of spring 2000. A significant number of the positions are not germane to maintenance, although they may be deemed necessary for the efficient operation of the organization. These positions include hazardous waste technicians, resource and quality advisers, computer and local-area network managers, augmentees for security police, honor guards for veterans' funerals, and even assignees to the base museum.

Table 6.1

Out-of-Hide Positions Filled by Maintainers in the 60th AMW Logistics Group, Spring 2000

Out-of-Hide Position	Maintainers Assigned	Average Grade[a]	Full-/ Part Time	Source of Requirement
Training Manager/Monitor	9	SSgt	F/T	Sqn, Flt
Hazardous Waste Technician	8	SrA	F/T	Grp, Sqn
Security Police Augmentee	8	A1C	P/T	Wg
Computer Systems	7	SSgt	F/T	Sqn, Flt
Self-Help Team	5	TSgt	F/T	Grp
Dorm/Facility Manager	4	MSgt	F/T	Wg, Sqn
Production Superintendent	4	MSgt	F/T	Sqn
Quality Adviser	4	SSgt	F/T	Sqn
Repairable Assets Control Center	4	SSgt	F/T	Flt
Safety	4	TSgt	F/T	Grp, Sqn
Vehicles	4	SSgt	F/T	Sqn
Aircraft Repair Enhancement Program	3	TSgt	F/T	Wg
Other Administration	3	SrA	F/T	Grp, Sqn, Flt
Resource Adviser/Manager	3	SSgt	F/T	Sqn
Unit Deployment Manager	3	TSgt	F/T	Sqn
Assistant Unit Deployment Manager	2	SrA	F/T	Sqn
Environmental Manager	2	SSgt	F/T	Wg, Flt
Museum	2	MSgt	F/T	Wg
Protocol	2	SSgt	F/T	Wg
Technical Order Distribution Office	2	SSgt	F/T	Sqn
Contractor-Operated Main Base Supply Liaison	1	TSgt	F/T	Grp
Honor Guard	1	SrA	F/T	Wg
Retention Manager	1	SSgt	F/T	Sqn

[a]TSgt = technical sergeant; MSgt = master sergeant.

At the time, there were 86 maintainers assigned out of hide; the second column in Table 6.1 shows the number of maintainers in each position. Except for security police augmentees, all positions were full time. Sources for out-of-hide requirements spanned the wing organization from the wing, group, and squadron and down to the flight.

Although only 86 maintainers were in out-of-hide positions (out of a maintenance force of roughly 1370 3-, 5-, and 7-levels in the generation and maintenance squadrons), these tended to be more experienced technicians. The average grade was E-5 Staff Sergeant (SSgt), typically a senior 5-level or a 7-level technician, because most of these duties could not be assigned to junior personnel. Thus, out-of-hide positions actually account for a drop in senior maintainers as a proportion of total maintainers. For primary-assigned 5-levels, the fill rate diminished from 79 to 74 percent as a result of out-of-hide obligations. Crew chiefs were the largest source, filling about half of the out-of-hide positions, while engine troops were the second-largest source at 14 percent of such positions.

A recent Air Staff sampling of eight bases in ACC and AMC suggests that about 4 percent of the maintenance population is assigned out of hide. Experienced maintainers may constitute more than 90 percent of the total in out-of-hide positions. With about 50,000 assigned 5- and 7-levels, more than 2600 experienced maintainers could potentially be returned to the flight line and to duties as OJT trainers.

Out-of-hide duties are thus responsible for a significant drift of people away from maintenance and sortie generation. For those who remain, the effect is a higher workload and an increase in duty hours. Moreover, the organization loses an important pool of trainers. Since crew chiefs have one of the highest M-UTEs in LCOM, their reassignment to nonmaintenance tasks may have a disproportionate effect on them.

Many out-of-hide functions appear useful and even important for a unit commander to support. The question for the Air Force is whether it is by now time to explicitly authorize and fill positions that are essential for base and community support so that the drift of skilled technical personnel to other duties can be minimized. At the present time, there is widespread sentiment in the field that the balance between sortie generation support, training of young enlisted personnel, and nonmaintenance tasks has been lost. When unit personnel are under severe pressure to meet their essential tasks, the constant loss of people to what are viewed as less important tasks has a highly detrimental effect on morale and unit cohesiveness.

ESTIMATING THE ADEQUACY OF THE WHITE BOX

Using the above treatment of white-box activities as background, we now explore the adequacy of the size of the white box under various assumptions. Is the manpower community's assumption correct that once LCOM and manpower rules are taken into account, enough time remains in the duty day to complete all other activities? Although the data available on these issues are incomplete, there is value in attempting to estimate the adequacy of the white box. If that box is large enough to provide ample time for units to perform all other activities that are demanded of them in their daily duties, then it may be reasonable to conclude that current problems relate not to insufficient authorizations of maintenance manpower but rather to other sources. On the other hand, if the box turns out to be smaller than is required to perform other important tasks, the Air Force may have to look at the relevance of those tasks as well as authorizations.

Recall that the white box is bounded by the man-hour rules in the blue box on the one hand and by LCOM direct maintenance tasks in the red box on the other. The blue box is static and applies to all occupations and experience levels, allowing 163.2 hours per month in peacetime for direct labor activities (the red box plus the white box), indirect labor, and overtime. The size of the white box thus depends on the M-UTEs that LCOM produces. Since these rates differ for every specialty and work center, so too does the size of the white box.

Below we illustrate the adequacy of the white box for alternative M-UTEs associated with a majority of maintenance specialties. For each M-UTE, we define a range of assumptions for the level of effort dedicated to white-box activities. We also define assumptions for other critical factors such as less-than-perfect personnel fill rates, productivity differentials due to declining experience, and "friction" caused by inefficiencies during the workday.

Table 6.2 gives the production hours per month for each 5 percent increment between M-UTEs of 10 to 50 percent. For an LCOM-derived M-UTE of 10 percent, for example, the number of hours per month dedicated to direct maintenance would be 163.2 × 0.10 = 16.3 hours. The third column in Table 6.2 gives the hours per day remaining for white-box activities. This is calculated by subtracting direct maintenance hours from direct labor hours (using ACC's indirect labor factor of 0.78) and then dividing by workdays per month (20.91). Again, for a 10 percent M-UTE, this is given as (127.3 – 16.3) ÷ 20.91 = 5.3 hours per day. At higher M-UTEs, there are fewer hours per day remaining for white-box activities.

Table 6.3 gives the range of assumptions for each factor. First, let us account for the "friction" factor. LCOM accounts only for direct maintenance man-hours. The LCOM concept is that parts break and aircraft require servicing; LCOM offers an estimate of the time needed to undertake these precise tasks. In reality, however, no work can be done with 100 percent efficiency. It takes time to travel from a shift "stand-up" to the work area, move between work stations, wait for someone else's prior job to be finished before beginning one's own, take breaks, correct mistakes, wait for parts or people, and the like—all of which interrupt the flow of maintenance actions. There should be allowances for such inefficiencies. Absent time studies

Table 6.2

Unassigned Hours for Various M-UTEs

M-UTE (%)	Direct Maintenance Hours/ Month, LCOM	Available Hours/Day, White Box
50	81.6	2.2
45	73.4	2.6
40	65.3	3.0
35	57.1	3.4
30	49.0	3.7
25	40.8	4.1
20	32.6	4.5
15	24.5	4.9
10	16.3	5.3

Table 6.3

**Best-Case and Worst-Case Assumptions for Factors
Affecting White-Box Workload**

Factor	Best Case (%)	Mean (%)	Worst Case (%)
Indirect labor	22	22	22
Friction	5	5	5
Personnel fill rate	90	85	80
Experience mix	90	85	80
OJT	15	23	30
Out of hide	4	6	8
High OPTEMPO	10	15	20
Added maintenance duties	10	20	30

that can offer quantification, we postulate a rather conservative friction factor of 5 percent of direct labor hours.[14]

Next, the analysis needs to account for the fact that the utilization rates based on LCOM assume full shift manning. LCOM derives a requirement for maintenance man-hours and computes the shift load and manpower authorizations to match that requirement. This is not the number that is actually available to perform daily maintenance in the Air Force. During programming and budgeting in MAJCOMs and at the Air Staff, manpower programmers check stated requirements to see if they are valid. The Air Force typically validates and programs manpower on the basis of LCOM simulations, but not necessarily nonsimulated manpower positions based on other methods or standards. Furthermore, the personnel system typically fills validated positions to only 90 percent, which at the outset puts FSs at low C-1 readiness status in the Status of Resources and Training System (SORTS) reporting system. Very often, when recruiting and retention rates are falling, the personnel system cannot meet its 90 percent goal, so units may actually be manned to lower fill rates. Our computations adjust the per-person maintenance workload under the premise that when personnel fill rates fall below 100 percent, the same workload must be distributed over a smaller number of

---

[14]Friction also affects indirect labor. However, we are taking the conservative view that this reduces the amount of indirect labor accomplished rather than the 22 percent of primary duty hours allocated for indirect labor.

people.[15] We assume a range of 80 to 90 percent for personnel fill rates.

Declining experience affects the overall productivity of the force. Generally, less experienced technicians take more time to complete tasks than their more experienced counterparts. Junior maintainers may make more mistakes and are more likely to encounter problems they have never seen before. As reported in Chapter Two, the experience mix among 3-, 5-, and 7-levels has declined, as has the experience of 5-levels in particular. For analytical purposes, productivity is assumed to be between 80 and 90 percent of "normal" values.[16] In Chapter Seven, we analyze the effects of declining experience mix in more detail.

We base our assumptions about the level of effort applied to each white-box activity on the results of our wing-level research. Teaching and learning together constitute a significant portion of the duty day—between about 15 and 30 percent. Out-of-hide positions consume between 4 and 8 percent of assigned personnel. Duty hours during high-OPTEMPO periods seem to rise by roughly 15 percent on average; we assume a range of 10 to 20 percent in our calculations. Finally, with no reliable estimate of increases in workload caused by additional, "unfunded" maintenance duties associated with canning, MC rates, and others, we use a range of 10 to 30 percent for illustrative purposes.

Table 6.4 gives the total number of direct labor hours worked per day for each M-UTE based on *mean values* for the factors laid out in Table 6.3. Programmed direct labor should total 5.8 hours per day, so any additional time worked would be overtime that is not programmed or funded. Table 6.4 also shows the net hours available per

---

[15]This adjustment (dividing the work by the fill rate) is applied to maintenance production work only. It can be argued that the same amount of out-of-hide duty also needs to be divided among fewer people, but with an increased maintenance workload there will be pressures to reduce some of this extra activity. We have thus elected to ignore any impact of fill rate on the per-person out-of-hide workload.

[16]This is interpreted as the amount of work accomplished in a given time. Thus, if a task takes time T given normal productivity, it will require a time $T \times (100/P)$ to accomplish a given productivity P (percent). This factor affects not only maintenance production tasks but also the requirement for OJT and the pool of maintainers available for out-of-hide duties. Despite this, we assume no impact on OJT (either teaching or learning) or on out-of-hide functions.

Table 6.4

Net Hours Available for White-Box Activities, Assuming Mean Values for Factors

M-UTE (%)	Total Direct Hours/Day	Net Direct Hours/Day
50	9.5	−3.7
45	8.7	−3.0
40	8.0	−2.2
35	7.3	−1.5
30	6.6	−0.8
25	5.8	0.0
20	5.1	0.7
15	4.4	1.4
10	3.6	2.2

day for other (white-box) activities. When net hours are negative (designated by numbers in white cells), maintainers with the corresponding M-UTE must work more hours than programmed—meaning that the size of the white box is inadequate. In Table 6.4, maintenance specialties with M-UTEs greater than 25 percent would be working more hours per day than programmed. According to LCOM results for F-16 Block 40 squadrons, specialties with such M-UTEs include crew chief (52 percent, flight line only), avionics (30 to 36 percent depending on the work center), structures (31 percent), and engines (28 to 31 percent depending on the work center). Crew chiefs would be working nearly ten hours per day just on direct labor alone, giving them a net of −4.0 hours per day, or 20 hours per week beyond what is programmed.

Table 6.5 shows the results for best-case, mean, and worst-case values. Even under the best assumptions, it is not possible to accomplish all tasks within the normal workday (including the 7.7 percent MAF overtime) when the M-UTE reaches 40 percent. Under the worst-case assumptions, extra overtime can be avoided only in specialties whose M-UTE is below about 12 percent.

One core consideration, of course, is that all the factors considered are subject to random variations that can cause wide swings in workload. That is why LCOM uses a Monte Carlo approach to account for demands arising in bunches. This analysis does not take these variations into the strict account that they deserve. However,

Table 6.5

Net Hours Available for White-Box
Activities Under Best-Case, Mean,
and Worst-Case Assumptions

M-UTE (%)	Extreme Combined Parameter Estimates		
	Best	Mean	Worst
50	−1.4	−3.7	−6.2
45	−0.9	−2.9	−5.3
40	−0.3	−2.2	−4.4
35	0.3	−1.5	−3.5
30	0.9	−0.8	−2.6
25	1.4	0.0	−1.7
20	2.0	0.7	−0.7
15	2.6	1.4	0.2
10	3.2	2.2	1.1

the worst-case assumptions in Table 6.3 are consistent with, and sometimes more optimistic than, what is often reported from the field during the most stressful times.

Second, it is unlikely that the unassigned residual hours actually come in useful segments. An average of three hours of dead time per day can be spread out over eight working hours in six half-hour segments in uneven and unforeseen intervals that may not constitute very useful time. Also, owing to the variation in workload from day to day, it may not be known at the beginning of the working shift how much time will really be available for other duties. Thus, an average unassigned time period may appear significant on paper but in reality may not be usefully applied. Dead time is unavoidable in any occupational activity, and it would be unrealistic for the Air Force to set a goal of driving unassigned hours to zero. Taking this into account would tend to increase required man-hours.

The implication of the above is that the time available in the white box may be inadequate for certain AFSCs in high-demand work centers, especially when variations drive working hours up. It is important that the Air Force carefully evaluate how much time is really available by work center and AFSC as well as how much all the added tasks affect total working hours and any residual that may in fact exist. This is even more important when one considers that LCOM may underestimate the M-UTEs for some or all maintenance specialties.

The examples here suggest that there is a plausible degree of stress on maintenance technicians that merits high-level attention.

SUMMARY

The size of the white box is determined by manpower rules governing direct labor hours on the one hand and by direct maintenance hours as ascertained by LCOM on the other. Any activities maintainers perform that are not considered in LCOM or man-hour rules end up by default in the white box. The tasks performed in the white box—those related to OJT, high-OPTEMPO periods, additional maintenance duties, and out-of-hide positions—result from decisions at all levels of the Air Force: Air Force headquarters, MAJCOMs, wing, group, squadron, and flight. However, the Air Force does not systematically track and evaluate the levels of effort its maintainers expend on these activities. Without such knowledge, decisionmakers can neither control the tasks that maintainers must accomplish nor assess whether the size of the white box leaves sufficient time for maintainers to complete all required tasks.

In manpower programming, it has been assumed that once LCOM results and manpower rules are taken into account, there will be sufficient time during the duty day for maintainers to complete any other tasks that remain. This assumption need not have been questioned during the 1980s and early 1990s. Our assessment, however, is that the white box may be "bursting at the seams." The environment has changed enough in the mid- to late 1990s to warrant a close examination of white-box activities. This examination should strive to determine current levels of effort relating to OJT, high-OPTEMPO tasks, out-of-hide activities, and workload arising from direct maintenance duties that are inadequately captured in programming. More critically, the Air Force should seek to establish functional, analytically derived standards for these activities so that they can be explicitly accounted for in programming processes.

The Air Force should take a close look at what tasks are actually carried out by maintainers and others in the field. The migration of skilled maintainers out of their career fields is a serious issue. These people represent a considerable investment in human capital for the Air Force. The service is having difficulty meeting its own standards regarding MC rates and sortie goals. Certain occupational skills are most critical to the central task of getting the aircraft to fly reliably. In the context of these facts, it appears unacceptable to have a significant portion of exactly those critical skills detailed to all the tasks referred to in Table 6.1. In short, the time has come for the Air Force to revisit the core methodology by which maintenance manpower requirements are estimated—informed by empirical data from the field.

In summary, the lack of knowledge regarding the totality of tasks maintenance technicians (and many other specialties) are actually performing during their regular duty days is quite vexing. The Air Force cannot yet answer with any certainty the question of whether the tasks by now add up to more than should reasonably be expected of its personnel. In our research at fighter and mobility wings, we have accumulated some evidence that the shortfalls many have heard about anecdotally are real and may be reaching alarming levels. We now turn to a preliminary assessment of the magnitude of these shortfalls.

Chapter Seven

A PRELIMINARY ASSESSMENT OF SHORTFALLS

In this chapter, we evaluate potential shortfalls arising from or related to two factors: duty hours observed in the field and a deteriorating experience mix. To gain insight into these issues, the analyses use manpower calculations merely as a surrogate for the stress that maintainers in the field are experiencing. We express an index of stress in terms of "manpower equivalents."[1] However, care is taken not to translate this measure into remedies that involve increased authorizations. In practical terms, the Air Force could define alternative remedies to shortfalls that do not require changes in manpower authorizations. Thus, if the present analyses identify a 10 percent shortfall in a given area, it should be interpreted as a statement about added, unfunded workload that existing manpower must bear—*not* that adding manpower is necessarily the preferred solution to correct this shortfall.

A CALCULUS OF OVERTIME-INDUCED SHORTFALLS

The first analysis compares the duty hours that 5- and 7-level maintainers state they are working with the programmed hours embodied in the Air Force's MAFs. If actual duty hours are greater than programmed hours, we apply the percentage of excess hours to the number of maintainers assigned to yield a shortfall in manpower

---

[1]This is quite different from the trainer equivalents introduced in Chapter Six. The purpose of that metric was to give a sense of capacity through a straight calculation of manning, time allocation, and effectiveness. Manpower equivalents are used to express the point that today's maintainers are doing the work of larger numbers of technicians.

equivalents. Supplementing assigned maintainers by this percentage theoretically brings actual duty hours to the same level as programmed duty hours. If added manpower equivalents bring the total assigned to a number that is less than the total authorized, the stress from duty hours is deemed related only to fill-rate problems. If the supplemented number of technicians exceeds total authorizations, the source of stress is related both to a low fill rate and to inadequate authorizations.

There are two major caveats to keep in mind. First, long duty hours may reflect inefficiencies that could be reduced by changing the way maintenance operations are organized and conducted. For example, the Air Force could reduce overall duty hours by shifting some workload to maintenance specialties that seem underutilized (e.g., AFSCs that receive very low M-UTEs in LCOM). Second, maintainers may not complete all necessary tasks despite working longer hours; some lower-priority tasks could be left undone in favor of pursuing more immediate missions such as sortie generation. Backlogs may thus arise, be they postponed maintenance actions or delayed, less systematic OJT. Note that inefficiencies in maintenance and the inability to accomplish all tasks tend to be offsetting influences: More efficient operations would tend to lower duty hours, while clearing backlogs would tend to raise them.

Figure 7.1 depicts 5- and 7-level duty hours per day in the fighter and mobility wings based on responses to our questionnaires. For each wing, hours are reported for the mid-1990s under "normal" OPTEMPO (left column), current "normal" OPTEMPO (middle column), and "high" OPTEMPO (right column). Maintainers believe that their duty hours have increased over the past three to five years. FW technicians recall that their hours were relatively high in the mid-1990s (nearly ten hours per day) but that these hours have risen by close to 8.5 percent. Maintainers in the AMW report the same increase, but from fewer duty hours per day in the mid-1990s. Technicians also report increases in duty hours during high-OPTEMPO periods—by 12 percent in the FW and 21 percent in the AMW.

The two horizontal lines in Figure 7.1 represent the man-hour availability factors for peacetime (the lower line, at 8.6 hours per day) and wartime sustained (the higher line, at 10.1 hours per

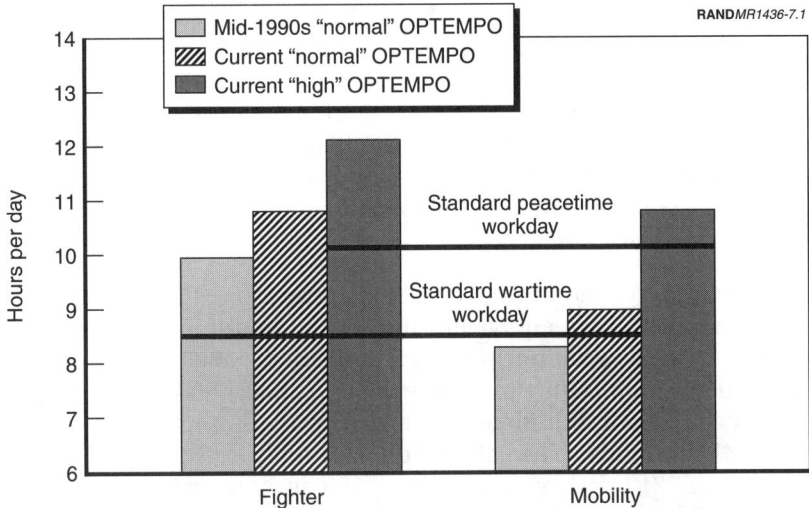

Figure 7.1—Duty Hours per Day in Fighter and Mobility Wings

day).[2] The peacetime MAF applies to the two normal-OPTEMPO columns for each wing, while the wartime MAF should be considered in relation to the high-OPTEMPO columns.

The maintainers at the FW recall that even in the mid-1990s, their duty days were considerably longer—by 16 percent—than the MAF would suggest. Current hours in the FW during normal OPTEMPO exceed the peacetime MAF by 25 percent. Conversely, maintainers in the AMW believe that their hours fell short of the MAF by about 4 percent in the mid-1990s but that current hours during normal OPTEMPO surpass the MAF by 4 percent. Actual hours during high-OPTEMPO periods exceed the wartime MAF by 20 percent in the FW and by 7 percent in the AMW.

---

[2]We use the wartime sustained MAF rather than the higher wartime surge MAF. In addition, we spread the 50.5 hours per week over five days rather than the six days used in AFI 38-201, yielding 10.1 hours per day. This is because many of the high-OPTEMPO activities occur at home station and together total up to six months a year or more.

Figure 7.2 gives the number of authorized and primary-assigned 5- and 7-level maintainers at the 388th FW and the 60th AMW.[3] These numbers include only those maintainers who are authorized and assigned to the fighter, aircraft generation, and maintenance squadrons. Note that the two wings face very different circumstances with regard to fill rate. The fill rate for primary-assigned 5- and 7-levels in the 388th FW is about 85 percent, while the 60th AMW is filled to 102 percent.

In Figure 7.3, two additional columns appear for each wing. These columns portray the equivalent number of maintainers needed to bring reported working hours to authorized levels. The cross-hatched/upward-sloping bars represent normal-OPTEMPO periods, and the cross-hatched/downward-sloping bars portray high-OPTEMPO periods. The calculation is as follows: In the 388th FW, there were 761 primary-assigned and 895 authorized 5- and 7-levels in FY 1999, when the survey was administered. Their normal-

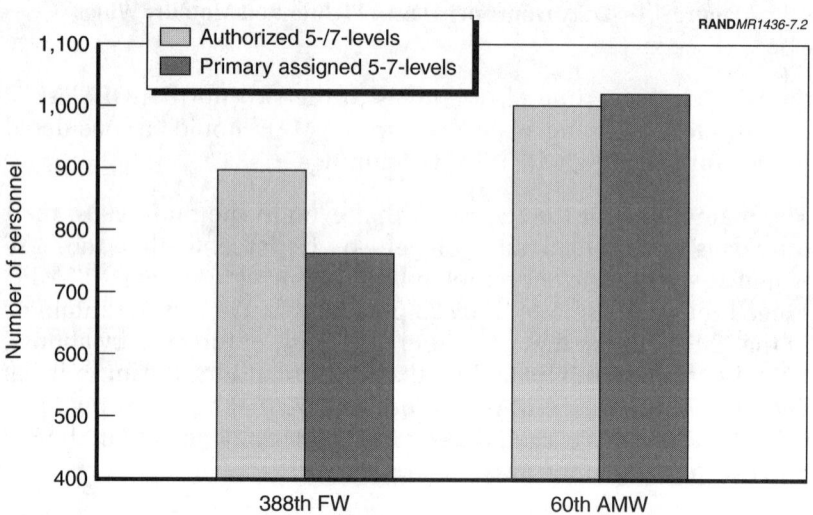

Figure 7.2—Authorized and Assigned 5- and 7-Levels, 388th FW and 60th AMW

---

[3]The numbers reflect the years during which RAND administered the questionnaires: FY 1999 for the FW and FY 2000 for the AMW.

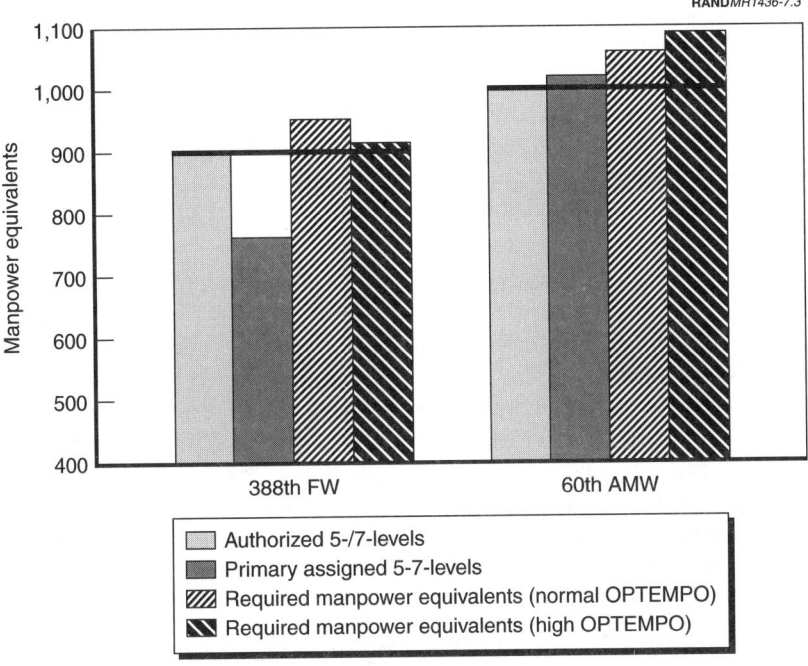

RAND*MR1436-7.3*

Figure 7.3—Manpower Equivalents Needed in the 388th FW and the 60th
AMW to Meet Programmed Duty Hours

OPTEMPO duty days were one-quarter longer than the peacetime
MAF (10.8 hours versus 8.6 hours). Adding 25 percent in manpower
equivalents would yield 761 + (761 × 0.25) = 954, which is 7 percent
higher than the authorized 895. High-OPTEMPO duty weeks are 20
percent longer than the wartime MAF (12.1 hours versus 10.2 hours),
yielding manpower equivalents (913) only 2 percent higher than
authorized. In the 60th AMW, maintainers reported that they worked
4 percent longer than the peacetime MAF, bringing the 1018 assigned
5- and 7-levels to 1060 manpower equivalents. This is 6 percent
higher than the authorized 1001. The 7 percent high-OPTEMPO
supplement would yield 1091, which is 9 percent higher than
authorized.

This analysis suggests that the longer duty hours may result not only
from too few available personnel but also from authorization inade-

quacies. Having a fill rate that is less than 100 percent of authorizations only makes the overtime problem worse. The analysis reinforces the implication drawn in Chapter Six that the white box does not provide adequate time to complete all of the tasks required of maintainers. Consequently, it is imperative that the Air Force gain insight into actual duty hours across the force and to examine the validity of all the activities in which maintainers are engaged.

A CALCULUS OF EXPERIENCE-INDUCED SHORTFALLS

Let us now turn to an assessment of how the decline in experience and skill mix affects the ability of maintainers to perform direct maintenance and other white-box-related tasks.[4] The Air Force, like the other military services, largely hires into entry positions—i.e., rarely is there lateral entry at any grade. Moreover, only a small percentage of careers last more than 20 years. Thus, the Air Force has a high requirement for OJT, especially in hands-on occupations such as aircraft maintenance.

Maintaining a Balanced Inventory of Personnel

For the reasons outlined above, it is of critical importance that the Air Force strive for a balanced inventory of skills—i.e., that it manage the ratio of experienced to inexperienced personnel. When this inventory becomes unbalanced, severe problems can occur. The challenge of creating and maintaining a balanced inventory of personnel has been studied extensively in the Air Force in relation to pilots. Given the fact that there are always conflicting objectives, however, severe imbalances nonetheless occur. During the drawdown in the early 1990s, for example, the Air Force leadership decided it would be unfair and generally bad for morale to force out midlevel pilots who wanted to stay, and they thus reduced under-

---

[4]Our library research suggests that the most recent time the Air Force had to face similar problems with the skill mix of the maintenance force was in the late 1970s. See L. D. Howell, *Manpower Forecasts and Planned Maintenance Personnel Skill Level Changes,* Technical Report ASD/TR 81-5018, Washington, D.C.: Air Force Systems Command, 1981, and R. Garcia and J. P. Racher, Jr., *An Investigation into a Methodology to Incorporate Skill Level Effects into the Logistics Composite Model,* Wright-Patterson Air Force Base, OH: Air Force Institute of Technology, 1981.

graduate pilot production by about half for several consecutive years. This was followed by a combination of unanticipated stress from increased contingency deployments and growth in airline hiring. The midlevel pilots came to the end of their service commitment, and many left for jobs in the civilian sector. The cohorts immediately behind them were then too small to fill the gaps. Through a combination of poor management decisions (however reasonable they may have seemed at the time) and external pressures, the Air Force is thus looking at a growing pilot shortage that will soon become the worst in the service's history.[5]

The point here is that it is critical to pay careful attention to the management of the personnel inventory. This holds equally true for the enlisted maintainer force. Like pilots, qualified maintainers represent an expensive investment in human capital as well as a critical productive resource for flying units. Without an adequate number of skilled maintainers, the sortie generation capacity of units declines, and operational and training problems manifest themselves over time.

Because it takes time to train 5-levels, 7-levels, and 9-levels, there is a necessary relationship between the functional requirement for skills and the shape of the personnel inventory. The three pairs of graphs in Figure 7.4 illustrate this relationship heuristically in a notional wing of three fighter squadrons. The graphs in Figure 7.4a portray a healthy experience mix and a supportive personnel inventory. The graph on the left shows a desired balance between the different skill levels, with the majority being 5-levels and a large proportion being 7-levels. This is a force that is productive and knowledgeable, with adequate supervisory capacity and a sufficient production of 3-levels that can mature over time into senior journeymen, craftsmen, and supervisors.

Maintaining this qualified and sustainable inventory of functional skills requires an equally balanced and sustainable inventory of personnel, as illustrated in the right-hand graph in Figure 7.4a. The horizontal axis shows the number of years in a military career, and

---

[5]See Taylor et al., 2000.

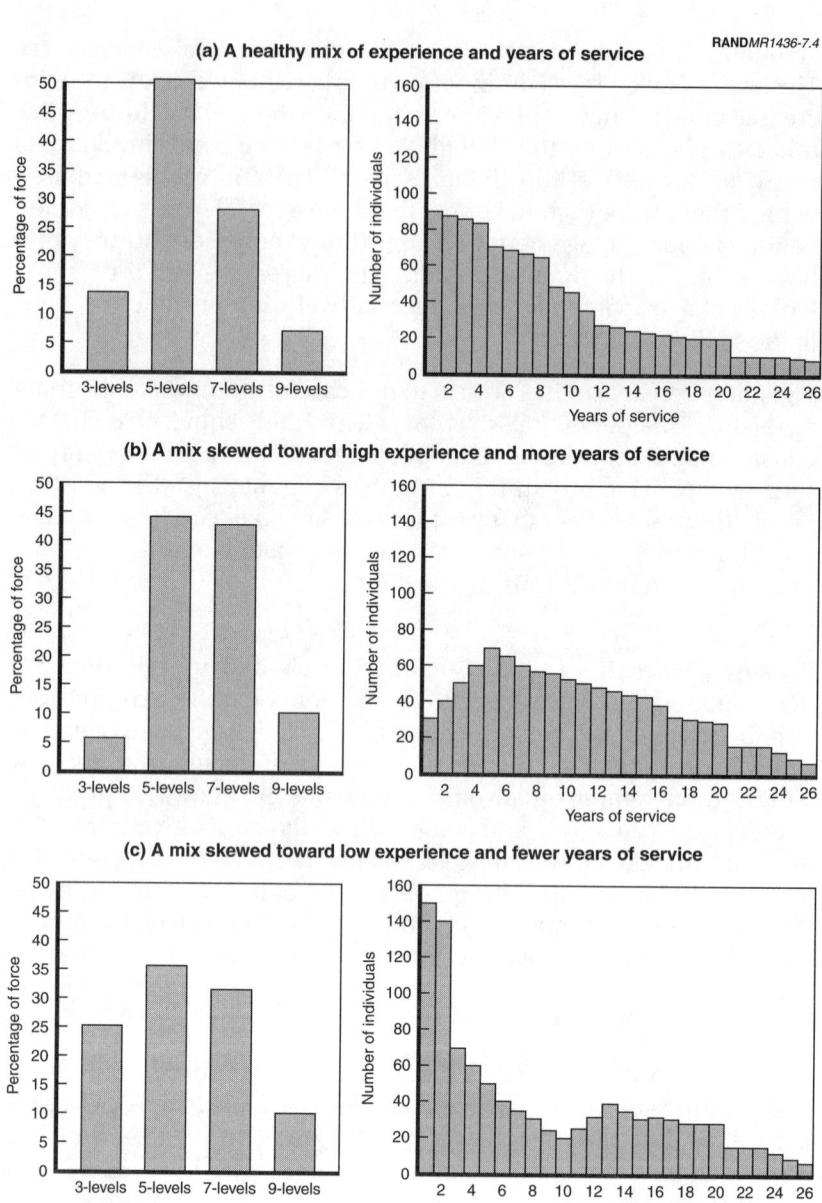

Figure 7.4—Functional Skill Requirements and the Personnel Inventory

the vertical axis indicates the numbers in each yearly cohort. The personnel inventory profile reflects certain critical aspects of the personnel system. First, most careers in the enlisted force are short. On average, an Air Force enlisted career is six to seven years. In other words, a large portion of the force is very junior. They come for a four-year tour, and no more than about 55 percent can be expected to sign up for a second four-year tour. After the second tour, at most 75 percent can be expected to enter the career force, about 95 percent of whom plan to stay until retirement at 20 years of service. A very small percentage of the force stays beyond 20 years to make up the most senior supervisors of the enlisted force.

The pairs of charts in Figure 7.4b and Figure 7.4c show alternative unbalanced skill mixes and personnel inventory profiles. Figure 7.4b illustrates a force that is highly experienced, much like the one that characterized the Air Force in the mid-1990s. Given that a senior force is more productive than a junior force, the Air Force deliberately increased the seniority of the maintenance force during the drawdown of the 1990s. However, this did not prove sustainable.[6] As the force aged and as the economy pulled, the exit rates of senior personnel grew—and since the only way to replace exiting personnel is to hire from the bottom, the Air Force had to increase the proportion of first-termers. As illustrated in Figure 7.4c, these imbalances can persist for years once they have become established. The result is that the Air Force has to make do with a workforce that is more junior and inexperienced. Thus, unless careful attention is paid to setting the right *analytically or experientially based requirements* for the proper skill mix of the maintenance force, difficult functional problems cannot be avoided.

Figure 7.5 demonstrates the effect that a more unfavorable experience mix can have on the capacity to produce. Specifically, Figure 7.5 illustrates the reduction in production capacity in an AMW as 5-level manning has come down. We calculate a surrogate for production capacity called "producer equivalents" as the product of the

---

[6]A glance at the second graph in Figure 7.4b shows more personnel in older annual cohorts. So long as recruits enter only at the bottom of the ladder, any sustainable mix must exhibit a steadily declining membership as one moves toward older annual cohorts. The situations depicted can be created, but they cannot be sustained.

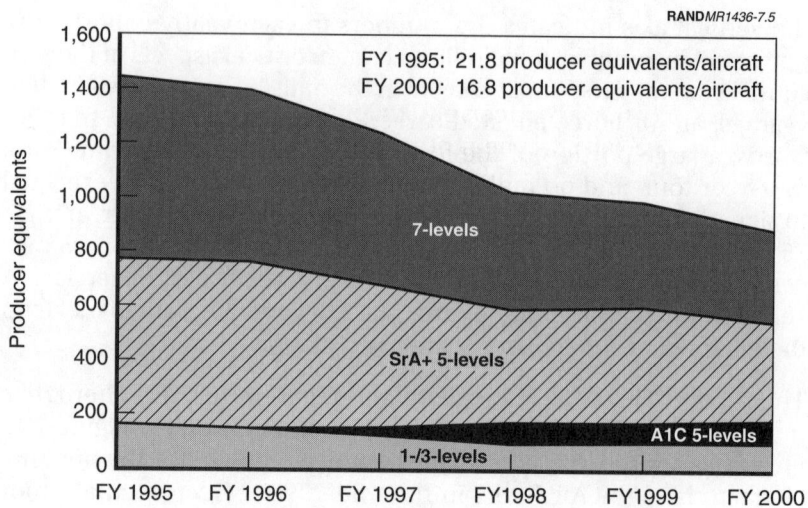

Figure 7.5—Producer Equivalents in a Mobility Wing

number of primary-assigned 7-levels, 5-levels, and 3-levels over time and the relative productivity of each skill level according to the wing's senior maintainers.[7] Thus, for example, if 5-levels are twice as productive as 3-levels and the number assigned of each is equal, then there are twice as many 5-level *producer equivalents* as 3-level *producer equivalents.*

Figure 7.5 shows that the current production capacity of the wing is only about 60 percent of that observed in FY 1995. This is due in part to a 30 percent decrease in total assigned, which followed reduced authorizations because of a 21 percent reduction in the number of aircraft at Travis Air Force Base. The remainder of the drop has resulted from a deteriorating experience mix. The 3-levels and junior 5-levels have become more prominent as a proportion of the force, increasing from 30 percent to 39 percent. As a proportion of production capacity in Figure 7.5, these less experienced technicians rose

---

[7]We asked maintainers in a survey how long it takes for each skill level to complete maintenance tasks compared to other skill levels (given tasks they can do independently). Using 7-levels as the standard (1.0), senior 5-levels were assessed at 0.91 of a 7-level, junior 5-levels at 0.56, and 3-levels at 0.27.

from 11 percent to 20 percent. The number of senior 5-levels assigned diminished by 34 percent, and 7-levels by 44 percent. The production capacity per aircraft actually declined by 23 percent—from 21.8 to 16.8 producer equivalents—thereby increasing the workload, especially for the more experienced maintainers. This in part causes the increased duty hours field technicians report.

Also recall from Chapter Six that the declining experience mix has had a negative effect on the capacity to absorb junior personnel. The number of trainer equivalents declined by 32 percent in the FW and the number of trainees per trainer equivalent rose by 71 percent, from 2.1 to 3.6. This was due to increases in 3-levels and junior 5-levels as a proportion of the maintenance force. It was also due to reductions in the amount of time 5- and 7-levels devote to teaching in favor of production to compensate for falling productivity.

Estimating the Manpower Implications of Diminished Experience

The heart of the analysis expresses the effects of swings in the experience mix in terms of additional manpower equivalents required to negate shortfalls in production and training. The analysis attempts to answer the following: Using the mid-1990s authorized and assigned experience mixes as baselines, how many manpower equivalents would be needed given the current experience mix to maintain the mid-1990s level of production *and* conduct appropriate teaching and learning while completing other necessary duties? The results can provide insight into the potential experience-induced shortfalls in production and OJT capacity in a wing.

This analysis is supported by a model described in detail in Appendix D. The model determines the minimum manpower required, under the current experience mix, to meet the production capacity inferred from the mid-1990s experience mix. The implied training requirement must also be satisfied. It does this by changing both manpower and the time each skill level allocates to production, teaching, and administrative duties. Time allocated to learning remains constant. Inputs to this analysis include numbers of authorized and assigned maintainers by skill level, how they allocate time to various tasks, and effectiveness in accomplishing these tasks.

Table 7.1

Authorizations and Primary Assignments at Hill and Travis Air Force Bases, FY 1994 and FY 2000 (fighter, generation, and maintenance squadrons only)

Level	388th FW				60th AMW (C-5 Only)			
	FY 1994 Authorized	FY 1994 Share (%)	FY 2000 Authorized	FY 2000 Share (%)	FY 1994 Authorized	FY 1994 Share (%)	FY 2000 Authorized	FY 2000 Share (%)
3-Levels	267	22	318	25	216	21	219	24
5-Levels	675	57	713	56	612	60	553	60
7-Levels	249	21	237	19	200	19	144	16
Total	1191		1268		1028		916	
	FY 1994 Assigned	FY 1994 Share (%)	FY 2000 Assigned	FY 2000 Share (%)	FY 1994 Assigned	FY 1994 Share (%)	FY 2000 Assigned	FY 2000 Share (%)
3-Levels	288	25	341	31	226	20	204	24
5-Levels	385	33	374	34	494	44	364	42
7-Levels	479	42	382	35	397	36	295	34
Total	1152		1097		1117		863	

level maintainers as well as the share of the total for each skill level. The three fighter squadrons and the maintenance squadron are included in the 388th FW totals. The 60th AMW numbers refer only to C-5 technicians in the C-5 AGS, the EMS, and the CRS.[8] As can be seen, both the authorized and the assigned skill mixes have changed. Junior maintainers represent a larger portion of the force, rising three percentage points in authorizations and four to six percentage points in assignments. The largest reductions in shares have come largely from 7-levels. Also note the preponderance of 7-levels among primary-assigned maintainers. This is because most SSgts are primary-assigned 7-levels, unlike authorizations and control assignments, which prohibit the attainment of 7 level until the rank of technical sergeant (TSgt). Recall that primary AFSCs represent the duties an individual is best qualified to perform, while control AFSCs are used to make enlisted assignments based on authorized positions.[9]

The next step is to determine how maintainers at different skill levels allocate their time to production, teaching, learning, and other

---

[8]The source of authorization data is AF/XPM.

[9]See Chapter Two, footnote 1.

(including administrative) tasks. Figure 7.6 shows the current distribution of productive time, based on our findings at Travis Air Force Base, across several different skill levels. This is reasonably representative (within 10 percent) of the results obtained at Hill Air Force Base, where technicians allocated a somewhat greater share of time than did those at Travis to teaching and "other" tasks and devoted less time to learning and production. For the purposes of this analysis, we divide 3- and 5-levels into three sublevels that define relative experience within the overall skill level. A "minus" skill refers to brand-new entrants into that level; a "plus" skill refers to the most senior maintainers within that level; and all others have intermediate experience within that skill level.[10]

Figure 7.6 illustrates the general principle that junior personnel spend most of their time learning while also producing. The more experience they gain on the job, the less time they spend learning and the more producing. Midgrade personnel spend most of their time producing, but senior 5-levels spend more and more time teaching. Senior supervisors at the 7 level spend a somewhat greater part of their time teaching but do more administrative tasks; in addition, they spend a much greater part of their "production" time supervising than "turning wrenches" on aircraft.

Figure 7.7 illustrates assumptions about relative productivity and teaching effectiveness by skill. As can be seen from this figure, a skilled craftsman's productivity is set at one; journeymen have lower productivity levels, and apprentices lower still. Note that there are many production tasks that 3-levels cannot do independently and that this varies depending on the technical requirements of the AFSC.

Armed with authorizations and skill mix, current time distributions by skill mix across key activities, and productivity and teaching differentials, a notional picture can now be drawn of authorized and assigned conditions in the wing. We use these assumptions as inputs

---

[10]We differentiate these skill sublevels by grade. For example, among primary-assigned 5-levels, an A1C is considered a "5-minus," an SrA a "5," and an SSgt a "5-plus."

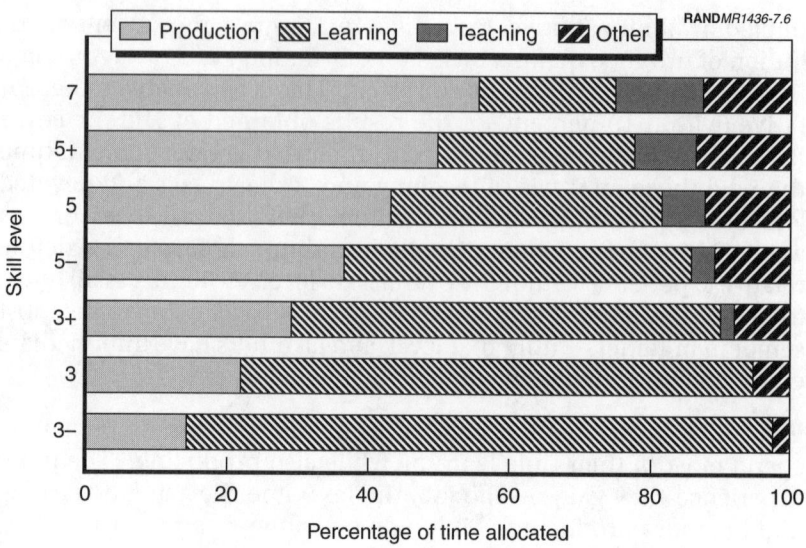

Figure 7.6—Time Shares in Maintenance Activities by Skill Sublevel at the 60th AMW

into the model described in Appendix D. The last issue to consider is that of desired level of task accomplishment. What are the "right" levels of production, OJT, and administrative duties against which to measure task accomplishment and thus the number of manpower equivalents needed? LCOM's utility lies in defining appropriate production levels, but it does not differentiate experience. Moreover, as stated, the Air Force does not have adequate OJT standards and is just beginning to recognize problems associated with other duties such as out-of-hide tasks. For the purposes of the present analysis, we therefore assume that the mid-1990s workforce was able to perform all the required tasks—i.e., that the "right" level of task accomplishment is that inferred by the experience mix and time distributions prevailing in the mid-1990s. An exception to this is 3-level learning, which, absent well-defined OJT standards, is based on how long maintainers say it *does* take for 3-levels to become 5-levels as opposed to how long it *should* take. On average, maintainers say this takes nearly 50 percent longer than it should. We thus assume that

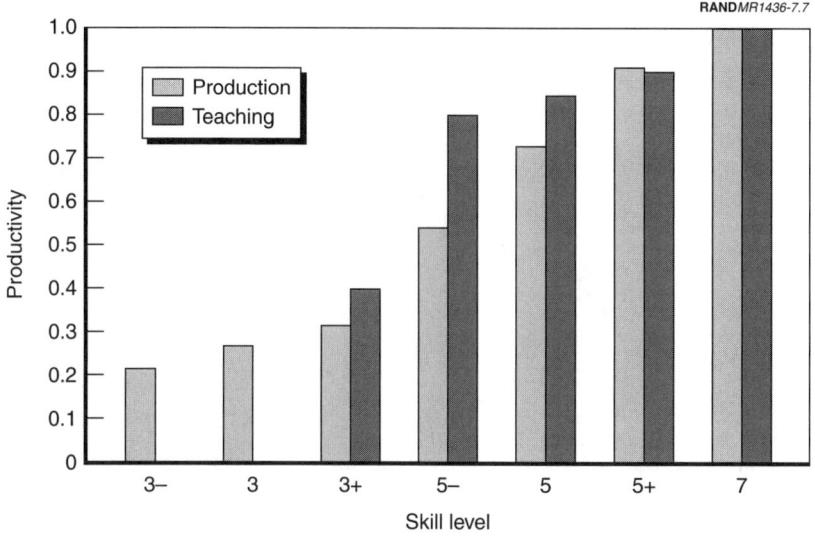

**Figure 7.7—Relative Productivity and Teaching Effectiveness
by Skill Sublevel**

the "right" time share that 3-levels dedicate to learning is, on average, around 70 percent.

There is a major catch here, however. In order to obtain increased
production, it is possible to simply specify an increased workforce
with the current skill mix. In the case of teaching and learning, it is
not possible to correct the shortfall this way because adding people
with the same skill mix does not change the teacher-to-student ratio
at all. Instead, it is necessary to make an adjustment in the fraction
of time senior people spend teaching. This increased teaching time
can come only at the expense of other work.

The model results are presented in Figure 7.8. The analysis uses FY
1994 authorized and primary-assigned numbers as baselines for each
wing.

The analysis indicates that today's less favorable experience mix
causes a potential shortfall in authorized manpower equivalents—
when compared with FY 1994 authorizations—of 12 percent at Hill

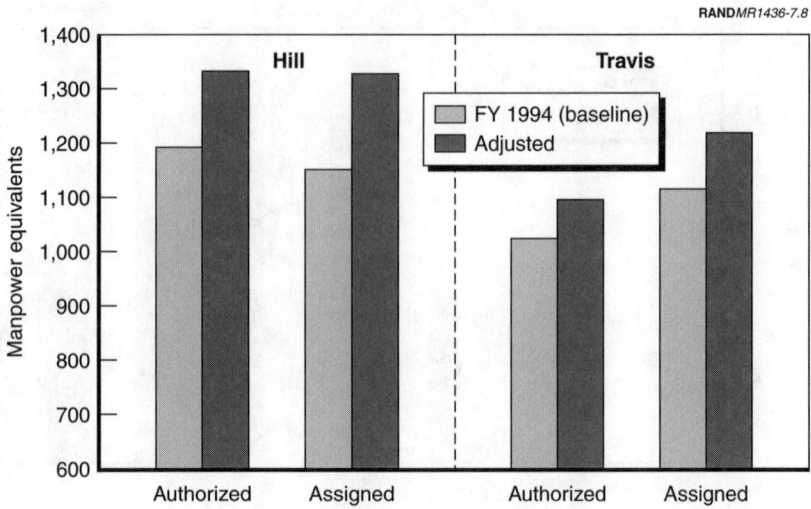

RAND*MR1436-7.8*

Figure 7.8—Manpower Equivalents at Hill and Travis Air Force Bases,
Adjusted for Loss of Experience

Air Force Base and 7 percent for Travis Air Force Base C-5s. The experience-induced shortfall for primary-assigned maintainers is somewhat worse: 15 percent at Hill and 9 percent at Travis. This reflects the requirement for more producer equivalents and for more OJT as the experience mix deteriorates, suggesting a certain level of stress in the maintenance force. As expected, 3-levels constitute about two-thirds of the increase in manpower equivalents because their share of the current experience mix is larger than in the baseline.

Figure 7.9 provides some insight into how the share of workload changes. This figure shows the baseline and adjusted percentage of overall capacity that each skill level contributes in each of the four activities. Capacity is calculated by the product of the number of maintainers in the skill level, the percentage of time they devote to a given activity, and their effectiveness in performing the activity. The case shown involves manpower authorized for Hill Air Force Base.

The 3-levels constitute a larger adjusted percentage of capacity in each of the activities because of their increased numbers. However,

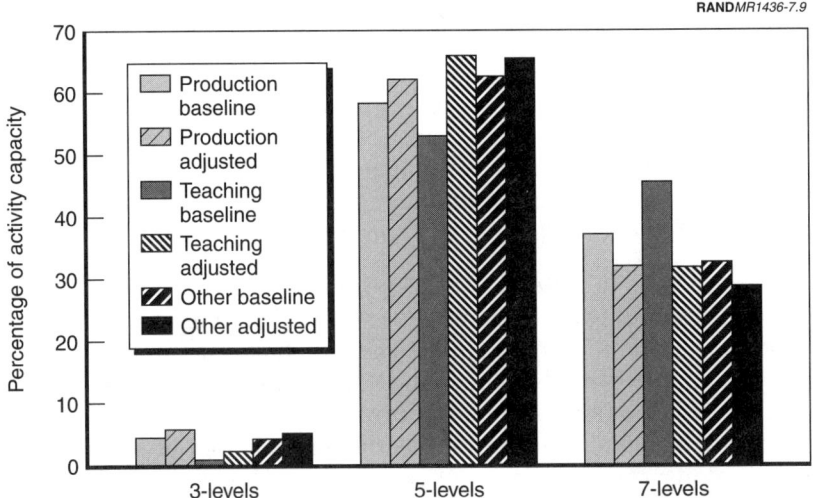

RAND*MR1436-7.9*

Figure 7.9—Percentage of Activity Capacity Contributed by Each Skill
Level, Baseline and Adjusted, Hill Authorized

their effectiveness in producing, teaching, and doing other tasks is
assumed to be so low that their contribution remains small. In fact,
the time share each 3-level dedicates to production diminishes
slightly, while the more experienced 3-levels ("3-plus") spend a bit
more of their time teaching. Meanwhile, 5-levels substantially increase the time they devote to teaching, while 7-levels reduce their
teaching time. Overall, the wing's teacher equivalents rise by 20 percent to service the less favorable experience mix.

An excursion to this analysis added only 3-levels to the force. The excursion showed that production goals could be met only by accept-
ing chronic shortfalls in the accomplishment of OJT and administrative goals. This is despite the result showing senior maintainers increasing the share of their time teaching. In the longer term, the only
way to absorb the additional 3-levels would be to change the concepts for how OJT is accomplished. Moreover, this excursion allowed 3-levels the ability to complete all production tasks independently, although at a lower level of efficiency compared with senior
maintainers. In fact, 3-levels in most maintenance career fields can

do only a minority of tasks without supervision; thus, production goals would likely not be met in reality.

In sum, this analysis suggests that the less favorable experience mix prevalent in wings today may contribute to the stress reported from the field. It also supports the concept that the less experienced a force becomes, the more manpower it needs to maintain required levels of production, training, and administration.

It is important to note that our computations are based only on consideration of the effects of falling skill mix, holding total authorizations constant. As noted in the discussion in Chapter Four on the nonstationarity of contingency- and ASD-related break rates, empirical data suggest that current authorizations may be too low. Thus, the use of current authorizations as the baseline for our calculations yields a conservative estimate of experience-induced shortfalls.

Experience Mix as a Determinant of Manpower Requirements

The Air Force defines total maintenance requirements on the basis of LCOM and manpower standards. Once these requirements are defined, the manpower community divides these requirements among the various skill levels as part of the programming process. The manpower side is charged with determining the number of spaces *for each skill level* needed to meet the units' tasks (e.g., operational readiness and rejuvenation). The personnel side then finds the right "faces," or people, to fill the spaces.

Personnel managers cannot meet the requirements for providing the right kind and number of people *unless the functional managers in maintenance can first determine the appropriate inventory of various skill levels that must be sustained over time.* That is to say, a basic functional requirement that must be determined is the desirable mix of apprentices, journeymen, craftsmen, and supervisors for each maintenance specialty. Only after this mix has been ascertained can the personnel system determine how to fill these functional requirements in the most appropriate way.

In reality, however, it is mainly *career progression* that determines the authorized skill mix. The pyramid on the left-hand side of Figure 7.10 graphically represents the general shape of a personnel

RAND*MR1436-7.10*

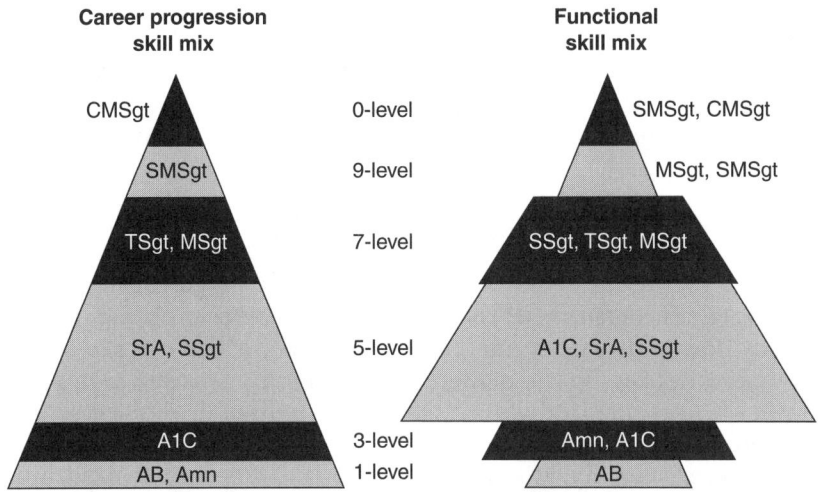

**Figure 7.10—Shapes of Personnel Inventories Emphasizing Career
Progression vs. Functional Requirements**

inventory in which career progression is emphasized. Personnel
enter the force at the bottom as 1- and 3-levels and reach the highest
positions as 9- and 0-level supervisors and managers. The pyramid
allows individuals to progress at a predetermined rate that is highly
grade-oriented. An individual can be awarded a 5-level only when he
has also attained the grade of SrA and can be awarded a 7-level only
when he reaches the grade of TSgt.[11] This pyramid is applied across
the Air Force regardless of career field. In fact, control AFSCs
(CAFSCs) are based on this progression in the same way as authorizations.

Alternatively, the shape on the right-hand side of Figure 7.10 is representative of a skill mix that might suit the functional requirements of
a technical field such as maintenance. This is one where there are
fewer apprentices and more experienced journeymen and craftsmen.
Under a functionally oriented skill mix, grade is less critical than

---

[11]See U.S. Department of the Air Force, AFI 36-2101, May 1, 1998, p. 33.

professional knowledge and experience. Thus, an A1C can be a 5-level if he has received his required OJT and passed his career development tests; similarly, an SSgt can achieve 7-level. Generally, the pool of potential 5- and 7-levels is larger here than in the career progression skill mix. This characterizes primary AFSCs (PAFSCs), which are awarded to an individual on the basis of his demonstrated capabilities.

Another important way to define these inventories is in terms of recruiting and retention. The career progression experience mix suggests a "recruiting force" that is notable for its high turnover rate among junior personnel. This is a force that relies on bringing in a steady flow of new personnel both to handle the high exit rate of junior personnel at the end of their service commitment and to provide a pool from which individuals can be promoted to replace senior personnel who are lost to separations and retirements. To keep such an inventory healthy, junior-level training must be emphasized, and total manpower must account for the higher number of trainers and supervisors needed. Such a force shape is most appropriate for career fields that require physical strength and endurance ("youth and vigor") and relatively low grade skills. Typically, this force shape is sought primarily by light infantry forces that place a high premium on physical abilities.

The functional skill mix required in a technically qualified force such as aircraft maintenance, on the other hand, suggests a "retention force," which is noted for its much lower turnover rate. The health of this force is based on building and retaining experience by keeping separations to a minimum. The need to bring in inexperienced personnel is reduced, as is the amount of entry-level training associated with their advancement. The retention force is more senior and therefore highly productive and—as long as care is taken to avoid sudden dips in retention—is relatively stable over time, with a much lower turnover rate of the personnel inventory. Fields that require highly technical skills are better served by an emphasis on retention because such skills take a long time to acquire. In the opinion of both maintenance and manpower specialists consulted in the course of this study, most Air Force maintenance career fields should be managed as a retention force.

Each type of force is associated with its own kind of risk. In a recruiting force, the high turnover rate of more junior personnel leads shortfalls in recruiting new personnel to be felt immediately because productive output rapidly declines. Once recruitment gets back on track, however, productive output can be recovered relatively quickly because junior positions require a shorter training pipeline.

The risk for a retention force, on the other hand, is that of unexpectedly high turnover rates on the part of senior personnel. Yet this risk is not manifested in a rapid drop in productive output. As senior members leave the force, the remaining senior members increase their working hours and potentially forgo lower-priority tasks, including the training of junior personnel, and thus the primary productive output remains constant—but only for a while. Over time, this creates a snowball effect whereby more and more senior members find greater incentive to leave as a result of the gradually increasing stress—and at some point one notices a drop in productive output that may even become precipitous. The most insidious manifestation of the risk, however, is that fewer trainers are available to upgrade junior personnel (who now make up a higher share of the force) to take the place of lost senior personnel. By then, the force has "dug itself into a hole" from which it takes years to climb out.

By implication, the risk-mitigating strategies for the two classes of forces are different. To remain healthy, a recruiting force must have available—on demand—various tools to raise the inflow of new personnel. Typically, this means being able to increase the number of recruiters in the field and to make various bonuses or other financial incentives (e.g., college funds) available to potential recruits. If these tools can be rapidly applied, a recruiting force can be sustained even when the propensity to enlist drops. For a retention force, the task is more difficult. Any loss of senior personnel can be harmful both to the productivity of the force (as every unanticipated exit causes a loss of human capital that it will take years to replace) and to the training capacity of the force (as all senior personnel are actual or potential OJT trainers). For such a force to avoid high sensitivity to unanticipated exits, it may prove necessary to build in buffers by creating extra positions at the mid- and high levels so that a degree of unwanted exits is not allowed to cause too much disruption in the force. Although this is a more expensive risk mitigation strategy, it is more than offset by meeting the technically demanding requirements associated with many aircraft maintenance occupations. A recruiting force is simply not compatible with many maintenance career fields and is therefore not an option.

Yet research for this report indicates that the maintenance force shows signs of "morphing" into the shape of a recruiting force as senior personnel exit and junior maintainers become proportionally larger. This predicament has not been alleviated by authorizations that are too skewed toward the personnel community's career progression pyramid and that do not account sufficiently for fluid functional requirements in maintenance. In addition, the maintenance community has not adequately telegraphed its functional requirements to the manpower community. A quick comparison of the control skill mix (that which the personnel community recognizes for making assignments to authorized positions) and the primary skill mix (that which gives an indication of actual qualifications in the field) is instructive.

Figure 7.11 provides the mix of 3-, 5-, and 7-level primary and control assignments in FY 2000. The count is limited to operational units (sortie generation and maintenance squadrons) in ACC, AMC, PACAF, and USAFE. This figure shows that control-assigned 3-levels have increased over the period as a percentage of the total, yet primary-assigned 3-levels have actually remained constant (after rising slightly in FY 1995 and FY 1996). At the same time, the share of primary-assigned 5-levels has risen while that of control-assigned 5-levels has fallen. This is due in part to an increase in A1Cs from 6 percent of primary 5-levels to about 17 percent, whereas a maintainer cannot receive a control 5-level until reaching the grade of SrA. The starkest difference, however, is between control- and primary-assigned 7-levels. Control 7-levels constituted some 20 to 22 percent of the force between FY 1994 and FY 2000, yet primary 7-levels were 36 to 39 percent of the force. The reason for this is that most SSgts in the units were awarded primary 7-level but are prohibited from receiving control 7-level.

The primary skill mix provides some insight into preferred functional requirements for maintenance manpower as well as into how units respond to personnel shortfalls. To offset a 22 percent reduction in SrAs—many of whom were lost to the civilian sector—increasing numbers of A1Cs were awarded their primary 5-level. While this

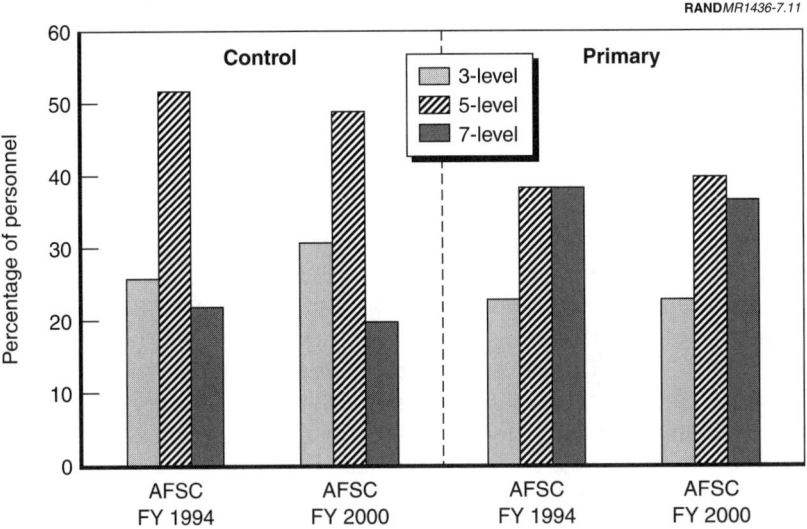

RAND*MR1436-7.11*

Figure 7.11—Shares of 3-, 5-, and 7-Levels in Primary and Control
Assignments in Operational Units, FY 2000

meant that the 5-level force was younger and less experienced, it also
allowed units to maintain the same level of technicians who were authorized to complete maintenance tasks somewhat independently.
Had the primary skill mix emulated the control skill mix—resulting in
a 13 percent increase in 3-levels and the same decrease in 5-levels—
the ability to generate sorties and repair jets would have been
severely degraded. In a similar manner, there were many more primary 7-levels than control 7-levels. Seven-levels have more supervisory responsibilities (including the authority to check off "red x's"
and certify that a plane is flyable) and spend more of their time
teaching than do 5-levels. When primary 7-levels can remain a large
proportion of the force, that force is better able to maintain production and absorb trainees.

In sum, the process for determining manpower requirements and
authorizations in maintenance should balance the functional requirements of maintenance with career progression in establishing
experience mix. Functional requirements vary with such factors as
maintenance occupation (AFSC), recruitment, retention, and train-

ing concepts. How variable manpower requirements should be as a result is a question that the manpower, personnel, and maintenance communities should address.

SUMMARY

The aim of the analyses in this chapter has been to give expression to the manpower-related stresses maintainers face in the field. Maintainers—particularly senior 5-levels and 7-levels—report that their duty hours are longer than what is assumed in the MAFs. The first analysis suggests that technicians are working longer hours not only because of low fill rates, but also because of shortfalls in authorizations. This analysis provides further evidence that the residual activities associated with the white box must be explicitly addressed in manpower processes. It is no longer safe to assume that low M-UTEs allow sufficient time during a normal duty day for maintainers to complete all valid Air Force tasks.

The experience mix of 3-, 5-, and 7-levels has deteriorated significantly in assignments and less so in authorizations. Manpower processes have not adequately incorporated the effects of this decline on productivity and OJT training capacity. The second analysis in this chapter indicates that were a maintenance force with the current experience mix to take on the workload capacity implied by the more experienced mix of the mid-1990s, the current force would need higher levels of manpower than those for which it is authorized. This means either that maintainers in the field must work harder to maintain productivity and training capacity or that they must delay or forgo the completion of tasks deemed lower priority in the context of their day-to-day missions.

The results of these analyses do not suggest that adding manpower is necessarily the appropriate solution to remedying these shortfalls. Since the inventory can be expanded only through the introduction of new blood from the bottom, simply adding manpower can make the situation even worse. Remedies should thus reach beyond manpower to new concepts both for organizing wings and squadrons and for conducting maintenance production and training. More fundamentally, manpower (and personnel) processes are in need of renewed emphasis on a force management that balances career progression with functional requirements. As a technically demanding

career field in which skills take years to develop, aircraft maintenance must necessarily be more retention-oriented than recruit-
ment-oriented. This functional requirement can be at odds with the
goals of career progression, which allow for larger cohorts and higher
turnover at lower skill levels.

Chapter Eight

RECOMMENDATIONS AND CONCLUSIONS

This concluding chapter recommends a set of actions that the Air Force can take to deepen its corporate knowledge of the requirements for maintenance manpower. The recommendations are intended to provide the insight the Air Force needs to develop appropriate concepts for restoring the maintenance force to a state of health.

To summarize, our research has indicated problems in critical processes for determining the requirements for maintenance manpower. There is reason to believe that maintenance manpower is underestimated. However, the solution is not to hire more 3-levels, as this would exacerbate the current imbalance in the skill mix. Rather, a series of steps must be put in place that lead to more completely stated requirements and to better integration of requirements and personnel policies.

LCOM, the core of the red box, is a highly data-intensive model, yet the data available from automated systems are found to be wanting. This is compounded by the model's current application, which may not be based on the most stressful maintenance scenarios and which is limited by policy. While this raises questions about the manpower estimates derived from LCOM, no better substitute for LCOM has been identified. Moreover, LCOM is not the only, or even the most important, problem associated with current manpower processes.

Man-hour rules residing in the blue box apply the same standards across the Air Force—officer and enlistee, chief master sergeant and airman basic, avionics specialist and security police. The generality applied in the blue box seems inconsistent with the extreme detail in the red box. Moreover, the hours assumed for activities during non-available periods may severely underestimate the hours maintainers actually dedicate. In particular, there is no mention of the time it takes to teach and learn via OJT, a key element of the maintainer's skill progression.

The residual hours in the white box may be inadequate for many maintainers to accomplish the myriad valid Air Force tasks that are not covered in the other boxes. Efforts associated with OJT, high OPTEMPO, direct maintenance duties beyond policy guidelines, and out-of-hide positions are very time-consuming. These activities are compounded by deteriorating experience, which has led to a significant decline in productivity and to an increase in the requirement for OJT capacity. Yet the Air Force lacks insight into the actual level of effort maintainers apply to these tasks, and it does not exercise appropriate oversight over them. As a result, maintainers in the field accomplish their missions only by working longer hours and by postponing some activities.

RECOMMENDATIONS FOR ANALYSIS AND POLICY

The analyses and investigations in this study result in numerous implicit and explicit suggestions for improving the processes for setting maintenance manpower requirements. This section outlines the most important ones.

Develop a richer scenario set that addresses the prevailing conditions maintainers see during peacetime. LCOM studies should be based on the most stressful scenarios. The new Expeditionary Aerospace Force (EAF), which is characterized by lengthy deployments and split ops with considerable home station resource shortages coupled with very significant shortfalls in flying hours (especially for junior pilots) and time-consuming peacetime tasks, could actually be even more stressful for the maintenance force.[1] A richer scenario set that includes EAF needs to be analyzed in LCOM studies.

_____

[1]Other RAND research (see Taylor et al., 2000) has suggested that the flying-hour program is insufficient to provide enough sorties to absorb junior pilots at the desired rate. If enough sorties were in fact programmed, the requirement for maintenance manpower would likely increase.

Incorporate LCOM into maintenance management analyses conducted within the logistics community. LCOM has the ability to characterize new network and business rule alternatives that may or may not represent superior and less manpower-intensive methods of maintaining aircraft and repairing components. LCOM could thus become a very useful construct for analytically based studies of various alternatives for the process reengineering of all aspects affecting wing-level aircraft maintenance. The logistics community needs to avail itself of this potential; which is to say that LCOM cannot be left to the manpower community alone. Maintenance specialists already participate in LCOM manpower studies; it is now time for the logistics community to adopt LCOM for its own efforts to improve business processes.

A similar issue arises with regard to using LCOM to perform comparisons between written policies and actual field practice. When policy is not capable of being observed in practice, LCOM can at least serve to estimate the maintenance man-hour implications of this difference. This may or may not affect the funding of various resources, including manpower, but it is a natural and obvious extension of the model's capabilities that will yield benefits in programming as well as in initiating reviews of various policies and regulations.

Make the impact of minimum crew size explicit in LCOM reports. Since minimum crew size often emerges as a binding constraint on LCOM shift manning estimates, it is important to make these constraints obvious to outsiders. Changes in work rules may be capable of reducing minimum crew sizes in many areas. It is not always necessary to use a specialist to perform every task; often it may be sufficient to rely on an alternative AFSC as long as each person is at least trained to a safe level in the particular task that requires an unusually large crew size. This is a question that only the maintenance community can resolve, and therefore it is important that LCOM analysts constantly educate logistics managers regarding the role of minimum crew sizes inside the model.

Introduce variable skill mix and OJT into LCOM-related analyses. LCOM needs to focus on the implications of changing skill mix in a much more explicit fashion. If LCOM is a sound model with adequate data inputs and the LCOM process is an accepted methodology for estimating manpower requirements in the Air Force, then

LCOM should also be the preferred vehicle for determining whether production can be met when important changes in the available personnel inventory occur over time. This means that the LCOM process, in addition to computing required man-hours for maintenance to meet flying schedules, should also provide exact manning numbers by skill level. The current version of LCOM does not allow for simulation of the effect of skill-mix changes on productivity, but the model could certainly be expanded to address this issue more directly.

The LCOM model is not suited to accomplishing the entire task of estimating trainer/trainee man-hours. Much analysis needs to be done offline to set the right levels of OJT trainers and trainees. Such analysis would use expected retention rates and training requirement information to determine an appropriate and sustainable skill-level distribution. Once such analyses are available, the LCOM model can be modified to express a required number of explicit OJT tasks. Opportunities for OJT would be driven by break rates, which would in turn drive a time requirement for both trainers and trainees in LCOM. LCOM could then be employed to determine manpower levels that support the production of both sorties and well-trained maintainers over time.

Initiate a wide-ranging effort to collect and analyze detailed data on aircraft break rates and associated factors. LCOM is a highly data-intensive model. Correctly estimating the manpower requirement at the AFSC level by work center requires data on the tasks performed by each occupational skill—even down to subspecializations within each AFSC, as in the case of crew chiefs, avionics, and propulsion. That requires associating maintenance tasks with each occupational category, which in turn requires linking five-digit WUC data in the technical order to the manpower resource that will perform the work. If the data do not exist at this level of detail, no relief can be found in running the model at the three-digit level, since the three-digit level is simply an aggregation of work performed at the five-digit level. If the data do not exist at the five-digit level, they cannot be "fudged" at the three-digit level. Therefore, there is a high payoff in manpower analysis to obtaining correct and timely data on breaks by aircraft tail number. Furthermore, higher-quality data at the five-digit level are likely to have a significant payoff for a supply system that is now modeled only by inventory demands using models that all include costs. Finally, better data on break rates directly off the aircraft are essential to understanding the aging process of complex systems.

A particular challenge for such a data collection effort is to allow for quick, easy, and accurate entries of five-digit WUC, reason code, failure code, and fix time—at a minimum. Since a technician assigned to follow up on a pilot-reported discrepancy often does not know the exact part that has failed but must instead search for it, the data system will have to allow easy entries of how the failure is identified and track fix times for the entire operation, from initial failure report to precise diagnosis, replacement, and repair.

High-quality data are a prerequisite to understanding the statistical properties of the break process. Aside from stationarity considerations, this distribution is likely to be exponential for large fleets—and this is an important observation for the supply system, as it helps predict breaks and demand rates off the aircraft. However, the Air Force today deploys in smaller UTCs, and it is a leap of faith simply to assume that an exponential distribution is appropriate regardless of the size of the deploying unit. Neither current automated data systems nor the audits are sufficient to allow us to perform the required statistical work to test these issues; thus, a significantly better data system is necessary.

The same statement holds true for achieving a proper understanding of two related and critical issues. First, in keeping with the principle of focusing on the most demanding scenario, it appears of paramount importance to gain a better understanding of how the MTBF is dependent on specific sortie scenarios. LCOM allows maintenance man-hours to vary with higher sortie rates and ASDs but assumes that the failure rates are linear in sorties and flying hours. Data from real-world contingencies indicate that this is not a correct assumption. Rather, the mean failure rate appears to be highly nonstationary, and therefore the higher break rate during stressful scenarios needs to be analyzed and included in LCOM estimations. Second, even in the context of a linear approximation to the effect of higher ASDs, there is important evidence to suggest that the magnitude of the effect is higher than that included in current LCOM simulations. Only better and more systematic data analysis can determine the actual effect of longer sortie durations on break rates and therefore on maintenance man-hours.

Absent automated data, expand field audits to capture high-OPTEMPO conditions and to observe the performance of selected maintenance tasks. In the absence of high-quality data off the aircraft, field audits are undoubtedly an acceptable second-best option. These audits appear to be of sufficient quality to ensure that peacetime data can be used to calibrate the model. However, the audits do not give an accurate picture of wartime or high-OPTEMPO conditions, instead reflecting the typical working environment. Therefore, they are not sufficient to allow for better estimates of high-demand conditions. Special audits with maintenance personnel who have recently returned from deployments may be of value for certain weapon systems. Another difficulty is that it is not known to what extent the audit data represent pure maintenance work—i.e., servicing and fixing systems or parts—and to what extent they miss all the inefficiencies that cause drag in fix times. It would be highly valuable to undertake an audit of the audit data—e.g., to follow and observe a few critical AFSCs in the performance of their daily tasks to enhance the understanding of how they actually perform their maintenance tasks.

Evaluate the relevance of established MAFs in light of observed practices. Such a reality check of the LCOM audit data is also an essential part of the difficult task of assessing the realism of the factors that determine the official Air Force MAFs. These highly technical factors attain great importance both in LCOM analyses of manpower requirements and in all areas where manpower standards are used to determine requirements. It does not appear reasonable to apply the same factor to all occupations and grades. It is now appropriate to reevaluate the factors on the basis of actual data. This is an issue that goes well beyond maintenance, extending into all support occupations in the Air Force.

Assess varied indirect labor factors by grade and function. The indirect labor factor also stands in need of considerable analytical revision. At present, the tasks and activities listed as indirect labor are quite general, and it is left up to the MAJCOMs to determine how the factor applies to them. A more satisfactory approach would be to note that the indirect labor factor includes activities that are supervisory in nature as well as activities that are "hands-on." This suggests that there should be different indirect labor assumptions by grade and function inside maintenance organizations. It also suggests that there may be good reasons indirect labor factors should be different in different organizations. For example, the time it takes to clean up a work area is much higher when many parts and tools must be sorted and cleaned before the floor can be swept, as compared to a deskbound analyst shutting off the computer and putting some papers away—yet the same indirect labor assumption applies to both.

Determine actual working hours of maintainers in the field. These somewhat arcane details regarding the MAF and indirect labor are critical because they have great leverage in determining how much time remains for maintainers after they have completed all their maintenance tasks. LCOM suggests that maintenance man-hours are a relatively small share of total duty hours and that there should be a sufficient amount of time left to perform all other tasks required of personnel in maintenance organizations. The MAF and the indirect labor assumption bounds this statement from the other end— i.e., they determine how much time manpower programmers can assume is available for all the other duties. Yet the Air Force has no real data on which to base any statements regarding whether the remaining time is sufficient to perform all other duties. This was not a critical issue only a few years ago, when personnel fill rates were higher, operational demands lower, and experience mix adequate. Now, however, when these critical external factors affecting the duty days of maintainers have changed so much, it has become paramount to obtain better information about how maintainers really spend their time. To gain insight into this type of information, we conducted preliminary field surveys at three wings in the same vein as the LCOM field audits. Our surveys yielded consistent results, but much more needs to be done to assess how much time is really demanded of maintainers across the force.

Define explicitly the set of valid Air Force tasks for which maintainers are responsible beyond direct maintenance and training. Again, while there are some preliminary data on these issues, the Air Force needs to take a much closer look at these tasks. Are they or are they not valid Air Force tasks? If so, how should they be funded and staffed? Absent such a formal review, we have repeatedly observed how training junior personnel becomes the bill payer. By not paying sufficient attention to the total duty time and the totality of tasks assigned to maintenance personnel, the Air Force is currently running a significant risk of shortchanging the training of its junior maintenance personnel, both officers and enlistees. The implications for flying safety, equipment failures, system aging rates, and short-term break rates are potentially significant. Ultimately, the quality of human capital is the most important asset of any organization. The Air Force needs to pay closer attention to the quality of the maintenance training that is now being provided in operational units. The difficulty in protecting training lies in the practice of putting off training when pressures mount to perform immediate tasks. It is possible to recover the time needed to train, but only by providing sufficient personnel to perform all the other tasks first. Only then will training be reinstated to the level that is critical to the long-term goals of the Air Force. The problem is complex and will take time to resolve.

Reevaluate skill-mix standards relevant to a "recruiting" force versus a "retention" force. Over the last few years, as pressure has mounted on Air Force maintenance organizations, retention rates have fallen and experience mix has declined. The clearly stated goal of personnel managers, going in to the drawdown after the Cold War, was to maintain a career force of highly skilled and experienced personnel. Now, owing to a series of external factors, this goal is in danger of no longer being achievable. Experience mix has fallen, and retention rates have plunged along with them—just when high retention rates have become even more critical. It therefore appears likely that the Air Force will have to adapt to an experience mix in the maintenance force that is lower than the stated goal.

To put the problem in starker perspective, the Air Force seems to be shifting, as a matter of practical reality, from managing a career force of high-quality, experienced maintainers to facing a recruiting force with a much higher flow-through of junior personnel, to be managed by a smaller share of senior NCOs. If that is the reality of the future, it has significant implications for the manner in which OJT is conducted and for the way maintenance is performed and managed. This issue is worthy of senior-level discussion and focus. It is not clear that this is the right direction for the Air Force, but it is clear that there is no easy way to reestablish a stable and healthy career force. To begin with, such a force must be clearly defined by setting policy parameters regarding the desired skill mix and the train-up time required to progress from one level to the next. These standards are now set through a combination of personnel and functional constraints and goals. However, the functional requirement for a healthy experience mix and for an efficient train-up schedule for maintainers must be set first, before the personnel system can apply its own rules to fill the spaces in the most appropriate manner.

Reassess appropriate personnel fill rates for maintenance occupations. The recognition of higher maintenance manpower requirements does nothing for a stressed maintainer on the flight line or in a back shop unless these higher requirements are funded as valid manpower authorizations and are then actually filled by the personnel system. The research in this report suggests that authorizations are too low as a result of a deteriorating skill mix and other pressures (including higher OPTEMPO, out-of-hide responsibilities, and the like). Until the Air Force directly determines what tasks maintainers should validly perform—and until it provides authorizations and personnel outside of maintenance to perform those tasks that maintainers should not perform—there will continue to be personnel and manpower problems in maintenance.

Develop concepts for maintenance reorganization at the wing level. Finally, a high payoff is likely to be derived from continued process reengineering of wing-level maintenance organizations. The LCOM data suggest what is often reported anecdotally: that there are significant differences between various work centers with regard to effective manpower utilization factors. Some work centers are very busy; others are less busy. The question of minimum crew sizes for many tasks needs to be analyzed in great detail, as this is often a determining factor for manpower requirements. This demands in turn that maintenance managers carefully examine all the business rules at the wing level to determine the most efficient work flow from one center and one occupation to the next as well as to ascertain who needs to be task-trained sufficiently to become useful as a backup for another AFSC, perhaps in another work center. One way to attain higher levels of efficiency in maintenance is through determined process reengineering and experimentation over a longer period of time, giving local unit commanders the flexibility to attempt new management techniques—learning by failure and success what efficiencies can be found in maintenance. These methods have proven highly successful in the commercial sector and need to be applied continuously in all Air Force maintenance organizations, from the flight level up.

As noted previously, the recommendations in this report point to a number of areas in which the Air Force lacks critical information. The real difficulty lies in how to engineer a transition from an inventory of maintenance personnel that is unbalanced in various ways to an objective inventory that can be sustained over time. How to apply the correct force management tools to enable this transition is a challenging analytical and policy agenda.

CONCLUSIONS

In sum, LCOM should be based on better data on break rates and on a more complete understanding of the statistical properties of these data. LCOM should be expanded to address the implications stemming from the functional requirement for balancing the skill mix of the personnel inventory over time, and more analytical attention should be paid to the requirements of OJT. As long as these factors remain unheeded, there is a great danger that the Air Force will authorize too few manpower positions in aircraft maintenance.

Improved quality of data is at the core of future LCOM developments. Given better data on aircraft break rates, tracked over time, many analytical issues that require a deeper understanding than that which currently prevails may prove tractable. As noted, LCOM is a conceptually and analytically sophisticated modeling approach that demands high-quality data. With today's computer technologies, programming the model to perform intricate tasks is much less demanding than providing the many kinds of data that the model can incorporate. Assembling data is expensive, and data can be difficult to keep current. Yet if the Air Force is willing to make the investments required, the payoff is likely to be high in many analytical areas that can lead to improved policymaking with potentially significant results for more efficient resource management.

More generally, current manpower processes should more systematically take force management into account. This report proposes several steps in this area, including paying much more careful attention to OJT and to the functionally required experience mix of 3-, 5-, and 7-level maintainers. The Air Force lacks appropriate standards in these areas, and it is therefore easy to slip into problems when changes occur, such as increased OPTEMPO and unexpected personnel losses. The tasks and duties represented by the red, white, and blue boxes must surely be reanalyzed in all areas, but this analysis must be combined with close attention to setting the standards and guidelines for what the force shape should be. Both manpower and logistics communities agree that the technical requirements of aircraft maintenance demand a strong career force—i.e., one that is made up of a greater share of journeymen and craftsmen than is the case in many other Air Force occupations. This means that the career progression pyramid used by the personnel community must be balanced against the functional requirements of maintenance—and that manpower requirements must be carefully coupled with personnel management tools and practices that support these principles.

In the end, it can therefore be concluded that while the Air Force need not abandon its basic processes for determining manpower requirements, some of the underlying principles and applications thereof should be critically examined. Do these processes fully account for the three requirements set forth in Chapter Two? Our research in this area has led to the conclusion that they do not. Specifically, they do not adequately account for key operational requirements of combatant commanders—namely, the rotational deployments that encourage split ops. They do not appropriately address the requirement of rejuvenation—especially OJT—at a time when the experience mix is unfavorable. They do not sufficiently represent other Air Force tasks such as out-of-hide responsibilities. The three boxes must thus be evaluated in light of the force shape required to sustain a proper mix of skill levels that can be adequately trained via OJT. Finally, the correct skill mix needs to be carefully supported by personnel management tools that recognize the specific requirements for a more senior career progression pyramid than is appropriate for other Air Force careers. These are all significant challenges that cannot be met overnight. While there is a shortage of maintainers in the Air Force, this cannot be quickly remedied simply by hiring more entry-level maintainers. It will take several years before the Air Force can again feel secure that the maintenance force has attained a degree of stability and robustness consistent with operational requirements. Only a close cooperative relationship between the logistics, manpower, and personnel communities can attain this goal.

Forthcoming changes both in U.S. military strategy and in Air Force roles present important opportunities to remedy some of these deficiencies in manpower processes. The corporate Air Force needs to gain systematic insight into all challenges maintainers face in the field. This is a necessary first step toward establishing a better match between requirements and resources and building a rejuvenated, sustainable maintenance force.

THE EXPONENTIAL FLEET CLOCK

We examined the fidelity of an exponential fleet clock for failure times using a simple model in which aircraft have a single breakable part, fly until they break, and then join a queue for repair. This is illustrated in Figure A.1.

Repair times are constant. Breaks are postulated to occur, for each aircraft, according to a normal distribution in flying hours. This corresponds to case "A" in Figure 3.2. Breaks are generated using one of two cases. The first case is labeled "exact" because it exactly corresponds to the model assumption of a normal distribution (since

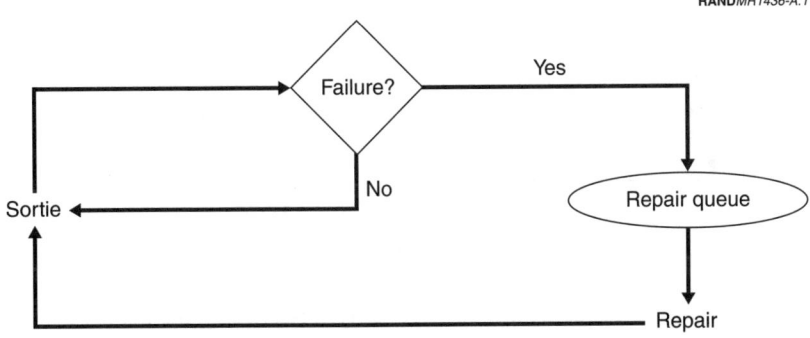

RAND*MR1436-A.1*

Figure A.1—Simple "Fly-When-Ready" Model Used to Study LCOM's Exponential Fleet-Clock Approximation

previous repair) for each individual aircraft.[1] The second case, labeled "exponential," uses the LCOM approach: A fleet exponential distribution where the MTBF is that of an individual aircraft—i.e., the mean of the postulated normal distribution—divided by the number of aircraft currently in service. The results are presented in Figure A.2.

Figure A.2, which is typical of the results, indicates that there is some difference between the break distributions under the LCOM exponential fleet clock treatment and an exact treatment given a normal break-time distribution for each part. However, the difference does not look large (the exact case has a larger tail—that is, there are more long intervals until the next break and fewer cases of breaks coming close together).

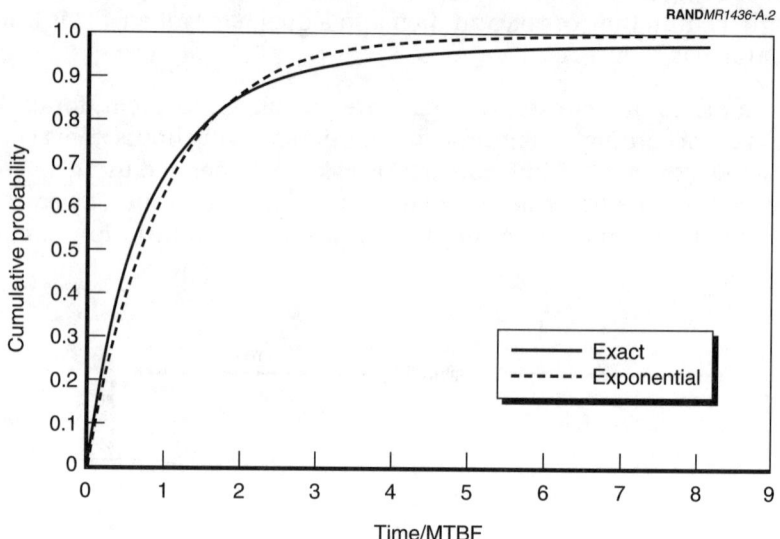

**Figure A.2—Cumulative Probability of Time to Next Failure
Repair Time = 1.25 MTBF, 10 Aircraft Fleet**

---

[1]As noted, this model is for illustrative purposes only. We do not believe that individual aircraft break times follow a normal distribution, although the break times (as opposed to flying hours) for certain parts *may* very nearly do so.

It is important to evaluate the *operational* impact of this result from Figure A.2. Since the exponential fleet-clock case has a higher probability of short break intervals (but the same average interval), one might infer that it is more stressful on maintenance. Examination of the MC rate for both cases bears this expectation out (see Figure A.3).

Figure A.3 shows that the MC rate varies somewhat depending on whether the exact break distribution or the fleet exponential distribution is used. While it is never very large (5 percent difference), the case where the difference is largest—repair time = 1.25 MTBF, 10 aircraft fleet—is one where the repair capacity is severely stressed to keep up with the breaks. For this case, the repair facility utilization rate (assuming that all tasks require the same crew size) would be 44 percent. This is in the realistic range, especially considering that when different crew sizes are required for different tasks, the above utilization rate would decline.

This LCOM break-modeling procedure also assumes that failures on different subsystems of the same aircraft are independent of one another. In the real world, correlated failures are common; for

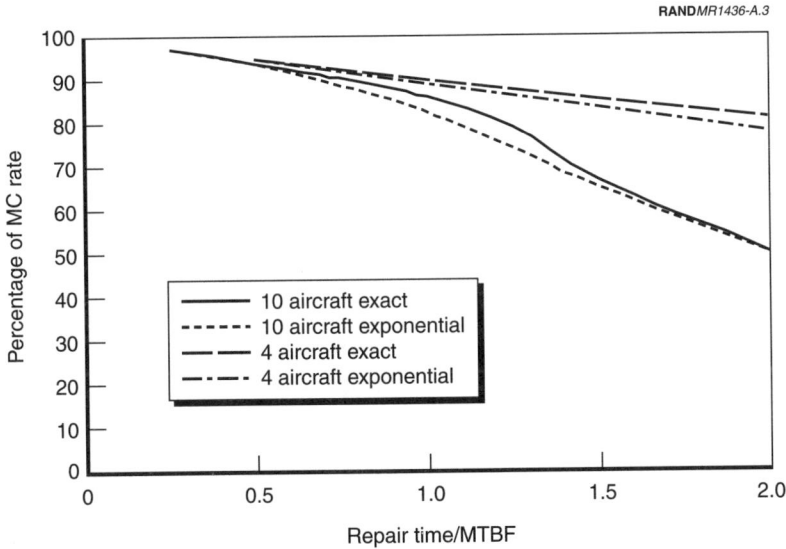

Figure A.3—MC Rate Under LCOM's Fleet Exponential Distribution

instance, an electrical event can trigger multiple failures. However, since in practice it is too demanding to assemble data on correlated failures, the LCOM model has settled for using a single fleet clock for each failure type.

THE BREAK PROCESS IN THE REAL WORLD AND IN LCOM

This appendix discusses the nature of the break process itself. We noted in Chapter Three that LCOM uses exponential distributions to represent the break process. Now we ask whether the nature of the actual data is consistent with this representation.

The choice of an exponential distribution corresponds to an *analytical assumption* about the break process over the fleet of aircraft to be simulated in LCOM. It is a plausible assumption both when the fleet size is large and when breaks on different aircraft are truly independent. When these conditions hold, fleet breaks would in fact be exponentially distributed, independent of what the distribution happens to be for each aircraft.[1] However, no statistical test has yet been performed on the data to demonstrate that exponential distributions appropriately represent breaks for actual aircraft fleets, where neither the assumption of large numbers of aircraft nor that of independent breaks necessarily holds. This statistical work could be undertaken by using CAMS/GO-81 data from REMIS for all aircraft

---

[1]To see this, consider that as the number of aircraft increases, the probability that two successive breaks (across the fleet) are from different aircraft approaches 1.0. If breaks on different aircraft are independent, however, then the probability that the second break will occur in a specified time interval, assuming that break has not already occurred, cannot depend on how much time has elapsed since the first break. This characteristic is consistent only with an exponential distribution (see, for example, William Feller, *An Introduction to Probability Theory and Its Applications,* Vol. 1, New York: John Wiley & Sons, 1971, Chapter 13, p. 9).

types in the inventory.[2] In addition, the analysis should be extended to aggregations of aircraft that are representative of various UTC packages that the Air Force is likely to deploy. It is probable that the results will indeed, at least for fairly large UTCs, be consistent with exponential distributions, but this needs to be confirmed by extensive data analysis. Note, however, the empirical examination discussed in Chapter Three, which indicates the *probable* adequacy of the exponential distribution.

There appears to be no documentation to suggest that there was ever any empirical basis for choosing an exponential distribution to represent break rates. One might speculate on why the early developers of the model made this particular choice and on why they chose a lognormal distribution for fix times. The correctness of the exponential distribution in the large-fleet, independent-break limit offers a reasonable hypothesis. Additionally, it was noted in Chapter Three that for an exponential distribution, a majority of the breaks are associated with smaller-than-average break intervals. This would tend to be associated with a higher frequency of backlogs. Similarly, a lognormal fix-time distribution would be associated with backups when the occasional task takes a long time. Since a basic feature of the Monte Carlo approach is to include the impact of occurrences worse than average, it makes sense, in the absence of specific empirical knowledge, to provide a safety margin as it were. Thus, choosing the exponential for break rates and the lognormal for fix times adds some safety, at least when compared to the standard normal distribution, because the exponential yields more shorter-interval breaks and the lognormal more longer-interval fix times. On the other hand, neither distribution is very extreme, and other classes exist that would yield even greater shares of below- or above-average draws. Thus it was not unreasonable, at a time when the model was still being developed, to make the indicated choices in anticipation of a time when more precise estimates of the real properties of break rates and fix times could be made. Currently, the data are available

---

[2]Chapter Four discusses problems with data integrity in CAMS/GO-81 and REMIS. However, we have also suggested that there are perhaps many five-digit WUCs that are quite adequately represented in the systems, i.e., those that are fairly frequent and with which technicians become very familiar over time. If these more accurate WUCs can be identified, then it would be possible to undertake the statistical tests suggested above on a partial sample of codes.

but seem not to have been analyzed properly. It may be that the exponential and the lognormal seemed safe to the early developers of the model, while reality is worse or better than the model assumes. Without the proper statistical analysis, however, this question will remain unanswered. Such an analytical effort might examine detailed actual break data over time to test hypotheses about break statistics, including the manner in which mean break rates may vary over time.

TIME DEPENDENCE OF THE BREAK DATA

The choice of a distribution with fixed parameters, such as the exponential, to represent break intervals raises a critical issue: that the distribution has a fixed mean, amounting to an assumption that the MTBF is *constant* over time. If this property is not consistent with actual data, then the use of a single exponential distribution (or any other time-independent distribution) is not appropriate.

Real-world factors can cause the average break rate or the MTBF to vary with time. This occurs, for example, if breaks increase in frequency as aircraft age; if maintenance processes change to improve quality control; if the skill level of the maintenance force changes; or if a change is made in a subsystem. Changes in the way aircraft are used can also affect the MTBF even if the sortie rates and average durations remain the same.

Even if it were possible to demonstrate that the *long-term* MTBF is roughly constant over many years, changes such as those enumerated above can cause variations in the MTBF that can last for weeks or months, especially during stressful wartime missions. It should be obvious that if the MTBF decreases—or, equivalently, if the failure rate increases—then the rate at which potential backlogs occur must increase. If conflicts cause increases in failure rates, then a maintenance capability sized for the long-term average rate cannot, by definition, perform adequately; relative to the average, a level of slack must be provided to enable maintenance organizations to meet peak demands.

It is interesting to note that a time-dependent break rate will generate more overall bottlenecks than will a stationary break rate with the same long-term MTBF. That is to say, the impact of high-bottleneck periods will not be compensated for, even in the long term, by low-bottleneck periods. To illustrate this, suppose (simplistically) that a backlog situation occurs whenever two failures occur within a critical time T_c. Also suppose that the failure rate R is half the time above the mean R_0 by an amount δ and half the time below average by the same amount. Finally, assume that the rates remain at one of the two extreme states for a time long enough to expect several failures. That is, the phenomenon of the failure rate changing between failures is ignored for the purposes of this analysis.

Given the above, the probability that a failure will occur within T_c of the previous failure is given by $1-e^{-RT_c}$ (for an exponentially distributed failure interval). Multiplying by the failure rate R gives the rate of backlog events: $R(1-e^{-RT_c})$. The average backlog rate is then

$$\frac{1}{2}[R_+(1-e^{-R_+T_c})+R_-(1-e^{-R_-T_c})]$$

where $R_+ = R + \delta$ and $R_- = R - \delta$. This is larger than $R_0(1-e^{-RT_c})$ for cases where the MTBF is larger than T_c—that is, for cases in which an even distribution of failures can be handled without causing a backlog. As a numerical illustration, take $R_0 = 1.0$ failure/day and $\delta = 0.5$ failure/day. Thus, the failure rate is 1.5/day during "bad" periods and only 0.5/day during "good" periods. Assume $T_c = 0.2$ day. Then the rate of backlog events in the stationary case is 0.181 event/day, while in the nonstationary case the long term average rate rises to 0.218 event/day. That is, the effect of a nonstationary MTBF is to increase the stress on the system, potentially implying the need for additional resources.

SHOULD THE EFFECT OF NON-STATIONARITY OF MEAN BREAK RATES BE INCLUDED IN LCOM?

The answer to the question posed above is that it depends on the circumstances. In particular, if the most demanding maintenance scenario can be associated with a significant shift up in break rates, then this would make the most demanding scenario even more demanding, and LCOM must then account for its effect in order to ensure that all planned sorties can be successfully executed. If this is not done, then the LCOM simulation will estimate too few maintenance man-hours to support the required sorties.

Wartime scenarios are usually assumed to be among the most demanding maintenance scenarios. It is therefore of critical importance to investigate whether there are reasons to believe that the MTBF shows a statistically significant positive correlation with wartime flying patterns. If, through the Monte Carlo simulation approach, LCOM is going to capture the worst-case scenarios, it is insufficient to use CAMS/GO-81 data from shorter periods to capture this. Rather, the simulation scenarios should use mean failure rates that are representative of the most stressful break rates observed in wartime. Currently, some sample data from Kosovo can be used to estimate the effects of current operational practices on break rates, but this knowledge, while important, is clearly incomplete.

THE EMPIRICAL ISSUE OF STATISTICAL NONSTATIONARITY AND THE ASD

RAND research has shown that the MTBF, as a function of flying hours and sortie count, is in general highly unstable.[3] One interpretation of this finding is that in addition to being dependent on flying hours and sortie counts, break rates are quite sensitive to the operating environment. Variables include both the kinds of sorties that are flown (combat, training, inspections, sortie duration, etc.) and various environmental factors (temperature, humidity, dust, runway conditions, etc.). This is illustrated in a series of figures based on recent RAND research.[4]

The particular focus of this research was the so-called deceleration factor, which is really a complicated way of describing a failure rate formula that is a linear combination of sortie count and flying hours.[5] By Air Force instruction, a value of 0.1 is used for each addi-

---

[3]See Crawford, 1988.

[4]See Amatzia Feinberg et al., *Supporting Expeditionary Aerospace Forces: Lessons from the Air War over Serbia*, MR-1263-AF, Santa Monica: RAND, 2002.

[5]The term *deceleration factor* arose in the context of adjusting for sortie durations beyond one hour in a context of determining how many parts need to be stocked in the readiness spares package (RSP) kit to support given sortie generation scenarios. The deceleration factor (DCF) is the coefficient of flying hours in a formula giving removal

tional flying hour over one—i.e., each extra hour after the first one adds a 10 percent increase in parts for the kit. The deceleration factor is not used for all parts but applies to avionics in F-16s, F-15C/Ds, and F-15Es.

To study whether the assumption of a linear relationship between failure rates and ASD is realistic and, if the relationship is linear, whether the deceleration factor of 0.1 is accurate, RAND compared break rates prior to and during the Kosovo contingency (Operational Noble Anvil [ONA]). Figure B.1 illustrates their methodology. The horizontal axis in Figure B.1 measures average sortie durations, and the vertical axis displays the actually experienced removal rates, all based on CAMS. The dashed line indicates the expected removal

RAND*MR1436-B.1*

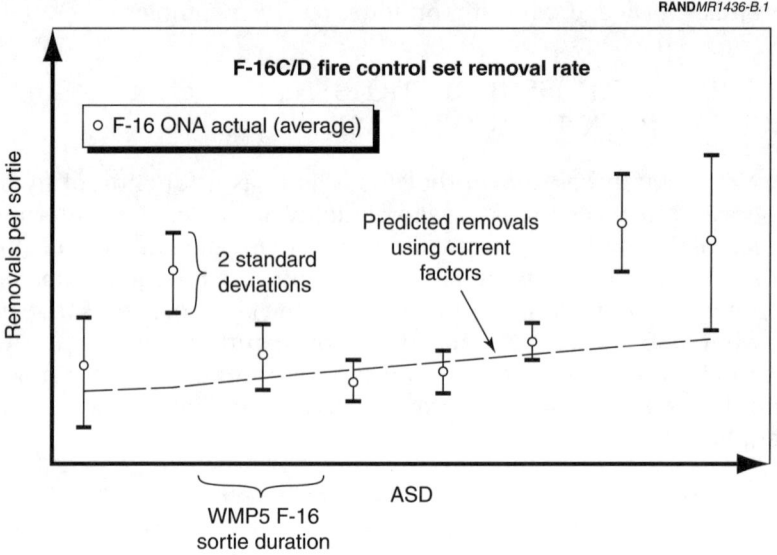

Figure B.1—Methodology for Charts Below

rate (RR) per sortie: $RR = RR_1[1 + DCF \times (H - 1)]$, where RR_1 is the removal rate for an average sortie duration of one hour and H is the actual duration. This is completely equivalent to the formula $RR = RR_S + RR_H \times H$, where $RR_S = RR_1 - DCF$ and $RR_H = RR_1 \times DCF$.

rates given the Air Force's current assumptions about the deceleration coefficient as explained above. The graphs will thereby compare the actual removal rates against the officially assumed removal rates for the purposes of stocking parts inventories.

Figures B.2 through B.4 are organized as demonstrated in Figure B.1, with the addition that the distribution of sorties by length is also overlaid on the figure. The black circles are read on the scale on the right side of graph. Thus, in Figure B.2, about 500 of the sorties in the Spangdahlem Air Base sample were of five to six hours' duration, a little under 400 of four to five hours' duration, and around 300 three to four hours long—together accounting for the vast majority of the sorties flown by the Spangdahlem F-16s. The dashed line indicates the predicted removal rates, with noncontingency data and the official deceleration factor used to account for the effect of increasing average sortie duration. The removal rates for the 131 pod are indicated by the white circles, and the value for each circle is also indicated in the diagram, corresponding to the scale on the left. Finally, the confidence intervals around each removal rate are indicated by the small dashes and dots.

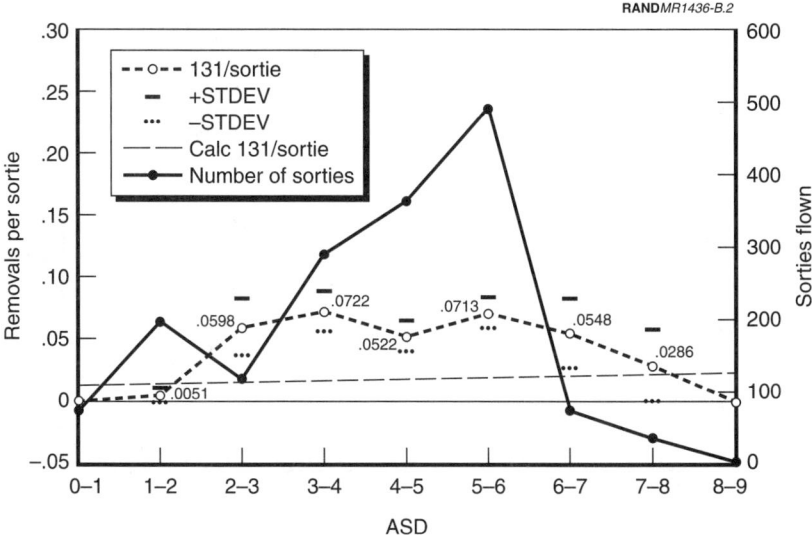

Figure B.2—Spangdahlem Air Base F-16 131 Pod Removals During ONA
(n = 83 removals)

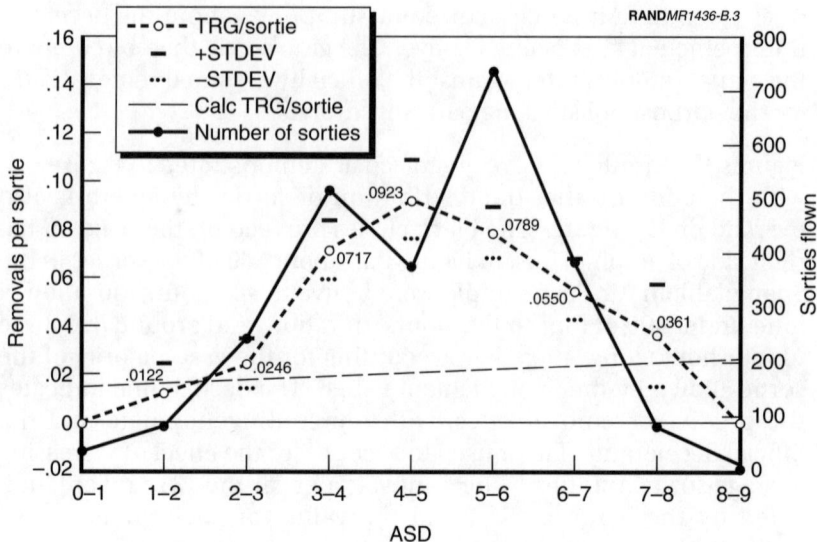

Figure B.3—Aviano Air Base F-16 LANTIRN Targeting Pod Removals During ONA (n = 161 removals)

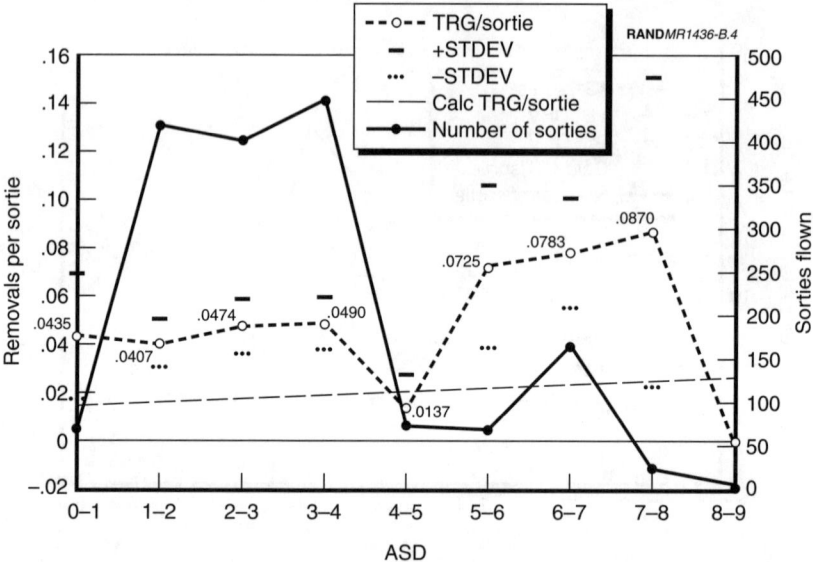

Figure B.4—Lakenheath Air Base F-15E LANTIRN Targeting Pod Removals (n = 82 removals)

The most important facts in Figure B.2 are the following: First, for shorter sortie durations—i.e., those less than one hour and between one and two hours—the actual removal rates were lower than predicted by the equation using the standard deceleration coefficient. Second, for all sortie durations in the interval two to three hours up to six to seven hours, actual removal rates were on average about five times greater than predicted. Third, for sortie durations of five to six hours or more, the removal rates actually declined. The explanation for this may lie in the nature of the sortie. For sorties up to four to five hours, our hypothesis is that the 131 pod was more likely to be used because the longer sorties probably indicate long loitering time on station waiting for targets of opportunity, with an increasing percentage of air-to-ground attacks canceled and the aircraft returned home still full up with missiles and bombs. This will remain a hypothesis until the nature of the sorties is further investigated.

Figure B.3 shows removal rates for the Low-Altitude Navigation and Targeting Infrared for Night (LANTIRN) pod in a similar diagram with data from the F-16s at Aviano Air Base. Here, the vast majority of the sorties are in the range of three to four up to six to seven hours' duration. For sortie durations up to two to three hours, removal rates were below or close to predicted. In the range where most of the flying was done—i.e., between three to four and six to seven hours' duration—the removal rates were again around five times higher than predicted values. As before, the removal rates for sorties beyond four to five hours decline with increased sortie duration, possibly reflecting sorties with more loitering and more returns with unused munitions.

Figure B.4 shows LANTIRN targeting pod removals from the F-15Es out of Lakenheath Air Base. The sortie durations for the F-15Es were shorter than those for the F-16s, with the vast majority falling in the range between one to two and four to five hours. With the exception of the removal rates for four to five hours and eight to nine hours, all actual removal rates were on the order of four times greater than predicted.

Figures B.5 and B.6 show removal rates for a few noncombat systems. Here the picture is more mixed. For some, removal rates were close to predicted, and for others they appear higher. The effect of

RAND*MR1436-B.5*

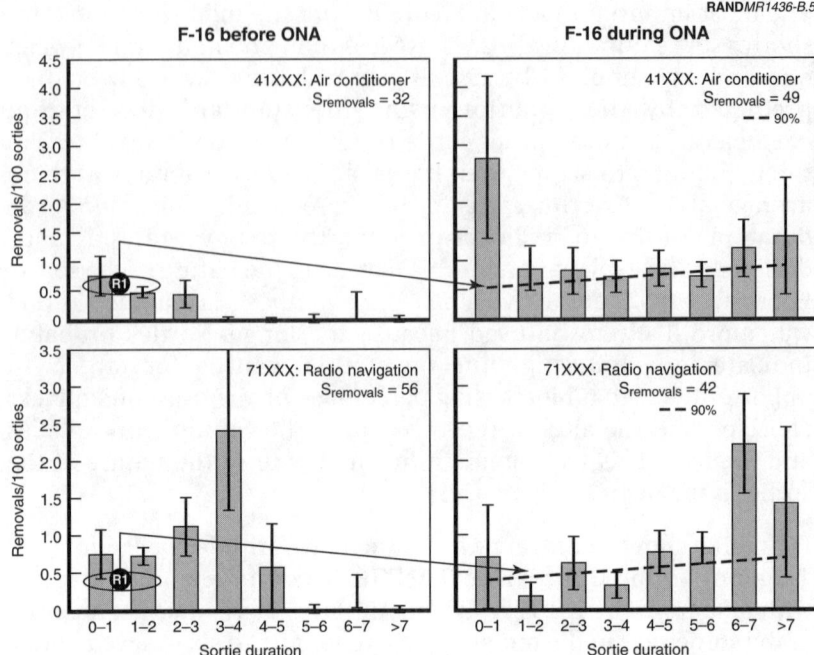

SOURCE: Analysis Decision Support System (ADSS), WMP5, LMI AF501MR2.

Figure B.5—Predicted vs. Actual Removals in ONA

RAND*MR1436-B.6*

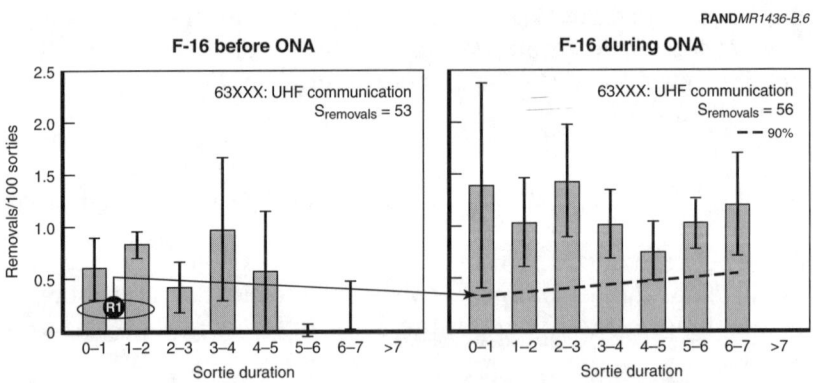

SOURCES: Analysis Decision Support System (ADSS), WMP5, LMI AF501MR2.

Figure B.6—Planned vs. Actual Requirements for Communications Radio

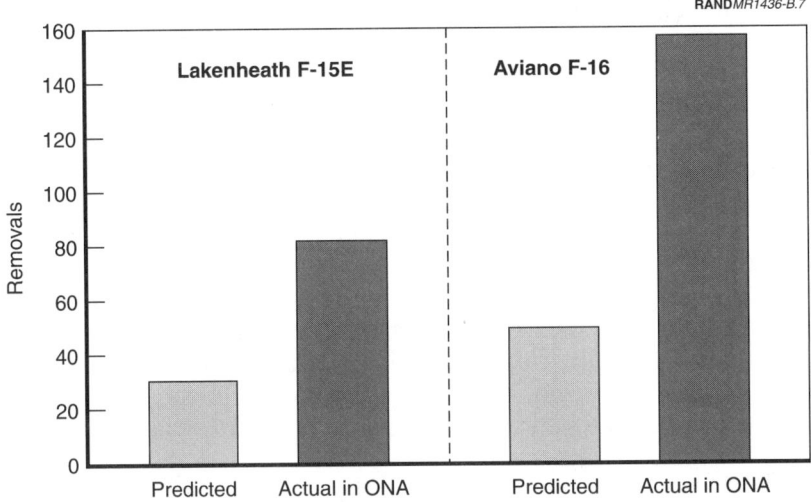

RAND*MR1436-B.7*

Figure B.7—Predicted vs. Actual LANTIRN Removals During ONA

longer sortie duration also appears more mixed, in some cases close to predictions and in others much less than expected. Figure B.7 summarizes the total experience for LANTIRN pods—i.e., without sorting removals by sortie duration. In all, actual removals were close to four times greater than predicted values.

From the perspective of trying to determine requirements for maintenance manpower, this is quite chilling. It indicates that the required manpower for LANTIRN maintenance is off by a large factor. The saving grace comes from two mitigating factors. First, not all units—or even most units—deploy at any given time. Thus, when an unexpectedly high demand for maintenance on a particular item occurs, it is possible to supplement the deployed force with personnel from nondeploying units. Second, not all subsystems exhibit higher-than-anticipated demands, and an AFSC services more than one single item type. Thus, the percentage increase in maintenance work hours for the AFSC as a whole is much less than that for the single item. Nevertheless, it clearly behooves the Air Force both to better understand how break rates will change under different conditions and to determine maintenance manpower requirements based on the most stressful scenarios for the maintenance force.

Recall the consequence of using a distribution with fixed parameters to generate break intervals, in particular the universal LCOM analysis practice of using a fleet exponential clock. The consequence is that the mean break rate (in suitable units—e.g., flying hours) is *constant over time*. What the data discussed in Figures B.2 through B.7 illustrate is the strong possibility that the mean break rate varies significantly over time, depending not only on conditions of use but potentially on the age of various systems as well. The implications for LCOM analysis are important. First, current planning factors that predict wartime and contingency removal rates as a function of longer sortie duration are likely to significantly underestimate actual removals—possibly raising required maintenance man-hours significantly. Second, the assumption of a linear relationship between failure rates and sortie duration is likely to be false.

Finally, of potentially greater significance is the fact that the temporal break rates (breaks per unit time) in any particular conflict cannot be expected to be related to prior long-term averages. That is, it may not be adequate to predict wartime rates on the basis of historical peacetime data. In other words, the average break rate is nonstationary over time and is highly context dependent in ways that are not currently known or adequately understood.

For purposes of computing manpower requirements for the most stressful realistic scenario, the temporal rate at which maintenance actions are generated is the critical variable to predict. The temporal break rate is computed from two separate inputs: first, an event break rate such as the breaks per sortie and breaks per flying hour, and second, the scenario that the simulation will support, i.e., a schedule of sorties and flying hours over the simulation period. Clearly, as wartime sortie rates and flying hours differ significantly from peacetime conditions, the long-term temporal break rate from maintenance data systems will not be representative of the wartime factors. Factors such as the daily sortie rate, variations in the daily sortie rate, environmental conditions, distance to final destinations, and refueling availability will be very different in war than in peace. The data from Kosovo illustrate just how far the break rates can be from their long-term averages. Furthermore, the Kosovo data strongly hint that attempts to predict the temporal rate *based on expected conditions* is a very difficult task that lies well beyond current analytical capabilities. First, it is clear that the simple linear dependence of break rate on ASD does not represent reality. Second, no credible quantitative information has been found on how other factors affect the break rate per sortie, in addition to ASD. Third, even if the quantitative dependence of break rates on these factors were known, there is no reliable method of predicting changes in those factors in the transition from peace to war.

Fourth, the data also suggest that not all systems behave in the same way. In other words, the question of whether actual break rate data do vary over time—that is, whether they are nonstationary—requires further investigation. Statistical tests exist for determining whether a data series is nonstationary, and considerable work must be done on five-digit-level WUCs from past CAMS/GO-81 data to determine which of the most important systems display significant levels of nonstationarity. As noted above, it may be possible to perform this type of work on a sample of five-digit WUCs that are sufficiently accurate for such purposes, assuming that these WUCs can be identified. When nonstationarity is found in the data, then LCOM must account for this in a manner currently not resorted to. Rather than looking at shorter-term CAMS/GO-81 data and updating some input files in LCOM, analysts must attempt to understand what the scenarios are that cause higher break rates. Then, instead of using the means for some CAMS/GO-81 base period, they must rely on the potentially much higher break rates. In some cases, the statistical tests and other analyses indicate that the factors that drive the break rates are largely unknown or unpredictable. For these cases, the best approach, in the sense of ensuring adequate manpower in the face of some large fraction of the expected cases, may be to use historical data to determine the highest historical rates and then to use values at or near these rates in the LCOM scenarios. As noted, this will reduce the MTBF and provide a very different point around which the Monte Carlo simulation will draw random samples.

The condition just discussed—that the mean and variance of a time series vary over time, possibly jumping up for a while during especially stressful scenarios and then coming back down—is known as statistical nonstationarity. The data shown from Kosovo illustrate the strong possibility that average break rates for many important systems on combat aircraft display this kind of nonstationarity during wartime scenarios. The data also suggest that not all systems behave this way. In other words, the question of whether actual break-rate data are nonstationary requires further investigation. Statistical tests exist for determining whether a data series is nonstationary, and considerable work must be done on five-digit-level WUCs from past CAMS/GO-81 data to determine which of the most important systems display significant levels of nonstationarity.

If, as the data above indicate, significant combat systems on Air Force aircraft are associated with above-normal break rates in wartime, then this has potentially important implications for estimating maintenance man-hours in LCOM. Depending on the minimum crew sizes and effective M-UTEs for different work centers and AFSCs, it is unclear if this also means that total manpower requirements are underestimated. Only further detailed data analysis can determine the extent to which this is important. In the context of performing such detailed data analyses, it would be important to focus on aging aircraft—which is also, at the core, an issue of the nonstationarity or time dependence of mean break rates.

RAND QUESTIONNAIRES FOR MAINTAINERS IN THE FIELD

When we first began looking at maintenance issues as part of our readiness research for the Air Force, it quickly became clear that there was a dearth of concrete information on how technicians in the field were actually spending their time under various conditions. Anecdotal evidence was mounting that pointed to an increasing level of stress caused by the taxing demands of high OPTEMPO combined with shortages in people and supplies. It was virtually impossible, however, to find any systematic quantification of this alleged stress— i.e., analyses on which the Air Force could base remedial actions. In some areas, the Air Force did not seem to be asking some important questions. We therefore developed questionnaires for maintainers at three wings where case studies were already being undertaken as part of ongoing readiness work: the 388th FW at Hill Air Force Base, the 60th AMW at Travis Air Force Base, and the 305th AMW at McGuire Air Force Base. Responses to these questionnaires are used throughout this report, particularly in Chapters Six and Seven.

The immediate purpose of these questionnaires was to test both the validity of the anecdotes and the feasibility of quantifying the core problems. We were aware of Air Force surveys that sought to determine why officers and enlisted personnel made decisions to reenlist or to separate.[1] The surveys included exhaustive lists of potential

---

[1]See, for example, U.S. Department of the Air Force, *Report on Career Decisions in the Air Force: Results of the 2000 USAF Careers and New Directions Surveys*, San Antonio, TX: Air Force Personnel Center, Survey Branch, Randolph Air Force Base, November 30, 2000, and U.S. Department of the Air Force, *2000 Follow-Up Quality of Life Survey*,

reasons, including the quality of unit leadership, opportunities for advancement, training opportunities, and deployments. We also surveyed all elements of the 8th Air Force to determine how ten types of operations—such as routine peacetime operations, inspections, and "operations other than war"—help or hurt readiness and quality of life.[2] Indeed, LCOM analysts have regularly used field surveys (or "audits") to serve as checks of automated reporting systems (CAMS, GO-81) as they populate the LCOM model with data on task times and break rates.

Our questionnaires focused solely on maintenance technicians in the operational squadrons—fighter, aircraft generation, and maintenance squadrons. The questions sought to illuminate, under various conditions and during different time frames, such issues as duty hours worked; percentage of time devoted to tasks such as OJT, production, and administration; and the relative productivity of different skill levels. Differences between the operations of fighter and mobility wings were also captured. Importantly, the questionnaires evolved for each wing; at Hill Air Force Base we garnered responses from 60 experienced 5- and 7-levels, while at Travis Air Force Base there were responses from over 900 active-duty 3-, 5-, and 7-levels and reserve technicians.

The questionnaires provide a solid foundation for further research by the Air Force into the problems facing maintainers today. The results of these questionnaires, while not statistically adequate for a definitive quantification of these problems across the Air Force, do yield important data that lend credence to the anecdotes emanating from the field. Just as the LCOM field audits provide a second-best yet necessary data source in lieu of accurate, automated information, so too do the questionnaires serve as an imperfect source of information that the Air Force has not heretofore gathered.

San Antonio, TX: Air Force Personnel Center, Survey Branch, Randolph Air Force Base, September 2000.

[2]See Thomas Fossen et al., *What Helps and What Hurts: How Ten Activities Affect Readiness and Quality of Life at Three 8AF Wings*, DB-223-AF, Santa Monica: RAND, 1997.

An example of one of the questionnaires is provided below. It was administered to 3-levels, 5-levels, and 7-levels at the 60th AMW. Supervisors answered a separate, more detailed questionnaire.

RAND QUESTIONS

60th AMW MAINTENANCE WORK CENTERS

3-Levels, 5-Levels, 7-Levels

SPRING 2000

RAND's Project AIR FORCE is conducting a study on USAF readiness sponsored by AF/XO. To help us inform USAF decisionmakers about the impact of heavy, competing demands on you as maintainers in the field, we are asking you to tell us how you spend your duty days under various operational circumstances.

RAND will use the information you provide for research purposes only. RAND will keep your responses strictly confidential. We will not disclose your identity or information that identifies you to anyone outside the research project, including USAF, except as required by law.

If you have any questions or concerns regarding these questions, you can contact the persons below for clarification. After you are finished, please put the form in the enclosed envelope and place in the RAND box.

Thank you, in advance, for your time, your honesty, and your input.

RAND
1333 H Street, N.W.
Washington, D.C. 20005-4707
(202) 296-5000
Attn.: David Thaler, ext. 5221, or Carl Dahlman, ext. 5231
E-mails: david_thaler@rand.org or carl_dahlman@rand.org

BACKGROUND

1. Please indicate the following information (for those answering both sets of questions, we need this again, please).

   Your squadron: _____

   Your work center: _____

   Your primary AFSC: _____ (what skill level you're performing at)

   Your special experience indicator (SEI), if applicable: _____

   How long have you worked on this aircraft? _____ YRS _____ MOS.

2. Are you:
   (Mark all that apply)

   ○ 1   Active (specify rank: _____)

   ○ 2   ART (specify rank: _____)

   ○ 3   Civilian (specify GS level: _____)

3. What is the length of your average duty week?

   ☐☐ . ☐ hours.

4. Did you work in a mobility wing 3-5 years ago?
   (Mark One)

   ○ 1   Yes

   ○ 2   No ➡ **Go to Question 7**

5. What was your AFSC 3–5 years ago? _____

6. Do you believe that the duty hours of someone in that position today has increased compared to when you held that job?

   ○ 1   Yes, roughly by _____ hours per week.

   ○ 2   No, the hours have not changed measurably.

7. We want to get a sense of how maintenance personnel spend their duty days during normal operations (local ops, channels). Please indicate, on average, what percentage of your time is spent on each of the following activities during a normal duty day.

Next, please also indicate what percentage of your time was spent on these activities during a normal duty day 3–5 years ago if you were in a mobility wing at that time.

Please make sure that your answers in each column add up to 100%.

	On average, what proportion of your time is spent on the following activities during a normal duty day?	What were these percentages 3–5 years ago? ☐ Does not apply, wasn't in a mobility wing 3–5 years ago.
Production (sortie generating, maintenance and repair, cann)	☐☐☐ %	☐☐☐ %
Formal education and training	☐☐☐ %	☐☐☐ %
Learning by OJT	☐☐☐ %	☐☐☐ %
Training others (including OJT)	☐☐☐ %	☐☐☐ %
Ancillary training	☐☐☐ %	☐☐☐ %
Administration (including GO-81)	☐☐☐ %	☐☐☐ %
Other (including out of hide, awaiting work assignment)	☐☐☐ %	☐☐☐ %
Supervision of production	☐☐☐ %	☐☐☐ %
TOTAL	**100%**	**100%**

8. We also want to get a sense of how the duty days of maintenance personnel change during deployments and rotations, MRT, and eight-hour surges.

    Please indicate what proportion of your time, on average, is spent on the following activities. Again, please make sure your answers add up to 100%. If you have not participated in one of these operations, indicate so and leave that column blank.

    Finally, please indicate the average length of a duty week for each of these operations.

	Preparation for contingency deployment, rotation, or exercise	Contingency deployment, rotation, or exercise— you are deployed	Contingency deployment, rotation, or exercise— you remain at home station	Recovery contingency deployment, rotation, or exercise	MRT	Surge
	☐ Does not apply; have not participated in this type of operation.	☐ Does not apply; have not participated in this type of operation.	☐ Does not apply; have not participated in this type of operation.	☐ Does not apply; have not participated in this type of operation.	☐ Does not apply; have not participated in this type of operation.	☐ Does not apply; have not participated in this type of operation.
Production (sortie generating, maintenance and repair, cann)	%	%	%	%	%	%
Formal education and training	%	%	%	%	%	%
Training others (including OJT)	%	%	%	%	%	%
Ancillary training	%	%	%	%	%	%
Administration (including GO-81)	%	%	%	%	%	%
Other (including out of hide, awaiting work assignment)	%	%	%	%	%	%
Supervision of production	%	%	%	%	%	%
TOTAL	**100%**	**100%**	**100%**	**100%**	**100%**	**100%**
Average length of a duty week for this operation	Hours/week	Hours/week	Hours/week	Hours/week	Hours/week	Hours/week

9. Is there anything else you would like to tell us about the impact of heavy, competing demands on you as a maintainer in the field?

    _____

    _____

    _____

    _____

    _____

**Please seal your completed survey in the envelope provided
and place in the RAND box.**

THANK YOU FOR YOUR TIME AND ASSISTANCE.

DESCRIPTION OF THE SKILL-MIX MODEL

This appendix describes the model used in Chapter Seven to simultaneously adjust both manpower and the way in which duty days are spent while leaving skill mix fixed at that given by current assignments.[1] The objective is to minimize the manpower needed while still generating the required sortie production and also providing good training (a correct teacher-to-student ratio). Administrative duties have also been considered. However, the model should be considered preliminary, with no pretense of comprehensively addressing this complex issue.

BASIC FORMULATION

Maintenance workers are divided into seven skill levels: 3–, 3 middle, 3+, 5–, 5 middle, 5+, and 7. Workers in a skill level have an efficiency associated with their ability to perform tasks relative to a 7-level. The efficiencies used for this paper are given in Table D.1.

These efficiencies are notional, although the productivity figures are based on our interviews. The efficiencies should be interpreted as the amount of work done per unit time relative to a 7-level. They have nothing to say about the quality of the work done, a factor that is not yet addressed in our model. Thus, the total maintenance production given by a middle 5-level working ten hours is what a 7-level could accomplish in eight hours.

---

[1]Several minor improvements to the model were added during the writing of this appendix, so the results presented here differ slightly from those given in Chapter Seven.

Table D.1

Task Efficiencies for Selected Skill Levels and Tasks

Task	Level						
	3–	3 middle	3+	5–	5 middle	5+	7
Teaching	0	0	0.4	0.8	0.85	0.9	1.0
Production	0.2	0.4	0.6	0.7	0.80	0.9	1.0
Other	0.5	0.7	0.8	0.9	0.90	0.9	1.0

Our model postulates that there is a certain requirement for learning, teaching, producing, and administrating in a unit. The authorized workforce is assumed to be able to perform all the required tasks. However, the skill mix has changed, resulting in a more junior workforce that has a larger requirement for teaching and a lower per-person productivity. The original and actual skill mixes are shown in Table D.2.

The objective is to find the way in which each skill-level cohort should spend its time so as to minimize the total manpower requirement while still getting the work done. This formulation is certainly simplistic; one would actually want to incorporate such factors as the differential cost of employing a more senior workforce versus a less skilled workforce. Such features can be added later; for now the skill mix is assumed to be fixed.

A little thought makes it clear that the amount of some of the work depends on the size of the force. We assume that the amount of maintenance production is a fixed number independent of the number of workers and depends only on the rate at which aircraft need to be prepared and repaired. The required amount of learning and teaching will vary in absolute amount but not in the amount per person so long as the skill mix is held constant. Finally, there should be two components to the category of "other," which includes not only administration but also any other activities demanded of the

Table D.2

Authorized and Actual Skill Mixes (%)

Skill Mix	Level						
	3–	3 middle	3+	5–	5 middle	5+	7
Authorized	8.9	8.9	8.9	19.0	19.0	19.0	16.3
Actual	11.0	11.0	11.0	18.5	15.7	14.8	18.0

maintenance workforce. One component scales with the workforce size (e.g., personnel administration) and one is independent of the size of the workforce (e.g., out-of-hide activities). In this analysis, it is assumed that under a force with current authorizations, this mix is equal.

Table D.3 shows how the required work in each category is calculated.

DEFINING AN "OPTIMAL" WORKFORCE TIME DISTRIBUTION

We assume that the skill mix has changed to a mix M_j. Thus, a given force size N^{Tot} yields $N_j = M_j N^{\text{Tot}}$. The problem is to adjust the time distributions $D_{i,j}$ (i indexes a task type) so as to "best" achieve the required output for all tasks. This suggests an objective function h given by:

$$h = \sum_i h_i$$
$$h_i = 0 \text{ if } W_i \geq W_i^*$$
$$= W_i - W_i^* \text{ when } W_i < W$$

where W_i^* represents the required work for task i. Thus, there is a simple linear penalty for work shortfalls and no reward for exceeding the required value. Alternatives are reasonable but are largely irrelevant, because the idea is to find the smallest workforce that can get all the work done. However, we added one additional term to the objective function.

Mechanical optimization of the above form will tend to give extreme results, such as certain cohorts spending *all* or *none* of their time in certain activities. In fact, the current time distributions should reflect many real-world considerations that are not explicit in our model. Thus, doing extreme violence to these distributions is likely to violate many real-world considerations as well. In order to avoid this, a term that penalizes deviations from the nominal time distributions has been added. It is of the form

Table D.3

Task Efficiencies for Various Skill Levels and Tasks

Task	Formula	Description
Production	$W_P = \sum_j N_j E_{P,j} D_{P,j}$	The sum over the workforce of the amount of work done by each individual per unit time. For an individual in cohort j, this is $E_{P,j} D_{P,j}$ where $E_{P,j}$ is the production efficiency of an individual in cohort j and $D_{P,j}$ is the fraction of time such an individual spends on maintenance production activities. For all cases other than learning, these need not equal the historic fraction, but the sum over all activities should equal 1.0.[a] When this formula is evaluated for the case of full authorizations at an authorized skill mix, it determines the required production that must be met.
Learning	$W_L = \sum_j N_j D_{L,j}^0$	The sum over cohorts of nominal learning shares. N_j is the number of people in cohort j, and $D_{L,j}^0$ is the fraction of time an individual in cohort j has historically spent his/her time learning. Since learning is an individual, per-person requirement, the learning share $D_{L,j}$ will always equal $D_{L,j}^0$.
Teaching	$W_T = \sum_j N_j E_{T,j} D_{T,j}$	The form of this formula is similar to that of production. However, the requirement for teaching is based on the idea that the teaching-to-learning ratio should equal the historic (based on authorizations) value. That is, the ratio should be given by $$\sum_j N_j^0 E_{T,j} D_{T,j}^0 \Big/ \sum_j N_j^0 D_{L,j}^0$$ where N_j^0 is the authorized number of individuals in cohort j.
Other	$W_A = \sum_j N_j E_{A,j} D_{A,j}$	The required "other" is sum of a fixed burden and a personnel administrative burden. It is thus given by $$W_A = W_A^0 + N^{Tot} W_A^P$$ The two coefficients are evaluated by computing the "other" using authorized levels and then by setting each of the two terms equal to half of this amount. This gives W_A^0 directly, and then W_A^P is obtained by dividing the personnel administration portion (half) by the total number of authorized personnel.

[a]This is acceptable as long as all individuals devote the same fraction of their time to activities that are not explicitly treated by the model. However, if this is not true—say that junior maintenance staff personnel spend a larger fraction of their time doing out-of-hide work—then it will be necessary to indicate, for each cohort, the fraction of their time collectively available for model-treated activities.

$$\text{penalty} = -\sum_{i,j}(D_{i,j} - D_{i,j}^0)^2$$

which leads to an overall objective function given by

$$H = \sum_i h_i - k\sum_{i,j}(D_{i,j} - D_{i,j}^0)^2$$

where the h_i given as above and k determines the relative importance of the two parts of the objective function. We found that $k = 0.5$ appeared to work well.

SOLVING FOR THE MINIMUM NECESSARY WORKFORCE

The overall procedure for determining the minimum workforce is as follows:

1. Use an automated procedure to optimize H, subject to the applicable constraints, to yield a set of work distributions $D_{i,j}$. Recall that the fraction of time spent learning, $D_{L,j}$, is not altered from the values we obtained by survey. The method used to optimize H employs generalized Lagrange multiplier methods, details of which are outside the scope of this appendix.

2. Make manual adjustments. Manual adjustments generally led to satisfying the entire production requirement and to equalize the percentage shortfall for teaching and "other." However, the manual adjustments were typically very small.

3. If shortfalls remain, increase the total manpower and repeat.

Table D.4 presents intermediate results starting from an authorized workforce of 1368.

Figure D.1 shows the shortfalls as the number of people rises from 1368 to 1592.

A final point of interest has to do with the relative value of individuals with various experience levels. These fall out of the optimization

Table D.4

Results as Workforce Size Increases

Workforce	Category	Level							
		3–	3 middle	3+	5–	5 middle	5+	7	Short-fall
1368 people, original time distribution	Teach	0.00	0.00	0.06	0.06	0.06	0.06	0.12	–19.9
	Production	0.18	0.23	0.25	0.38	0.43	0.48	0.56	–11.2
	Other	0.06	0.06	0.03	0.12	0.12	0.12	0.13	–11.1
1368 people, optimized time distribution	Teach	0	0	0	0.07	0.06	0.06	0.07	–37.6
	Production	0.17	0.22	0.27	0.38	0.49	0.60	0.63	0
	Other	0.07	0.07	0.07	0.12	0.07	0.01	0.10	–35.6
1440 people	Teach	0	0	0	0.07	0.07	0.07	0.10	–23.8
	Production	0.17	0.22	0.27	0.35	0.45	0.56	0.61	0
	Other	0.07	0.07	0.07	0.14	0.09	0.03	0.10	–23.9
1520 people	Teach	0	0	0	0.08	0.08	0.08	0.12	–11.0
	Production	0.17	0.22	0.27	0.32	0.42	0.52	0.58	0
	Other	0.07	0.07	0.07	0.16	0.11	0.06	0.10	–10.9
1592 people	Teach	0	0	0	0.09	0.09	0.09	0.14	–0.1
	Production	0.17	0.22	0.27	0.30	0.40	0.49	0.56	0
	Other	0.07	0.07	0.07	0.18	0.13	0.08	0.10	0

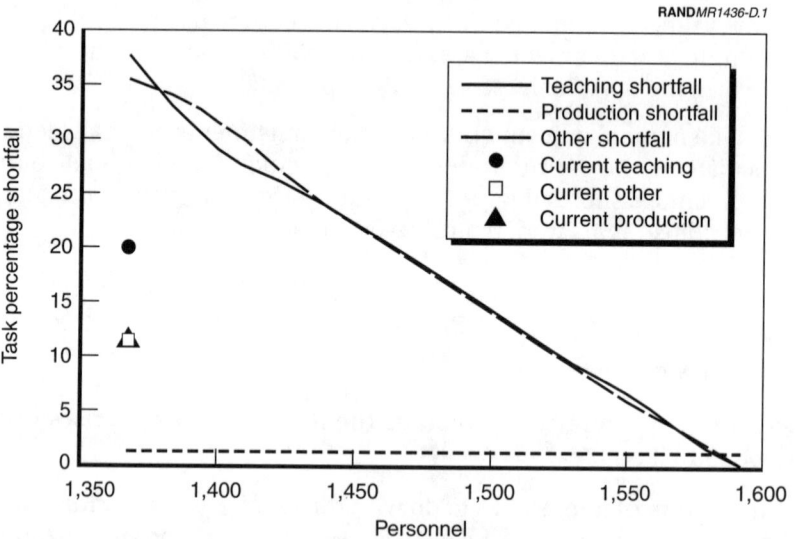

RAND*MR1436-D.1*

Figure D.1—Results as Workforce Size Increases

process (as Lagrange multipliers). As one might intuitively expect, they scale roughly with productivities (see Table D.5). Differences for different force sizes are very small, but there appears to be a trend. The differences might be related to the different relative emphasis that had to be put on various tasks for each force size in order to drive the production shortfall to zero and equalize the percentage shortfalls for teaching and administration.

Table D.5

Relative Personnel Values for Selected Force Sizes

Personnel	3–	3 middle	3+	5–	5 middle	5+	7
				Level			
1368	0.223	0.437	0.624	0.756	0.807	0.859	1.000
1440	0.218	0.428	0.610	0.767	0.819	0.870	1.000
1550	0.212	0.416	0.589	0.785	0.836	0.887	1.000
1592	0.210	0.411	0.582	0.791	0.842	0.892	1.000

BIBLIOGRAPHY

Crawford, G. B., *Variability in the Demands for Aircraft Spare Parts: Its Magnitude and Implications*, R-3318-AF, Santa Monica: RAND, 1988.

Crawford, G. B., and M. Kamins, "The Effect of High Sortie Rates on F-16 Avionics," internal document, Santa Monica: RAND, 1989.

Dahlman, Carl J., and David E. Thaler, *Assessing Unit Readiness: Case Study of an Air Force Fighter Wing*, DB-296-AF, Santa Monica: RAND, 2000.

Dahlman, Carl J., and David E. Thaler, "Ready for War But Not for Peace," in Zalmay Khalilzad and Jeremy Shapiro (eds.), *Strategic Appraisal: United States Air and Space Power in the 21st Century*, MR-1314-AF, Santa Monica: RAND, 2002.

Feinberg, Amatzia, et al., *Supporting Expeditionary Aerospace Forces: Lessons from the Air War over Serbia*, MR-1263-AF, Santa Monica: RAND, 2002.

Feller, William, *An Introduction to Probability Theory and Its Applications*, Vol. 1, New York: John Wiley & Sons, Chapter 13, 1971, p. 9.

Fishman, George S., *Monte Carlo: Concepts, Algorithms, and Applications*, New York: Springer, 1996.

Fossen, Thomas, et al., *What Helps and What Hurts: How Ten Activities Affect Readiness and Quality of Life at Three 8AF Wings*, DB-223-AF, Santa Monica, RAND, 1997.

Garcia R., and J. P. Racher, Jr., *An Investigation into a Methodology to Incorporate Skill Level Effects into the Logistics Composite Model,* Wright-Patterson Air Force Base, OH: Air Force Institute of Technology, 1981.

Howell, L. D., *Manpower Forecasts and Planned Maintenance Personnel Skill Level Changes,* Technical Report ASD/TR81-5018, Washington, D.C.: Air Force Systems Command, 1981.

HQ ACC/XP-SAS, *F-16C/D Block 40 Final Report,* Langley Air Force Base, VA, February 1998.

NMCM study (untitled), Maxwell Air Force Base, AL: Air Force Logistics Management Agency, p. iii.

Rubinstein, Reuven Y., *Simulation and the Monte Carlo Method,* Wiley Series in Probability and Mathematical Statistics, New York: John Wiley & Sons, 1981.

Slay, F. M., and C. C. Sherbrooke, *The Nature of the Aircraft Component Failure Process: A Working Note,* Report IR701R1, McLean, VA: Logistics Management Institute, 1988.

Slay, F. M., T. Bachman, R. Klein, T. J. O'Malley, F. Ichorn, and R. King, *Optimizing Spares: Support for the Aircraft Sustainability Model,* Report AF501MR1, McLean, VA; Logistics Management Institute, 1996.

Taylor, William, et al., *The Air Force Pilot Shortage: A Crisis for Operational Units?* MR-1204-AF, Santa Monica: RAND, 2000.

U.S. Department of the Air Force, *Classifying Military Personnel (Officers and Airmen),* AFI 36-2101, Washington, D.C., May 1, 1998.

U.S. Department of the Air Force, *Determining Manpower Requirements,* AFI 38-201, Washington, D.C., Table A2.1.

U.S. Department of the Air Force, *Report on Career Decisions in the Air Force: Results of the 2000 USAF Careers and New Directions Surveys,* San Antonio, TX: Air Force Personnel Center, Survey Branch, Randolph Air Force Base, November 30, 2000.

U.S. Department of the Air Force, *2000 Follow-Up Quality of Life Survey,* San Antonio, TX: Air Force Personnel Center, Survey Branch, Randolph Air Force Base, September 2000.

U.S. Department of Defense, *Department of Defense Dictionary of Military and Associated Terms,* Joint Publication 1-02, April 12, 2001, available at http://www.dtic.mil/doctrine/jel/new_pubs/jp1_02.pdf.